MYTHS AND MARVELS OF ASTRONOMY

RICHARD A. PROCTOR

GYAN

Published by

Gyan Publishing House
5, Ansari Road
Daryaganj, New Delhi-110002
Phone: 011-47034999, 9811692060
E-mail: books@gyanbooks.com

Distribution Network
gyanbooks.com
India, USA, Canada, UK, Australia, France

ISBN : 978-81-212-9486-7 (PB)
First Published, 1877

2nd Impression 2023

Printed at: Gyan Press, Delhi.

MYTHS AND MARVELS OF ASTRONOMY
Author: RICHARD A. PROCTOR

MYTHS AND MARVELS OF ASTRONOMY

LILLY'S HIEROGLYPHS (PUBLISHED IN 1651)

GREAT PLAGUE OF 1665.

GREAT FIRE OF LONDON, 1666.

MYTHS AND MARVELS OF ASTRONOMY

BY

RICHARD A. PROCTOR

AUTHOR OF "ROUGH WAYS MADE SMOOTH," "THE EXPANSE OF HEAVEN"
"OUR PLACE AMONG INFINITIES," "PLEASANT WAYS IN SCIENCE"
ETC. ETC.

THE : SILVER LIBRARY

NEW IMPRESSION

1903

PREFACE.

THE chief charm of Astronomy, with many, does not reside in the wonders revealed to us by the science, but in the lore and legends connected with its history, the strange fancies with which in old times it has been associated, the half-forgotten myths to which it has given birth. In our own times also, Astronomy has had its myths and fancies, its wild inventions, and startling paradoxes. My object in the present series of papers has been to collect together the most interesting of these old and new Astronomical myths, associating with them, in due proportion, some of the chief marvels which recent Astronomy has revealed to us. To the former class belong the subjects of the first four and the last five essays of the present series, while the remaining essays belong to the latter category.

Throughout I have endeavoured to avoid technical expressions on the one hand, and ambiguous phraseology (sometimes resulting from the attempt to avoid technicality) on the other. I have, in fact, sought to present my subjects as I should wish to have matters outside the range of my special branch of study presented for my own reading.

RICHARD A. PROCTOR.

CONTENTS.

MYTHS AND MARVELS
OF
ASTRONOMY

I.

ASTROLOGY.

Signs and planets, in aspects sextile, quartile, trine, conjoined, or opposite; houses of heaven, with their cusps, hours, and minutes; Almuten, Almochoden, Anahibazon, Catahibazon; a thousand terms of equal sound and significance.—*Guy Mannering.*

. . . . Come and see! trust thine own eyes.
A fearful sign stands in the house of life,
An enemy: a fiend lurks close behind
The radiance of thy planet—oh! be warned!—COLERIDGE.

ASTROLOGY possesses a real interest even in these days. It is true that no importance attaches now even to the discussion of the considerations which led to the rejection of judicial astrology. None but the most ignorant, and therefore superstitious, believe at present in divination of any sort or kind whatsoever. Divination by the stars holds no higher position than palmistry, fortune-telling by cards, or the indications of the future which foolish persons find in dreams, tea-dregs, salt-spilling, and other absurdities. But there are two reasons which render the history of astrology interesting. In the first place, faith in stellar influences was once so widespread that astrological terminology came to form a part of ordinary language, insomuch that it is impossible rightly to understand many passages of ancient and mediæval literature, or rightly to apprehend the force of many allusions and expressions, unless the significance of astrological teachings to the men of those times be recognised. In the second place, it is interesting to examine how the erroneous teachings of astrology were gradually abandoned, to note the way in which various orders of mind rejected these false doctrines or struggled to retain them, and to perceive how, with a large proportion of even the most civilised races, the superstitions of judicial astrology were long retained, or are retained even to this very day. The world has still to see some superstitions destroyed which are as widely received as astrology ever was, and which will probably retain their influence over many minds long after the reasoning portion of the community have rejected them.

Even so far back as the time of Eudoxus the pretensions of astrologers were rejected, as Cicero informs us ('De Div.' ii. 42). And though the Romans were strangely superstitious in such matters, Cicero reasons with excellent judgment against the belief in astrology. Gassendi quotes the argument drawn by Cicero against astrology, from the predictions of the Chaldæans that Cæsar, Crassus, and Pompey would die 'in a full old age, in their own houses, in peace and honour,' whose deaths, nevertheless, were 'violent, immature, and tragical.' Cicero also used an argument whose full force has only been recognised in modern times. 'What contagion,' he asked, 'can reach us from the planets, whose distance is almost infinite?' It is singular that Seneca, who was well acquainted with the uniform character of the planetary motions, seems to have entertained no doubt respecting their influence. Tacitus expresses some doubts, but was on the whole inclined to believe in astrology.

'Certainly,' he says, 'the majority of mankind cannot be weaned from the opinion that at the birth of each man his future destiny is fixed; though some things may fall out differently from the predictions, by the ignorance of those who profess the art; and thus the art is unjustly blamed, confirmed as it is by noted examples in all ages.'[1]

Probably, the doubt suggested by the different fortunes and characters of men born at the same time must have

[1] These reflections were suggested to Tacitus by the conduct of Thrasyllus (chief astrologer of the Emperor Tiberius), when his skill was tested by his imperial employer after a manner characteristic of that agreeable monarch. The story runs thus (I follow Whewell's version): 'Those who were brought to Tiberius on any important matter, were admitted to an interview in an apartment situated on a lofty cliff in the island of Capreæ. They reached this place by a narrow path, accompanied by a single freedman of great bodily strength; and on their return, if the emperor had conceived any doubts of their trustworthiness, a single blow buried the secret and its victim in the ocean below. After Thrasyllus had, in this retreat, stated the results of his art as they concerned the emperor, Tiberius asked him whether he had calculated how long he himself had to live. The astrologer examined the aspect of the stars, and while he did this showed hesitation, alarm, increasing terror, and at last declared that "The present hour was for him critical, perhaps fatal." Tiberius embraced him, and told him "he was right in supposing he had been in danger, but that he should escape it," and made him henceforward his confidential counsellor.' It is evident, assuming the story to be true (as seems sufficiently probable), that the emperor was no match for the charlatan in craft. It was a natural thought on the former's part to test the skill of his astrologer by laying for him a trap such as the story indicates—a thought so natural, indeed, that it probably occurred to Thrasyllus himself long before Tiberius put the plan into practice. Even if Thrasyllus had not been already on the watch for such a trick, he would have been but a poor trickster himself if he had not detected it the moment it was attempted, or failed to see the sole safe course which was left open to him. Probably, with a man of the temper of Tiberius, such a counter-trick as Galeotti's in *Quentin Durward* would have been unsafe.

occurred to many before Cicero dwelt upon it. Pliny, who followed Cicero in this, does not employ the argument quite correctly, for he says that, 'in every hour, in every part of the world, are born lords and slaves, kings and beggars.' But of course, according to astrological principles, it would be necessary that two persons, whose fortunes were to be alike, should be born, not only in the same hour, but in the same place. The fortunes and character of Jacob and Esau, however, should manifestly have been similar, which was certainly not the case, if their history has been correctly handed down to us. An astrologer of the time of Julias Cæsar, named Publius Nigidius Figulus, used a singular argument against such reasoning. When an opponent urged the different fortunes of men born nearly at the same instant, Nigidius asked him to make two contiguous marks on a potter's wheel which was revolving rapidly. When the wheel was stopped, the two marks were found to be far apart. Nigidius is said to have received the name of Figulus (the potter), in remembrance of the story; but more probably he was a potter by trade, and an astrologer only during those leisure hours which he could devote to charlatanry. St. Augustine, who relates the story (which I borrow from Whewell's 'History of the Inductive Sciences'), says, justly, that the argument of Nigidius was as fragile as the ware made on the potter's wheel.

The belief must have been all but universal in those days that at the birth of any person who was to hold an important place in the world's history the stars would either be ominously conjoined, or else some blazing comet or new star would make its appearance. For we know that some such object having appeared, or some unusual conjunction of planets having occurred, near enough to the time of Christ's birth to be associated in men's minds with that

event, it came eventually to be regarded as belonging to his horoscope, and as actually indicating to the Wise Men of the East (Chaldæan astrologers, doubtless) the future greatness of the child then born. It is certain that that is what the story of the Star in the East means as it stands. Theologians differ as to its interpretation in points of detail. Some think the phenomenon was meteoric, others that a comet then made its appearance, others that a new star shone out, and others that the account referred to a conjunction of Jupiter, Saturn, and Mars, which occurred at about that time. As a matter of detail it may be mentioned, that none of these explanations in the slightest degree corresponds with the account, for neither meteor, nor comet, nor new star, nor conjoined planets, would go before travellers from the east, to show them their way to any place. Yet the ancients sometimes regarded comets as guides. Whichever view we accept, it is abundantly clear that an astrological significance was attached by the narrator to the event. And not so very long ago, when astrologers first began to see that their occupation was passing from them, the Wise Men of the East were appealed to against the enemies of astrology,[1]—very much as

[1] The belief in the influence of the stars and the planets on the fortunes of the new-born child was still rife when Shakespeare made Glendower boast:

At my nativity
The front of heaven was full of fiery shapes
Of burning cressets; know, that at my birth
The frame and huge foundation of the earth
Shook like a coward.

And Shakespeare showed himself dangerously tainted with freethought in assigning (even to the fiery Hotspur) the reply:

So it would have done
At the same season, if your mother's cat
Had kittened, though yourself had ne'er been born.

Moses was appealed to against Copernicus and Galileo, and more recently to protect us against certain relationships which Darwin, Wallace, and Huxley unkindly indicate for the human race divine.

Although astronomers now reject altogether the doctrines of judicial astrology, it is impossible for the true lover of that science to regard astrology altogether with contempt. Astronomy, indeed, owes much more to the notions of believers in astrology than is commonly supposed. Astrology bears the same relation to modern astronomy that alchemy bears to modern chemistry. As it is probable that nothing but the hope of gain, literally in this case *auri sacra fames*, would have led to those laborious researches of the alchemists which first taught men how to analyse matter into its elementary constituents, and afterwards to combine these constituents afresh into new forms, so the belief that, by carefully studying the stars, men might acquire the power of predicting future events, first directed attention to the movements of the celestial bodies. Kepler's saying, that astrology, though a fool, was the daughter of a wise mother,[1] does not by any means present truly the relationship between astrology and astronomy. Rather we may say that astrology and alchemy, though foolish mothers,

In a similar vein Butler, in *Hudibras* ridiculed the folly of those who believe in horoscopes and nativities:

> As if the planet's first aspect
> The tender infant did infect
> In soul and body, and instil
> All future good and future ill;
> Which in their dark fatalities lurking,
> At destined periods fall a-working,
> And break out, like the hidden seeds
> Of long diseases, into deeds,
> In friendships, enmities, and strife,
> And all th' emergencies of life.

[1] Preface to the *Rudolphine Tables*.

gave birth to those wise daughters, astronomy and chemistry. Even this way of speaking scarcely does justice to the astrologers and alchemists of old times. Their views appear foolish in the light of modern scientific knowledge, but they were not foolish in relation to what was known when they were entertained. Modern analysis goes far to demonstrate the immutability, and, consequently, the non-transmutability of the metals, though it is by no means so certain as many suppose that the present position of the metals in the list of *elements* is really correct. Certainly a chemist of our day would be thought very unwise who should undertake a series of researches with the object of discovering a mineral having such qualities as the alchemists attributed to the philosopher's stone. But when as yet the facts on which the science of chemistry is based were unknown, there was nothing unreasonable in supposing that such a mineral might exist, or the means of compounding it be discovered. Nay, many arguments from analogy might be urged to show that the supposition was altogether probable. In like manner, though the known facts of astronomy oppose themselves irresistibly to any belief in planetary influences upon the fates of men and nations, yet before those facts were discovered it was not only not unreasonable, but was in fact, highly reasonable to believe in such influences, or at least that the sun, and moon, and stars moved in the heavens in such sort as to indicate what would happen. If the wise men of old times rejected the belief that 'the stars in their courses fought' for or against men, they yet could not very readily abandon the belief that the stars were for signs in the heavens of what was to befall mankind.

If we consider the reasoning now commonly thought valid in favour of the doctrine that other orbs besides our earth are inhabited, and compare it with the reasoning on which judicial astrology was based, we shall not find much to choose between the two, so far as logical weight is concerned. Because the only member of the solar system which we can examine closely is inhabited, astronomers infer a certain degree of probability for the belief that the other planets of the system are also inhabited. And because the only sun we know much about is the centre of a system of planets, astronomers infer that probably the stars, those other suns which people space, are also the centres of systems; although no telescope which man can make would show the members of a system like ours, attending on even the nearest of all the stars. The astrologer had a similar argument for his belief. The moon, as she circles around the earth, exerts a manifest influence upon terrestrial matter—the tidal wave rising and sinking synchronously with the movements of the moon, and other consequences depending directly or indirectly upon her revolution around the earth. The sun's influence is still more manifest; and, though it may have required the genius of a Herschel or of a Stephenson to perceive that almost every form of terrestrial energy is derived from the sun, yet it must have been manifest from the very earliest times that the greater light which rules the day rules the seasons also, and, in ruling them, provides the annual supplies of vegetable food, on which the very existence of men and animals depends. If these two bodies, the sun and moon, are thus potent, must it not be supposed, reasoned the astronomers of old, that the other celestial bodies exert corresponding influences? *We* know, but they did not know, that the moon rules the tides effectually because she is near to us, and that the sun is second only to the moon in tidal influence because of his enormous mass and attractive energy. We know also that his position as fire, light, and life of the earth and its inhabitants, is due directly to the tremendous heat

with which the whole of his mighty frame is instinct. Not knowing this, the astronomers of old times had no sufficient reason for distinguishing the sun and moon from the other celestial bodies, so far at least as the general question of celestial influences was concerned.

So far as particulars were concerned, it was not altogether so clear to them as it is to us, that the influence of the sun must be paramount in all respects save tidal action, and that of the moon second only to the sun's in other respects, and superior to his in tidal sway alone. Many writers on the subject of life in other worlds are prepared to show (as Brewster attempts to do, for example) that Jupiter and Saturn are far nobler worlds than the earth, because superior in this or that circumstance. So the ancient astronomers, in their ignorance of the actual conditions on which celestial influences depend, found abundant reasons for regarding the feeble influences exerted by Saturn, Jupiter, and Mars, as really more potent than those exerted by the sun himself upon the earth. They reasoned, as Milton afterwards made Raphaēl reason, that 'great or bright infers not excellence,' that Saturn or Jupiter, though 'in comparison so small, nor glist'ring' to like degree, may yet 'of solid good contain more plenty than the sun.' Supposing the influence of a celestial body to depend on the magnitude of its sphere, in the sense of the old astronomy (according to which each planet had its proper sphere, around the earth as centre), then the influence of the sun would be judged to be inferior to that of either Saturn, Jupiter, or Mars; while the influences of Venus and Mercury, though inferior to the influence of the sun, would still be held superior to that of the moon. For the ancients measured the spheres of the seven planets of their system by the periods of the apparent revolution of those bodies around the celestial dome, and so set the sphere of the moon innermost, enclosed by the sphere of Mercury, around which in turn was the sphere of Venus, next the sun's, then, in order, those of Mars, Jupiter, and Saturn. We can readily understand how they might come to regard the slow motions of the sphere of Saturn and Jupiter, taking respectively some thirty and twelve years to complete a revolution, as indicating power superior to the sun's, whose sphere seemed to revolve once in a single year. Many other considerations might have been urged, before the Copernican theory was established, to show that, possibly, some of the planets exert influences more effective than those of the sun and moon.

It is, indeed, clear that the first real shock sustained by astrology came from the arguments of Copernicus. So long as the earth was regarded as the centre round which all the celestial bodies move, it was hopeless to attempt to shake men's faith in the influences of the stars. So far as I know, there is not a single instance of a believer in the old Ptolemaic system who rejected astrology absolutely. The views of Bacon—the last of any note who opposed the system of Copernicus[1]—indicate the extreme limits to

[1] It is commonly stated that Bacon opposed the Copernican theory because he disliked Gilbert, who had advocated it. 'Bacon,' says one of his editors, 'was too jealous of Gilbert to entertain one moment any doctrine that he advanced.' But, apart from the incredible littleness of mind which this explanation imputes to Bacon, it would also have been an incredible piece of folly on Bacon's part to advocate an inferior theory while a rival was left to support a better theory. Bacon saw clearly enough that men were on their way to the discovery of the true theory, and, so far as in him lay, he indicated how they should proceed in order most readily to reach the truth. It must, then, have been from conviction, not out of mere contradiction, that Bacon declared himself in favour of the Ptolemaic system. In fact, he speaks of the diurnal motion of the earth as 'an opinion which we can demonstrate to be most false;' doubtless having in his thoughts some such arguments as misled Tycho Brahe.

which a Ptolemaist could go in opposition to astrology. It may be worth while to quote Bacon's opinion in this place, because it indicates at once very accurately the position held by believers in astrology in his day, and the influence which the belief in a central fixed earth could not fail to exert on the minds of even the most philosophical reasoners.

'Astrology,' he begins, 'is so full of superstition that scarce anything sound can be discovered in it; though we judge it should rather be purged than absolutely rejected. Yet if any one shall pretend that this science is founded not in reason and physical contemplations, but in the direct experience and observation of past ages, and therefore not to be examined by physical reasons, as the Chaldæans boasted, he may at the same time bring back divination, auguries, soothsaying, and give in to all kinds of fables; for these also were said to descend from long experience. But we receive astrology as a part of physics, without attributing more to it than reason and the evidence of things allow, and strip it of its superstition and conceits. Thus we banish that empty notion about the horary reign of the planets, as if each resumed the throne thrice in twenty-four hours, so as to leave three hours supernumerary; and yet this fiction produced the division of the week,[1] a thing so ancient and so universally received. Thus likewise we reject as an idle figment the doctrine of horoscopes, and the distribution of the houses, though these are the darling inventions of astrology, which have kept revel, as it were, in the heavens. And lastly, for the calculation of

[1] To Bacon's theological contemporaries this must have seemed a dreadful heresy, and possibly in our own days the assertion would be judged scarcely less harshly, seeing that the observance of the (so-called) Sabbath depends directly upon the belief in quite another origin of the week. Yet there can be little question that the week really had its origin in astrological formulæ.

nativities, fortunes, good or bad hours of business, and the like fatalities, they are mere levities, that have little in them of certainty and solidity, and may be plainly confuted by physical reasons. But here we judge it proper to lay down some rules for the examination of astrological matters, in order to retain what is useful therein, and reject what is insignificant. Thus, 1. Let the greater revolutions be retained, but the lesser, of horoscopes and houses, be rejected —the former being like ordnance which shoot to a great distance, whilst the other are but like small bows, that do no execution. 2. The celestial operations affect not all kinds of bodies, but only the more sensible, as humours, air, and spirits. 3. All the celestial operations rather extend to masses of things than to individuals, though they may obliquely reach some individuals also which are more sensible than the rest, as a pestilent constitution of the air affects those bodies which are least able to resist it. 4. All the celestial operations produce not their effects instantaneously, and in a narrow compass, but exert them in large portions of time and space. Thus predictions as to the temperature of a year may hold good, but not with regard to single days. 5. There is no fatal necessity in the stars; and this the more prudent astrologers have constantly allowed. 6. We will add one thing more, which, if amended and improved, might make for astrology—viz. that we are certain the celestial bodies have other influences besides heat and light, but these influences act not otherwise than by the foregoing rules, though they lie so deep in physics as to require a fuller explanation. So that, upon the whole, we must register as needed,[1] an astrology written

[1] In Bohn's edition the word 'defective' is here used, entirely changing the meaning of the sentence. Bacon registers an *Astrologia Sana* amongst the things needed for the advancement of learning, whereas he is made to say that such an astrology must be registered as defective.

in conformity with these principles, under the name of *Astrologia Sana.*'

He then proceeds to show what this just astrology should comprehend—as, 1, the doctrine of the commixture of rays; 2, the effect of nearest approaches and farthest removes of planets to and from the point overhead (the planets, like the sun, having their summer and winter); 3, the effects of distance, 'with a proper enquiry into what the vigour of the planets may perform of itself, and what through their nearness to us; for,' he adds, but unfortunately without assigning any reason for the statement, 'a planet is more brisk when most remote, but more communicative when nearest;' 4, the other accidents of the planet's motions as they pursue

> Their wand'ring course, now high, now low, then hid,
> Progressive, retrograde, or standing still;

5, all that can be discovered of the general nature of the planets and fixed stars, considered in their own essence and activity; 6, lastly, let this just astrology, he says, 'contain, from tradition, the particular natures and alterations of the planets and fixed stars; for' (here is a reason indeed) 'as these are delivered with general consent, they are not lightly to be rejected, unless they directly contradict physical considerations. Of such observations let a just astrology be formed; and according to these alone should schemes of the heavens be made and interpreted.'

The astrology thus regarded by Bacon as sane and just did not differ, as to its primary object, from the false systems which now seem to us so absurd. 'Let this astrology be used with greater confidence in prediction,' says Bacon, 'but more cautiously in election, and in both cases with due moderation. Thus predictions may be made of comets, and all kinds of meteors, inundations, droughts, heats, frosts, earthquakes, fiery eruptions, winds, great rains, the seasons of the year, plagues, epidemic diseases, plenty, famine, wars, seditions, sects, transmigrations of people, and all commotions, or great innovations of things, natural and civil. Predictions may possibly be made more particular, though with less certainty, if, when the general tendencies of the times are found, a good philosophical or political judgment applies them to such things as are most liable to accidents of this kind. For example, from a foreknowledge of the seasons of any year, they might be apprehended more destructive to olives than grapes, more hurtful in distempers of the lungs than the liver, more pernicious to the inhabitants of hills than valleys, and, for want of provisions, to monks than courtiers, etc. Or if any one, from a knowledge of the influence which the celestial bodies have upon the spirits of mankind. should find it would affect the people more than their rulers, learned and inquisitive men more than the military, etc. For there are innumerable things of this kind that require not only a general knowledge gained from the stars which are the agents, but also a particular one of the passive subjects. Nor are elections to be wholly rejected, though not so much to be trusted as predictions; for we find in planting, sowing, and grafting, observations of the moon are not absolutely trifling, and there are many particulars of this kind. But elections are more to be curbed by our rules than predictions; and this must always be remembered, that election only holds in such cases where the virtue of the heavenly bodies, and the action of the inferior bodies also, is not transient, as in the examples just mentioned; for the increases of the moon and planets are not sudden things. But punctuality of time should here be absolutely rejected. And perhaps

there are more of these instances to be found in civil matters than some would imagine.'

The method of inquiry suggested by Bacon as proper for determining the just rules of the astrology he advocated, was, as might be expected, chiefly inductive. There are, said he, 'but four ways of arriving at this science, viz.—1, by future experiments; 2, past experiments; 3, traditions; 4, physical reasons.' But he was not very hopeful as to the progress of the suggested researches. It is vain, he said, to think at present of future experiments, because many ages are required to procure a competent stock of them. As for the past, it is true that past experiments are within our reach, 'but it is a work of labour and much time to procure them. Thus astrologers may, if they please, draw from real history all greater accidents, as inundations, plagues, wars, seditions, deaths of kings, etc., as also the positions of the celestial bodies, not according to fictitious horoscopes, but the above-mentioned rules of their revolutions, or such as they really were at the time, and, when the event conspires, erect a probable rule of prediction.' Traditions would require to be carefully sifted, and those thrown out which manifestly clashed with physical considerations, leaving those in full force which complied with such considerations. Lastly, the physical reasons worthiest of being enquired into are those, said Bacon, 'which search into the universal appetites and passions of matter, and the simple genuine motions of the heavenly bodies.'

It is evident there was much which, in our time at least, would be regarded as wild and fanciful in the 'sound and just astrology' advocated by Bacon. Yet, in passing, it may be noticed that even in our own time we have seen similar ideas promulgated, not by common astrologers and fortune-tellers (who, indeed, know nothing about such matters), but by persons supposed to be well-informed in matters scientific. In a roundabout way, a new astrology has been suggested, which is not at all unlike Bacon's 'astrologia sana,' though not based, as he proposed that astrology should be, on experiment, or tradition, or physical reasons. It has been suggested, first, that the seasons of our earth are affected by the condition of the sun in the matter of spots, and very striking evidence has been collected to show that this must be the case. For instance, it has been found that years when the sun has been free from spots have been warmer than the average; and it has also been found that such years have been cooler than the average: a double-shotted argument wholly irresistible, especially when it is also found that when the sun has many spots the weather has sometimes been exceptionally warm and sometimes exceptionally cold. If this be not considered sufficient, then note that in one country or continent or hemisphere the weather, when the sun is most spotted (or least, as the case may be), may be singularly hot, while in another country, continent, or hemisphere, the weather may be as singularly cold. So with wind and calm, rain and drought, and so forth. Always, whether the sun is very much spotted or quite free from spots, something unusual in the way of weather must be going on somewhere, demonstrating in the most significant way the influence of sun-spots or the want of sun-spots on the weather. It is true that captious minds might say that this method of reasoning proved too much in many ways, as, for example, thus —always, whether the sun is very much spotted or quite free from spots, some remarkable event, as a battle, massacre, domestic tragedy on a large scale, or the like, may be going on, demonstrating in the most significant way the influence of sun-spots or the want of sun-spots on the passions of men—which sounds absurd. But the answer is twofold. First, such reasoning is captious, and secondly, it is not

certain that sun-spots, or the want of them, may not influence human passions; it may be worth while to enquire into this possible solar influence as well as the other, which can be done by crossing the hands of the new fortune-tellers with a sufficient amount of that precious metal which astrologers have in all ages dedicated to the sun.

That the new system of divination is not solely solar, but partly planetary also, is seen when we remember that the sun-spots wax and wane in periods of time which are manifestly referable to the planetary motions. Thus, the great solar spot-period lasts about eleven years, the successive spotless epochs being separated on the average by about that time; and so nearly does this period agree with the period of the planet Jupiter's revolution around the sun, that during eight consecutive spot-periods the spots were most numerous when Jupiter was farthest from the sun, and it is only by going back to the periods preceding these eight that we find a time when the reverse happened, the spots being most numerous when Jupiter was nearest to the sun. So with various other periods which the ingenuity of Messrs. De la Rue and Balfour Stewart has detected, and which, under the closest scrutiny, exhibit almost exact agreement for many successive periods, preceded and followed by almost exact disagreement. Here, again, the captious may argue that such alternate agreements and disagreements may be noted in every case where two periods are not very unequal, whether there be any connection between them or not; but much more frequently when there is no connection: and that the only evidence really proving a connection between planetary motions and the solar spots would be constant agreement between solar spot periods and particular planetary periods. But the progress of science, and especially the possible erection of a new observatory for finding out ('for a consideration') how sun-spots affect the weather, etc., ought not to be interfered with by captious reasoners in this objectionable manner. Nor need any other answer be given them. Seeing, then, that sun-spots manifestly affect the weather and the seasons, while the planets rule the sun-spots, it is clear that the planets really rule the seasons. And again, seeing that the planets rule the seasons, while the seasons largely affect the well-being of men and nations (to say nothing of animals), it follows that the planets influence the fates of men and nations (and animals). *Quod erat demonstrandum.*

Let us return, however, to the more reasonable astrology of the ancients, and enquire into some of the traditions which Bacon considered worthy of attention in framing the precepts of a sound and just astrology.

It was natural that the astrologers of old should regard the planetary influences as depending in the main on the position of the celestial bodies on the sky above the person or place whose fortunes were in question. Thus two men at the same moment in Rome and in Persia would by no means have the same horoscope cast for their nativities, so that their fortunes, according to the principles of judicial astrology, would be quite different. In fact it might happen that two men, born at the same instant of time, would have all the principal circumstances of their lives contrasted—planets riding high in the heavens of one being below the horizon of the other, and *vice versâ.*

The celestial sphere placed as at the moment of the native's birth was divided into twelve parts by great circles supposed to pass through the point overhead, and its opposite, the point vertically beneath the feet. These twelve divisions were called 'houses.'

Their position is illustrated in the following figure, taken from Raphaël's Astrology.

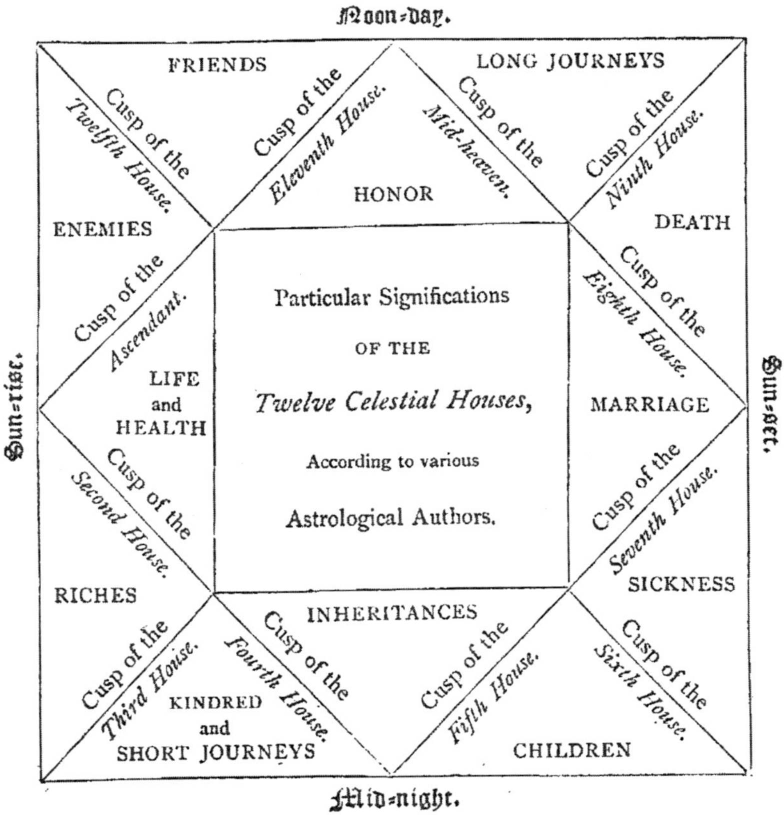

The first, called the Ascendant House, was the portion rising above the horizon at the east. It was regarded as the House of Life, the planets located therein at the moment of birth having most potent influence on the life and destiny of the native. Such planets were said to rule the ascendant, being in the ascending house; and it is from this usage that our familiar expression that such and such an influence is 'in the ascendant' is derived. The next house was the House of Riches, and was one-third of the way from the east below the horizon towards the place of the sun at midnight. The third was the House of Kindred, short journeys, letters, messages, etc. It was two-thirds of the way towards the place of the midnight sun. The fourth was the House of Parents, and was the house which the sun reached at midnight. The fifth was the House of Children and Women, also of all sorts of amusements, theatres, banquets, and merry-making. The sixth was the House of Sickness. The seventh was the House of Love and Marriage. These three houses (the fifth, sixth, and seventh) followed in order from the fourth, so as to correspond to the part of the sun's path below the horizon, between his place at midnight and his place when descending in the west. The seventh, opposite to the first, was the Descendant. The eighth house was the first house above the horizon, lying to the west, and was the House of Death. The ninth house, next to the mid-heaven on the west, was the House of Religion, science, learning, books, and long voyages. The tenth, which was in the mid-heaven, or region occupied by the sun at midday, was the House of Honour, denoting credit, renown, profession or calling, trade, preferment, etc. The eleventh house, next to the mid-heaven on the east, was the House of Friends. Lastly, the twelfth house was the House of Enemies.

The houses were not all of equal potency. The *angular* houses, which are the first, the fourth, the seventh, and the tenth—lying east, north, west, and south—were first in power, whether for good or evil. The second, fifth, eighth, and eleventh houses were called *succedents*, as following the angular houses, and next to them in power. The remaining four houses—viz. the third, sixth, ninth, and twelfth houses—were called *cadents*, and were regarded as weakest in influence. The houses were regarded as alternately masculine and feminine: the first, third, fifth, etc., being masculine; while the second, fourth, sixth, etc., were feminine.

The more particular significations of the various houses are shown in the accompanying figure from the same book.

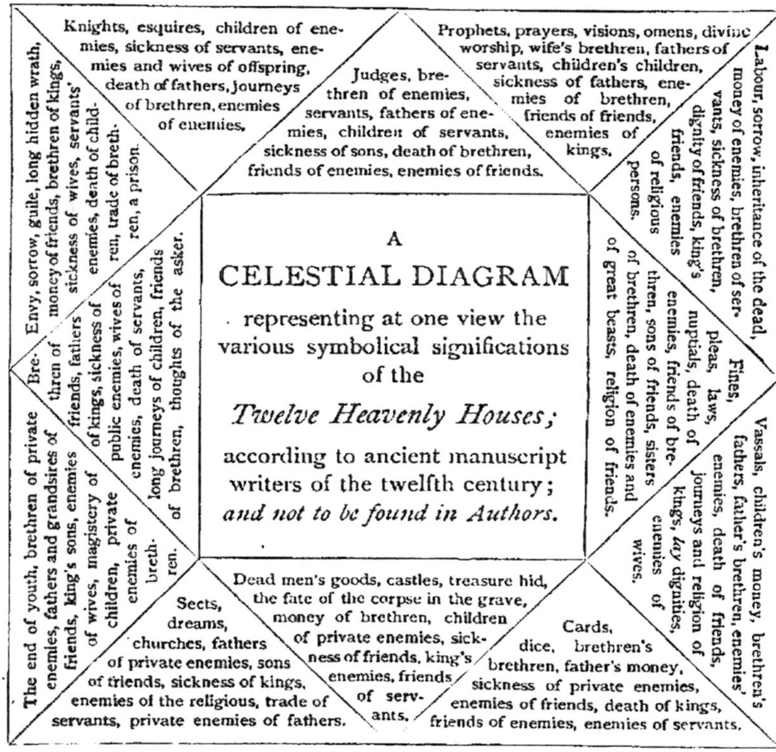

It will be easily understood how these houses were dealt with in erecting a scheme of nativity. The position of the planets at the moment of the native's birth, in the several houses, determined his fortunes with regard to the various matters associated with these houses. Thus planets of good influence in the native's ascendant, or first house, signified generally a prosperous life; but if at the same epoch a planet of malefic influence was in the seventh house, then the native, though on the whole prosperous, would be unfortunate in marriage. A good planet in the tenth house signified good fortune and honour in office or business, and generally a prosperous career as distinguished from a happy life; but evil planets in the ninth house would suggest to the native caution in undertaking long voyages, or entering upon religious or scientific controversies.

Similar considerations applied to questions relating to horary astronomy, in which the position of the planets in the various houses at some epoch guided the astrologer's opinion as to the fortune of that hour, either in the life of a man or the career of a State. In such inquiries, however, not only the position of the planets, etc., at the time had to be considered, but also the original horoscope of the person, or the special planets and signs associated with particular States. Thus if Jupiter, the most fortunate of all the planets, was in the ascendant, or in the House of Honour, at the time of the native's birth, and at some epoch this planet was ill-aspected or afflicted by other planets potent for evil in the native's horoscope, then that epoch would be a threatening one in the native's career.

The sign Gemini was regarded by astrologers as especially associated with the fortunes of London, and accordingly they tell us that the great fire of London, the plague, the building of London Bridge, and other events interesting to London, all occurred when this sign was in the ascendant, or when special planets were in this sign.[1]

[1] The astrologers were exceedingly ingenious in showing that their art had given warning of the great plague and fire of London. Thus, the star which marks the Bull's northern horn—and which is described by Ptolemy as like Mars—was, they say, exactly in that part of the sign Gemini which is the ascendant of London, in 1666. Lilly, however, for whom they claim the credit of predicting the year of this calamity, laid no claim himself to that achievement; nay, specially denied that he knew when the fire was to happen The story is rather curious. In 1651 Lilly had published his *Monarchy or no Monarchy*, which contained a number of curious hieroglyphics. Amongst these

The signs of the zodiac in the various houses were in the first place to be noted, because not only had these signs special powers in special houses, but the effects of the

were two (see frontispiece) which appeared to portend plague and fire respectively. The hieroglyphic of the plague represents three dead bodies wrapped in death-clothes, and for these bodies two coffins lie ready and two graves are being dug; whence it was to be inferred that the number of deaths would exceed the supply of coffins and graves. The hieroglyphic of the fire represents several persons, gentlefolk on one side and commonfolk on the other, emptying water vessels on a furious fire into which two children are falling headlong. The occurrence of the plague in 1665 attracted no special notice to Lilly's supposed prediction of that event, though probably many talked of the coincidence as remarkable. But when in 1666 the great fire occurred, the House of Commons summoned Lilly to attend the committee appointed to enquire into the cause of the fire. 'At two of the clock on Friday, the 25th of October 1666,' he attended in the Speaker's chamber, 'to answer such questions as should then and there be asked him.' Sir Robert Brooke spoke to this effect: 'Mr. Lilly, this committee thought fit to summon you to appear before them this day, to know if you can say anything as to the cause of the late fire, or whether there might be any design therein. You are called the rather hither, because in a book of yours long since printed, you hinted some such thing by one of your hieroglyphics.' Unto which he replied: 'May it please your honours, after the beheading of the late king, considering that in the three subsequent years the Parliament acted nothing which concerned the settlement of the nation's peace, and seeing the generality of the people dissatisfied, the citizens of London discontented, and the soldiery prone to mutiny, I was desirous, according to the best knowledge God had given me, to make enquiry by the art I studied, what might, from that time, happen unto the Parliament and nation in general. At last, having satisfied myself as well as I could, and perfected my judgment therein, I thought it most convenient to signify my intentions and conceptions thereof in forms, shapes, types, hieroglyphics, etc., without any commentary, that so my judgment might be concealed from the vulgar, and made manifest only unto the wise; I herein imitating the examples of many wise philosophers who had done the like. Having found, sir, that the great city of London should be sadly afflicted with a great plague, and not long after with planets in particular houses varied according to the signs in which the planets were situated. If we were to follow the description given by the astrologers themselves, not much insight would be thrown upon the meaning of the zodiacal signs. For instance, astrologers say that Aries is a vernal, dry, fiery, masculine, cardinal, equinoctial, diurnal, movable, commanding, eastern, choleric, violent, and quadrupedalian sign. We may, however, infer generally from their accounts the influences which they assigned to the zodiacal signs.

Aries is the house and joy of Mars, signifies a dry constitution, long face and neck, thick shoulders, swarthy complexion, and a hasty, passionate temper. It governs the head and face, and all diseases relating thereto. It reigns over England, France, Switzerland, Germany, Denmark, Lesser Poland, Syria, Naples, Capua, Verona, etc. It is a masculine sign, and is regarded as fortunate.

Taurus gives to the native born under his auspices a stout athletic frame, broad bull-like forehead, dark curly hair, short neck, and so forth, and a dull apathetic temper, exceedingly cruel and malicious if once aroused. It governs the neck and throat, and reigns over Ireland, Great Poland, part of Russia, Holland, Persia, Asia Minor, the Archipelago, Mantua, Leipsic, etc. It is a feminine sign, and unfortunate.

Gemini is the house of Mercury. The native of Gemini

an exorbitant fire, I framed these two hieroglyphics, as represented in the book, which in effect have proved very true.' 'Did you foresee the year?' said one. 'I did not,' said Lilly; 'nor was desirous; of that I made no scrutiny. Now, sir, whether there was any design of burning the city, or any employed to that purpose, I must deal ingenuously with you, that since the fire I have taken much pains in the search thereof, but cannot or could not give myself the least satisfaction therein. I conclude that it was the finger of God only; but what instruments He used thereunto I am ignorant.'

will have a sanguine complexion and tall, straight figure, dark eyes quick and piercing, brown hair, active ways, and will be of exceedingly ingenious intellect. It governs the arms and shoulders, and rules over the south-west parts of England, America, Flanders, Lombardy, Sardinia, Armenia, Lower Egypt, London, Versailles, Brabant, etc. It is a masculine sign, and fortunate.

Cancer is the house of the Moon and exaltation of Jupiter, and its native will be of fair but pale complexion, round face, grey or mild blue eyes, weak voice, the upper part of the body large, slender arms, small feet, and an effeminate constitution. It governs the breast and the stomach, and reigns over Scotland, Holland, Zealand, Burgundy, Africa, Algiers, Tunis, Tripoli, Constantinople, New York, etc. It is a feminine sign, and unfortunate.

The native born under Leo will be of large body, broad shoulders, austere countenance, with dark eyes and tawny hair, strong voice, and leonine character, resolute and ambitious, but generous, free, and courteous. Leo governs the heart and back, and reigns over Italy, Bohemia, France, Sicily, Rome, Bristol, Bath, Taunton, Philadelphia, etc. It is a masculine sign, and fortunate.

Virgo is the joy of Mercury. Its natives are of moderate stature, seldom handsome, slender but compact, thrifty and ingenious. It governs the abdomen, and reigns over Turkey both in Europe and Asia, Greece, and Mesopotamia, Crete, Jerusalem, Paris, Lyons, etc. It is a feminine sign, and generally unfortunate.

Libra is the house of Venus. The natives of Libra are tall and well made, elegant in person, round-faced and ruddy, but plain-featured and 'inclined to eruptions that disfigure the face when old; they' (the natives) 'are of sweet disposition, just and upright in dealing.' It governs the lumbar regions, and reigns over Austria, Alsace, Savoy,

Portugal, Livonia, India, Ethiopia, Lisbon, Vienna, Frankfort, Antwerp, Charleston, etc. It is a masculine sign, and fortunate.

Scorpio is, like Aries, the house of Mars, 'and also his joy.' Its natives are strong, corpulent, and robust, with large bones, 'dark curly hair and eyes' (presumably the eyes dark only, not curly), middle stature, dusky complexion, active bodies; they are usually reserved in speech. It governs the region of the groin, and reigns over Judæa, Mauritania, Catalonia, Norway, West Silesia, Upper Batavia, Barbary, Morocco, Valentia, Messina, etc. It is feminine, and unfortunate. (It would appear likely, by the way, that astrology was a purely masculine science.)

Sagittarius is the house and joy of Jupiter. Its natives are well formed and tall, ruddy, handsome, and jovial, with fine clear eyes, chestnut hair, and oval fleshy face. They are 'generally jolly fellows at either bin or board,' active, intrepid, generous, and obliging. It governs the legs and thighs,[1] and reigns over Arabia Felix, Spain, Hungary, Moravia, Liguria, Narbonne, Cologne, Avignon, etc. It is masculine, and of course fortunate.

Capricorn is the house of Saturn and exaltation of Mars. This sign gives to its natives a dry constitution and slender make, with a long thin visage, thin beard (a generally goaty aspect, in fact), dark hair, long neck, narrow chin, and weak knees. It governs, nevertheless, the knees and hams, and reigns over India, Macedonia, Thrace and Greece, Mexico, Saxony, Wilna, Mecklenburgh, Brandenburg, and Oxford. It is feminine, and unfortunate.

[1] Sir Toby Belch and Sir Andrew Aguecheek were evidently not well taught in astrology. 'Shall we set about some revels?' says the latter. 'What shall we do else?' says Toby; 'were we not born under Taurus?' 'Taurus, that's sides and heart,' says sapient Andrew. 'No, sir,' responds Toby, 'it's legs and thighs. Let me see thee caper.'

Aquarius also is the house of Saturn. Its natives are obust, steady, strong, healthy, and of middle stature; delicate complexion, clear but not pale, sandy hair, hazel eyes, and generally an honest disposition. It governs the legs and ankles, and reigns over Arabia, Petræa, Tartary, Russia, Denmark, Lower Sweden, Westphalia, Hamburg, and Bremen. It is masculine, and fortunate.

Pisces is the house of Jupiter and exaltation of Venus. Its natives are short, pale, thick-set, and round-shouldered (like fish), its character phlegmatic and effeminate. It governs the feet and toes, and reigns over Portugal, Spain, Egypt, Normandy, Galicia, Ratisbon, Calabria, etc. It is feminine, and therefore, naturally, unfortunate.

Let us next consider the influences assigned to the various planets and constellations.

Though we can understand that in old times the planets and stars were regarded as exercising very potent influences upon the fates of men and nations,[1] it is by no means easy to understand how astrologers came to assign to each planet its special influence. That is, it is not easy to understand how they could have been led to such a result by actual reasoning, still less by any process of observation.[2] There was a certain scientific basis for the belief in

[1] 'This is the excellent foppery of the world, that, when we are sick in fortune (often the surfeit of our own behaviour), we make guilty of our disasters the sun, moon, and stars: as if we were villains on necessity; fools by heavenly compulsion; knaves, thieves, and treacherous by spherical predominance; drunkards, liars, and adulterers, by inforced obedience of planetary influence; and all that we are, evil, by a divine thrusting on.'—SHAKESPEARE (*King Lear*).

[2] There are few things more remarkable, or to reasoning minds more inexplicable, than the readiness with which men undertook in old times, and even now undertake, to interpret omens and assign prophetic significance to casual events. One can understand that foolish persons should believe in omens, and act upon the ideas suggested by

the possibility of determining the special influences of the stars; and we should have expected to find some scientific process adopted for the purpose. Yet, so far as can be judged, the influences assigned to the planets depended on entirely fanciful considerations. In some cases we seem almost to see the line along which the fancies of the old astrologers led them, just as in some cases we can perceive how mythological superstitions (which are closely related to astrological ideas) had their origin; though it is not quite clear whether the planets were first regarded as deities with special qualities, and these qualities afterwards assigned to the planetary influences, or whether the planetary influences were first assigned, and came eventually to be regarded as the qualities of the deities associated with the several planets.

It is easy, for instance, to understand why astrologers should have regarded the sun as the emblem of kingly power and dignity, and equally easy to understand why, to the sun regarded as a deity, corresponding qualities should have been ascribed; but it is not easy to determine whether

their superstitions. The difficulty is to comprehend how these superstitions came into existence. For instance, who first conceived the idea that a particular line in the palm of the hand is the line of life; and what can possibly have suggested so absurd a notion? To whom did the thought first present itself that the pips on playing-cards are significant of future events; and why did he think so? How did the 'grounds' of a teacup come to acquire that deep significance which they now possess for Mrs. Gamp and Betsy Prig? If the believers in these absurdities be asked *why* they believe, they answer readily enough either that they themselves or their friends have known remarkable fulfilments of the ominous indications of cards or tea-dregs, which must of necessity be the case where millions of forecasts are daily made by these instructive methods. But the persons who first invented those means of divination can have had no such reasons. They must have possessed imaginations of singular liveliness and not wanting in ingenuity. It is a pity that we know so little of them.

the astrological or the Sabaistic superstitions were the earlier. And in like manner of the moon and planets. There seems to me no sufficient evidence in favour of Whewell's opinion, that 'in whatever manner the sun, moon, and planets came to be identified with gods and goddesses, the characters ascribed to these gods and goddesses, regulated the virtues and powers of the stars which bear their names.' As he himself very justly remarks, 'We do not possess any of the speculations of the earlier astrologers; and we cannot, therefore, be certain that the notions which operated in men's minds when the art had its birth, agreed with the views on which it was afterwards defended.' He does not say why he infers that, though at later periods supported by physical analogies, it was originally suggested by mythological beliefs. Quite as probably mythological beliefs were suggested by astrological notions. Some of these beliefs, indeed, seem manifestly to have been so suggested; as the character of the deity Mercury, from the rapid motions of the planet Mercury, and the difficulty of detecting it; the character of Mars from the blood-red hue of the planet when close to the horizon, and so forth.

Let us examine, however, the characteristics ascribed by astrologers to various planets.

It is unfortunate for astrology that, despite the asserted careful comparison of events with the planetary positions preceding and indicating them, nothing was ever observed which seemed to suggest the possibility that there may be an unknown planet ruling very strongly the affairs of men. Astrologers tell us now that Uranus is a very potent planet; yet the old astrologers seem to have got on very well without him. By the way, one of the moderns, the grave Raphaël, gives a very singular account of the discovery of Uranus, in a book published sixteen years before Neptune was discovered by just such a process as Raphaël imagined in the case of Uranus. He says that Drs. Halley, Bradley, and others, having frequently observed that Saturn was disturbed in his motion by some force exerted from beyond his orbit, and being unable to account for the disturbance on the known principles of gravitation, pursued their enquiry into the matter, 'till at length the discovery of this hitherto unknown planet covered their labours with success, and has enabled us to enlarge our present solar system to nearly double its bounds.' Of course there is not a word of truth in this; Uranus having been discovered by accident long after Halley and Bradley were in the grave. But the account suggests what might have been, and curiously anticipates the actual manner in which Neptune was discovered.

Astrologers agree in attributing evil effects to Uranus. But the evil he does is always peculiarly strange, unaccountable, and totally unexpected. He causes the native born under his influence to be of a very eccentric and original disposition, romantic, unsettled, addicted to change, a seeker after novelty; though, if the moon or Mercury have a good aspect towards Uranus, the native will be profound in the secret sciences, magnanimous, and lofty of mind. But let all beware of marriage when Uranus is in the seventh house, or afflicting the moon. And in general, let the fair sex remember that Uranus is peculiarly hostile to them, and very evil in love.

Saturn is the Greater Infortune of the old system of astrology, and is by universal experience acknowledged to be the most potent, evil, and malignant of all the planets. Those born under him are of dark and pale complexion, with small, black, leering eyes, thick lips and nostrils, large ears, thin face, lowering looks, cloudy aspect, and seemingly melancholy and unhappy; and though they have broad shoulders, they have but short lips and a thin beard,

They are in character austere and reserved, covetous, laborious, and revengeful; constant in friendship, and good haters. The most remarkable and certain characteristic of the Saturnine man is that, as an old author observes 'he will never look thee in the face.' 'If they have to love any one, these Saturnines,' says another old author, 'they love most constantly; and if they hate, they hate to the death.' The persons signified symbolically by Saturn are grandparents, and other old persons, day labourers, paupers, beggars, clowns, husbandmen of the meaner sort, and especially undertakers, sextons, and gravediggers. Chaucer thus presents the chief effects which Saturn produces in the fortunes of men and nations—Saturn himself being the speaker:—

. . . . quod Saturne
My cours, that hath so wide for to turne,
Hath more power than wot any man.
Min is the drenching in the sea so wan,
Min is the prison in the derke cote,
Min is the strangel and hanging by the throte,
The murmure and the cherles rebelling,
The groyning, and the prive empoysoning,
I do vengaunce and pleine correction,
While I dwell in the signe of the leon;
Min is the ruine of the high halles,
The falling of the toures and of the walles
Upon the minour or the carpenter:
I slew Sampson in shaking the piler.
Min ben also the maladies colde,
The derke tresons, and the castes olde:
My loking is the fader of pestilence.

Jupiter, on the contrary, though Saturn's next neighbour in the solar system, produces effects of an entirely contrary kind. He is, in fact, the most propitious of all the planets, and the native born under his influence has every reason to be jovial in fact as he is by nature. Such a native will be tall and fair, handsome and erect, robust, ruddy, and altogether a good-looking person, whether male or female. The native will also be religious, or at least a good moral honest man, unless Jupiter be afflicted by the aspects of Saturn, Mars, or Uranus; in which case he may still be a jolly fellow, no man's enemy but his own—only he will probably be his own enemy to a very considerable extent, squandering his means and ruining his health by gluttony and intoxication. The persons represented by Jupiter (when he is not afflicted) are judges, counsellors, church dignitaries, from cardinals to curates, scholars, chancellors, barristers, and the highest orders of lawyers, woollendrapers (possibly there may be some astral significance in the woolsack), and clothiers. When Jupiter is afflicted, however, he denotes quacks and mountebanks, knaves, cheats, and drunkards. The influence of the planet on the fortunes is nearly always good. Astrologers, who to a man reverence dignities, consider Great Britain fortunate in that the lady whom, with customary effusion, they term 'Our Most Gracious Queen,' was born when Jupiter was riding high in the heavens near his culmination, this position promising a most fortunate and happy career. The time has passed when the fortunes of this country were likely to be affected by such things; but we may hope, for the lady's own sake, that this prediction has been fulfilled. Astrologers assert the same about the Duke of Wellington, assigning midnight, May 1, 1769, as the hour of his birth. There is some doubt both as to the date and place of the great soldier's birth; but the astrologer finds in the facts of his life the means of removing all such doubts.[1]

[1] Wellington lived too long for the astrologers, his death within the year having unfortunately been predicted by them many times during the last fifteen years of his life. Some astrologers were more cautious, however. I have before me his horoscope, carefully calcu-

Next in order comes Mars, inferior only in malefic influence to Saturn, and called by the old astrologers the Lesser Infortune. The native born under the influence of Mars is usually of fierce countenance, his eyes sparkling, or sharp and darting, his complexion fiery or yellowish, and his countenance scarred or furrowed. His hair is reddish or sandy, unless Mars chances to be in a watery sign, in which case the hair will be flaxen; or in an earthly sign, in which case the hair will be chestnut. The Martialist is broad-shouldered, steady, and strong, but short,[1] and often bony and lean. In character the Martialist is fiery and

ated, *secundum artem*, by Raphaël in 1828, with results 'sufficiently evincing the surprising verity and singular accuracy of astrological calculations, when founded on the correct time of birth, and mathematically calculated. I have chosen,' he proceeds, 'the nativity of this illustrious native, in preference to others, as the subject is now living, and, consequently, all possibility of making up any fictitious horoscope is at once set aside; thus affording me a most powerful shield against the insidious representations of the envious and ignorant traducer of my sublime science.' By some strange oversight, however, Raphaël omits to mention anything respecting the future fortunes of Wellington, showing only how wonderfully Wellington's past career had corresponded with his horoscope.

[1] 'I have still observed,' says an old author, 'that your right Martialist doth seldom exceed in height, or be at the most above a yard or a yard and a half in height' (which is surely stint measure). 'It hath been always thus,' said that right Martialist Sir Geoffrey Hudson to Julian Peveril; 'and in the history of all ages, the clean tight dapper little fellow hath proved an overmatch for his burly antagonist. I need only instance, out of Holy Writ, the celebrated downfall of Goliath and of another lubbard, who had more fingers in his hand, and more inches to his stature, than ought to belong to an honest man, and who was slain by a nephew of good King David; and of many others whom I do not remember; nevertheless, they were all Philistines of gigantic stature. In the classics, also, you have Tydeus, and other tight compact heroes, whose diminutive bodies were the abode of large minds.'

choleric, naturally delighting in war and contention, but generous and magnanimous. This when Mars is well aspected; should the planet be evil aspected, then will the native be treacherous, thievish, treasonable, cruel, and wicked. The persons signified by Mars are generals, soldiers, sailors (if he is in a watery sign), surgeons, chemists, doctors, armourers, barbers, curriers, smiths, carpenters, bricklayers, sculptors, cooks, and tailors. When afflicted with Mercury or the moon, he denotes thieves, hangmen, and 'all cut throat people.' In fact, except the ploughboy, who belongs to Saturn, all the members of the old septet, 'tinker, tailor, soldier, sailor, apothecary, ploughboy, thief,' are favourites with Mars. The planet's influence is not quite so evil as Saturn's, nor are the effects produced by it so long-lasting. 'The influence of Saturn,' says an astrologer, 'may be compared to a lingering but fatal consumption; that of Mars to a burning fever.' He is the cause of anger, quarrels, violence, war, and slaughter.

The sun comes next; for it must be remembered that, according to the old system of astronomy, the sun was a planet. Persons born under the sun as the planet ruling their ascendant, would be more apt to be aware of the fact than Saturnine, Jovial, Martial, or any other folk, because the hour of birth, if remembered, at once determines whether the native is a solar subject or not. The solar native has generally a round face (like pictures of the sun in old books of astronomy), with a short chin; his complexion somewhat sanguine; curling sandy hair, and a white tender skin. As to character, he is bold and resolute, desirous of praise, of slow speech and composed judgment; outwardly decorous, but privately not altogether virtuous. The sun, in fact, according to astrologers, is the natural significator of respectability; for which I can discover no reason, unless it be that the sun travelling always in the ecliptic has no latitude, and so solar folk are allowed none. When the sun is ill aspected, the native is both proud and mean, tyrannical and sycophantic, exceedingly unamiable, and generally disliked because of his arrogance and ignorant pomposity. The persons signified by the sun are emperors, kings, and titled folk generally, goldsmiths, jewellers, and coiners. When 'afflicted,' the sun signifies pretenders either to power or knowledge. The sun's influence is not in itself either good or evil, but is most powerful for good when he is favourably aspected, and for evil when he is afflicted by other planets.

Venus, the next in order, bore the same relation to the Greater Fortune Jupiter which Mars bore to Saturn the Greater Ill-fortune. She was the Lesser Fortune, and her influence was in nearly all respects benevolent. The persons born under the influence of this planet are handsome, with beautiful sparkling hazel or black eyes (but another authority assigns the subject of Venus, 'a full eye, usually we say goggle-eyed,' by which we do not usually imply beauty), ruddy lips, the upper lip short, soft smooth hair, dimples in the cheek and chin, an amorous look and a sweet voice. One old astrologer puts the matter thus pleasantly :—'The native of Venus hath,' quoth he, 'a love-dimple in the chin, a lovely mouth, cherry lips, and a right merry countenance.' In character the native of Venus is merry 'to a fault,' but of temper engaging, sweet and cheerful, unless she be ill aspected, when her native is apt to be too fond of pleasure and amusement. That her influence is good is shown (in the opinion of Raphaël, writing in 1828) by the character of George IV., 'our present beloved monarch and most gracious majesty, who was born just as this benevolent star' was in the ascendant; 'for it is well known to all Europe what a refined and polished genuis, and what exquisite taste, the King of

England possesses, which therefore may be cited as a most illustrious proof of the celestial science; a proof likewise which is palpably demonstrable, even to the most casual observer, since the time of his nativity is taken from the public journals of the period, and cannot be gainsaid.' 'This illustrious and regal horoscope is replete with wonderful verifications of planetary influence, and England cannot but prosper while she is blessed with the mild and beneficent sway of this potent monarch.' Strengthened in faith by this convincing proof of the celestial science, we proceed to notice that Venus is the protectrice of musicians, embroiderers, perfumers, classic modellers, and all who work in elegant attire or administer to the luxuries of the great; but when she is afflicted, she represents 'the lower orders of the votaries of voluptuousness.'

Mercury is considered by astrologers 'a cold, dry, melancholy star.' The Mercurial is neither dark nor fair, but between both, long-faced, with high forehead and thin sharp nose, 'thin beard (many times none at all), slender of body, and with small weak eyes;' long slender hands and fingers are 'especial marks of Mercury,' says Raphaël. In character the Mercurial is busy and prattling. But when well affected, Mercury gives his subjects a strong, vigorous, active mind, searching and exhaustive, a retentive memory, a natural thirst for knowledge.[1] The persons signified by Mercury are astrologers, philosophers, mathematicians, politicians, merchants, travellers, teachers, poets, artficers, men of science, and all ingenious, clever men. When he is ill affected, however, he represents pettifoggers, cunning vile persons, thieves, messengers, footmen, and servants, etc.

The moon comes last in planetary sequence, as nearest

[1] It is likely that Swedenborg in his youth studied astrology, for in his visions the Mercurial folk have this desire of knowledge as their distinguishing characteristic.

to the earth. She is regarded by astrologers as a cold, moist, watery, phlegmatic planet, variable to an extreme, and, like the sun, partaking of good or evil according as she is aspected favourably or the reverse. Her natives are of good stature, fair, and pale, moon-faced, with grey eyes, short arms, thick hands and feet, smooth, corpulent and phlegmatic body. When she is in watery signs, the native has freckles on the face, or, says Lilly, 'he or she is blub-cheeked, not a handsome body, but a muddling creature.' Unless the moon is very well aspected, she ever signfies an ordinary vulgar person. She signifies sailors (not as Mars does, the fighting-men of war-ships, but nautical folk generally) and all persons connected with water or any kind of fluid; also all who are engaged in inferior and common offices.

We may note, in passing, that to each planet a special metal is assigned, as also particular colours. Chaucer, in the Chanones Yemannes' Tale, succinctly describes the distribution of the metals among the planets:—

> Sol gold is, and Luna silver we threpe;
> Mars iren, Mercurie silver we clepe:
> Saturnus led, and Jupiter is tin,
> And Venus coper, by my [the Chanones Yemannes'] faderkin.

The colours are thus assigned:—to Saturn, black; to Jupiter, mixed red and green; to Mars, red; to the sun, yellow or yellow-purple; to Venus, white or purple; to Mercury, azure blue; to the moon, a colour spotted with white and other mixed colours.

Again, the planets were supposed to have special influence on the seven ages of human life. The infant, 'mewling and puking in the nurse's arms,' was very appropriately dedicated to the moist moon; the whining schoolboy (did schoolboys whine in the days of good Queen

Bess?) was less appropriately assigned to Mercury, the patron of those who eagerly seek after knowledge: then very naturally, the lover sighing like furnace was regarded as the special favourite of Venus. Thus far the order has been that of the seven planets of the ancient astrology, in supposed distance. Now, however, we have to pass over the sun, finding Mars the patron of mid life, appropriately (in this respect) presiding over the soldier full of strange oaths, and so forth; the 'justice in fair round belly with good capon lined' is watched over by the respectable sun; maturer age by Jupiter; and, lastly, old age by Saturn.

Colours were also assigned to the twelve zodiacal signs —to Aries, white and red; to Taurus, white and lemon; to Gemini, white and red (the same as Aries); to Cancer, green or russet; to Leo, red or green; to Virgo, black speckled with blue; to Libra, black, or dark crimson, or tawny colour; to Scorpio, brown; to Sagittarius, yellow, or a green sanguine (this is as strange a colour as the *gris rouge* of Molière's *L'Avare*); Capricorn, black or russet, or a swarthy brown; to Aquarius, a sky-coloured blue; to Pisces, white glistening colour (like a fish just taken out of the water).

The chief fixed stars had various influences assigned to them by astrologers. These influences were mostly associated with the imaginary figures of the constellations. Thus the bright star in the head of Aries, called by some the Ram's Horn, was regarded as dangerous and evil, denoting bodily hurts. The star Menkar in the Whale's jaw denoted sickness, disgrace, and ill-fortune, with danger from great beasts. Betelgeux, the bright star on Orion's right shoulder, denoted martial honours or wealth; Bellatrix, the star on Orion's left shoulder, denoted military or civic honours; Rigel, on Orion's left foot, denoted honours; Sirius and Procyon, the greater and lesser Dog Stars, both implied wealth and renown. Star clusters seem to have portended loss of sight; at least we learn that the Pleiades were 'eminent stars,' but denoting accidents to the sight or blindness, while the cluster Præsepe or the Beehive in like manner threatened blindness. The cluster in Perseus does not seem to have been noticed by astrologers. The variable star Algol or Caput Medusæ, which marks the head of Gorgon, was accounted 'the most unfortunate, violent, and dangerous star in the heavens.' It is tolerably clear that the variable character of this star had been detected long before Montanari (to whom the discovery is commonly attributed) noticed the phenomenon. The name Algol is only a variation of Al-ghúl, the monster or demon, and it cannot be doubted that the demoniac, Gorgonian character assigned to this star was suggested by its ominous change, as though it were the eye of some fierce monster slowly winking amid the gloom of space. The two stars called the Aselli, which lie on either side of the cluster Præsepe, 'are said' (by astrologers) 'to be of a burning nature, and to give great indications of a violent death, or of violent and severe accidents by fire. The star called Cor Hydræ, or the serpent's heart, denotes trouble through women (said I not rightly that Astrology was a masculine science?); the Lion's heart, Regulus, implied glory and riches; Deneb, the Lion's tail, misfortune and disgrace. The southern scale of Libra meant bad fortune, while the northern was eminently fortunate.

Astrology was divided into three distinct branches—the doctrine of nativities, horary astrology, and state astrology. The first assigned the rules for determining the general fortunes of the native, by drawing up his scheme of nativity or casting his horoscope. It took into account the positions of the various planets, signs, stars, etc., at the time of the native's birth; and as the astrologer could calculate the movements of the planets thereafter, he could find when those planets which were observed by the horoscope to be most closely associated with the native's fortunes would be well aspected or the reverse. Thus the auspicious and unlucky epochs of the native's life could be predetermined. The astrologer also claimed some degree of power to rule the planets, not by modifying their movements in any way, but by indicating in what way the ill effects portended by their positions could be prevented. The Arabian and Persian astrologers, having less skill than the followers of Ptolemy, made use of a different method of determining the fortunes of men, not calculating the positions of the planets for many years following the birth of the native, but assigning to every day after his birth a whole year of his life and for every two hours' motion of the moon one month. Thus the positions of the stars and planets, twenty-one days after the birth of the native, would indicate the events corresponding to the time when he would have completed his twenty-first year. There was another system called the Placidian, in which the effects of the positions of the planets were judged with sole reference to the motion of the earth upon her axis. It is satisfactory to find astrologers in harmony amongst each other as to these various methods, which one would have supposed likely to give entirely different results. 'Each of them,' says a modern astrologer, 'is not only correct and approved by long-tried practice, but may be said to defy the least contradiction from those who will but take the pains to examine them (and no one else should deliver an opinion upon the subject). Although each of the above methods are different, yet they by no means contradict each other, but each leads to *true results*, and in many instances they each lead to the foreknowledge of the same event; in which respect they may be compared to the ascent of a mountain by different paths, where, although some paths are longer and more difficult than others, they notwithstanding all lead to the same object.' All which, though plausible in tone labours under the disadvantage of being untrue.

Ptolemy is careful to point out, in his celebrated work the 'Tetrabiblos,' that, of all events whatsoever which take place after birth, the most essential is the continuance of life. 'It is useless,' he says, 'to consider what events might happen to the native in later years if his life does not extend, for instance, beyond one year. So that the enquiry into the duration of life takes precedence of all others.' In order to deal properly with this question, it is necessary to determine what planet shall be regarded as the Hyleg, Apheta, or Lord of Life, for the native. Next the Anareta, or Destroyer of Life, must be ascertained. The Anaretic planets are, by nature, Saturn, Mars, and Uranus, though the sun, moon, and Mercury may be endowed with the same fatal influence, if suitably afflicted. The various ways in which the Hyleg, or Giver of Life, may be afflicted by the Anareta, correspond to the various modes of death. But astrologers have always been singularly careful, in casting horoscopes, to avoid definite reference to the native's death. There are but few cases where the actual day of death is said to have been assigned. One is related in Clarendon's 'History of the Rebellion.' He tells us that William Earl of Pembroke died at the age of fifty, on the day upon which his tutor Sandford had predicted his decease. Burton, the author of the 'Anatomy of Melancholy,' having cast his own horoscope, and ascertained that he was to die on January 23, 1639, is said to have committed suicide in order that the accuracy of his calculations might not be called in question. A similar story is related of Cardan by Dr. Young (Sidrophel Vapulans), on the authority of Gassendi, who, however.

says only that either Cardan starved himself, or, being confident in his art, took the predicted day for a fatal one, and by his fears made it so. Gassendi adds that while Cardan pretended to describe the fates of his children in his voluminous commentaries, he all the while never suspected, from the rules of his great art, that his dearest son would be condemned in the flower of his youth to be beheaded on a scaffold, by an executioner of justice, for destroying his own wife by poison.

Horary astrology relates to particular questions, and is a comparatively easy branch of the science. The art of casting nativities requires many years of study; but horary astrology 'may be well understood,' says Lilly, 'in less than a quarter of a year.' 'If a proposition of any nature,' he adds, 'be made to any individual, about the result of which he is anxious, and therefore uncertain whether to accede to it or not, let him but note the hour and minute when it was *first* made, and erect a figure of the heavens, and his doubts will be instantly resolved. He may thus in five minutes learn whether the affair will succeed or not: and consequently whether it is prudent to accept the offer made or not. If he examine the sign on the first house of the figure, the planet therein, or the planet ruling the sign, *will exactly describe the party making the offer*, both in person and character, and this may at once convince the enquirer for truth of the reality of the principles of the science. Moreover, the descending sign, etc., *will describe his own person and character*—a farther proof of the truth of the science.'

There is one feature of horary astrology which is probably almost as ancient as any portion of the science, yet which remains even to the present day, and will probably remain for many years to come. I refer to the influence which the planets were supposed to exert on the successive hours of every day—a belief from which the division of time into weeks of seven days unquestionably had its origin—though we may concede that the subdivision of the lunar month into four equal parts was also considered in selecting this convenient measure of time. Every hour had its planet. Now dividing twenty-four by seven, we get three and three over; whence, each day containing twenty-four hours, it follows that in each day the complete series of seven planets was run through three times, and three planets of the next series were used. The order of the planets was that of their distances, as indicated above. Saturn came first, then Jupiter, Mars, the Sun, Venus, Mercury, and the Moon. Beginning with Saturn, as ruling the first hour of Saturn's day (Saturday), we get through the above series three times, and have for the last three hours of the day, Saturn, Jupiter, and Mars. Thus the next hour, the first hour of the next day, belongs to the sun—Sunday follows Saturday. We again run three times through the series, and the three remaining hours are governed by the sun, Venus, and Mercury,—giving the moon as the first planet for the next day. Monday thus follows Sunday. The last three hours of Monday are ruled by the moon, Saturn, and Jupiter; leaving Mars to govern the next day—Martis dies, Mardi, Tuesday or Tuisco's day. Proceeding in the same way, we get Mercury for the next day, Mercurii dies, Mercredi, Wednesday or Woden's day; Jupiter for the next day, Jovis dies, Jeudi, Thursday or Thor's day; Venus for the next day, Veneris dies, Vendredi, Friday or Freya's day; and so we come to Saturday again.[1]

[1] It is singular that, when there is this perfectly simple explanation of the origin of the nomenclature of the days of the week, an explanation given by ancient historians and generally received, Whewell should have stated that 'various accounts are given, all the methods proceeding upon certain arbitrary arithmetical processes connected in some way

The period of seven days, which had its origin in, and derived its nomenclature from astrological ideas, shows by its wide prevalence how widely astrological superstitions were once spread among the nations. As Whewell remarks (though, for reasons which will readily be understood he was by no means anxious to dwell upon the true origin of the Sabbatical week), 'the usage is found over all the East; it existed among the Arabians, Assyrians, and Egyptians. The same week is found in India, among the Brahmins; it has there also its days marked by the names of the heavenly bodies; and it has been ascertained that the same day has, in that country, the name corresponding with its designation in other nations. . . . The period has gone on without interruption or irregularity from the earliest recorded times to our own days, traversing the extent of

with astrological views.' Speaking of the arrangement of the planets in the order of their supposed distances, and of the order in which the planets appear in the days of the week, he says, 'It would be difficult to determine with certainty why the former order was adopted, and how and why the latter was derived from it.' But, in reality, there is no difficulty about either point. The former arrangement corresponded precisely with the periodic times of the seven planets of the old Egyptian system (unquestionably far more ancient than the system adopted by the Greeks), while the latter springs directly from the former. Assign to the hours of the day, successively, the seven planets in the former order, continuing the sequence without interruption day after day, and in the course of seven days each one of the planets will have ruled the first hour of a day, in the order,—Saturn, the sun, the moon, Mars, Mercury, Jupiter, and Venus. What arbitrary arithmetical process there is in this it would be difficult to conceive. Arithmetic does not rule the method at all. Nor has any other method ever been suggested; though this method has been presented in several ways, some arithmetical and some geometrical. We need then have no difficulty in understanding what seems so preplexing to Whewell, the universality, namely, of the notions 'which have produced this result,' for the notions were not fantastic, but such as naturally sprang from the ideas on which astrology itself depends.

ages and the revolutions of empires; the names of ancient deities, which were associated with the stars, were replaced by those of the objects of the worship of our Teutonic ancestors, according to their views of the correspondence of the two mythologies; and the Quakers, in rejecting these names of days, have cast aside the most ancient existing relic of astrological as well as idolatrous superstition.

Not only do the names remain, but some of the observances connected with the old astrological systems remain even to this day. As ceremonies derived from Pagan worship are still continued, though modified in form, and with a different interpretation, in Christian and especially Roman Catholic observances, so among the Jews and among Christians the rites and ceremonies of the old Egyptian and Chaldean astrology are still continued, though no longer interpreted as of yore. The great Jewish Lawgiver and those who follow him seem, for example, to have recognised the value of regular periods of rest (whether really required by man or become a necessity through long habit), but to have been somewhat in doubt how best to continue the practice without sanctioning the superstitions with which it had been connected. At any rate two different and inconsistent interpretations were given in the earlier and later codes of law. But whether the Jews accepted the Sabbath because they believed that an All-powerful Being, having created the world in six days, required and took rest ('and was refreshed') on the seventh, as stated in Exodus (xx. 11 and xxxi. 17), or whether they did so in remembrance of their departure from Egypt, as stated in Deuteronomy (v. 15), there can be no question that among the Egyptians the Sabbath or Saturn's day was a day of rest because of the malignant nature of the powerful planet-deity who presided over that day. Nor can it be seriously doubted that the Jews descended from the old

Chaldeans, among whom (as appears from stone inscriptions recently discovered) the very word Sabbath was in use for a seventh day of rest connected with astrological observances, were familiar with the practice even before their sojourn in Egypt. They had then probably regarded it as a superstitious practice to be eschewed like those idolatrous observances which had caused Terah to remove with Abraham and Lot from Ur of the Chaldees. At any rate, we find no mention of the seventh day of rest as a religious observance until after the Exodus.[1] It was not their only religious observance having in reality an astrological origin. Indeed, if we examine the Jewish sacrificial system as de-

[1] The following remarks by the Astronomer-Royal on this subject seem to me just, in the main. They accord with what I had said earlier in my essay on Saturn and the Sabbath of the Jews ('Our Place among Infinities,' 11th essay). 'The importance which Moses attached to it [the hebdomadal rest] is evident; and, with all reverence, I recognise to the utmost degree the justice of his views. No direction was given for religious ceremonial' (he seems to have overlooked Numbers xxviii. 9, and cognate passages), 'but it was probably seen that the health given to the mind by a rest from ordinary cares, and by the opportunity of meditation, could not fail to have a most beneficial religious effect. But, to give sanction to this precept, the authority of at least a myth was requisite. I believe it was simply for this reason that the myth of the six days of creation was preserved. It is expressly cited in the first delivery of the commandments, as the solemn authority (Exodus xxxi. 17) for the command. It is remarkable that at the second mention of the commandment (Deuteronomy v.) no reference is made to the creation; perhaps, after the complete establishment of Jehovistic ideas in the minds of the Israelites, they had nearly lost the recollection of the Elohistic account, and it was not thought desirable to refer to it' (Airy, 'On the Early Hebrew Scriptures,' p. 17). It must be regarded as a singular instance of the persistency of myths, if this view be correct, that a myth which had become obsolete for the Jews between the time of Moses and that of the writer (whoever he may have been) who produced the so-called Mosaic book of Deuteronomy, should thereafter have been revived, and have come to be regarded by the Jews themselves and by Christians as the Word of God.

scribed in Numbers xxviii. and elsewhere, we shall find throughout a tacit reference to the motions or influences of the celestial bodies. There was the morning and evening sacrifice guided by the movements of the sun; the Sabbath offering, determined by the predominance of Saturn; the offering of the new moon, depending on the motions of the moon; and lastly, the Paschal sacrifice, depending on the combined movements of the sun and moon—made, in fact, during the lunation following the sun's ascending passage of the equator at the sign of Aries.

Let us return, however, after this somewhat long digression, to astrological matters.

Horary astrology is manifestly much better fitted than the casting of nativities for filling the pocket of the astrologer himself; because only one nativity can be cast, but any number of horary questions can be asked. It is on account of their skill in horary astrology that the Zadkiels of our own time have occasionally found their way into the twelfth house, or House of Enemies. Even Lilly himself, not devoting, it would seem, five minutes to inquire into the probable success of the affair, was indicted in 1655 by a half-witted young woman, because he had given judgment respecting stolen goods, receiving two shillings and sixpence, contrary to an Act made under and provided by the wise and virtuous King James, First of England and Sixth of Scotland.

State astrology relates to the destinies of kingdoms, thrones, empires, and may be regarded as a branch of horary science relating to subjects (and rulers) of more than ordinary importance.

In former ages all persons likely to occupy an important position in the history of the world had their horoscopes erected; but in these degenerate days neither the casting of nativities nor the art of ruling the planets flourishes as it should do. Our Zadkiels and Raphaëls publish, indeed, the horoscopes of kings and emperors, princes and princesses, and so forth; but their fate is as that of Benedict (according to Beatrice)—men 'wonder they will still be talking, for nobody marks them.' Even those whose horoscopes have been erected show no proper respect for the predictions made in their behalf. Thus the Prince of Wales being born when Sagittarius was in the ascendant should have been, according to Zadkiel, a tall man, with oval face, ruddy complexion, somewhat dusky, and so forth; but I understand he has by no means followed these directions as to his appearance. The sun, being well aspected, prognosticated honours—a most remarkable and unlooked-for circumstance, strangely fulfilled by the event; but then being in Cancer, in sextile with Mars, the Prince of Wales was to be partial to maritime affairs and attain naval glory, whereas as a field-marshal he can only win military glory. (I would not be understood to say that he is not quite as competent to lead our fleets as our battalions into action.) The House of Wealth was occupied by Jupiter, aspected by Saturn, which betokened great wealth through inheritance —a prognostication, says Professor Miller, which is not unlikely to come true. The House of Marriage was unsettled by the conflicting influences of Venus, Mars, and Saturn; but the first predominating, the Prince, after some trouble in his matrimonial speculations, was to marry a Princess of high birth, and one not undeserving of his kindest and most affectionate attention, probably in 1862. As to the date, an almanack informs me that the Prince married a Danish Princess in March 1863, which looks like a most culpable neglect of the predictions of our national astrologer. Again, in May 1870, when Saturn was stationary in the ascending degree, the Prince ought to have been injured by a horse, and also to have received a blow on the left side of the head, near the ear; but reprehensibly omitted both these ceremonies. A predisposition to fever and epileptic attacks was indicated by the condition of the House of Sickness. The newspapers described, a few years since, a serious attack of fever; but as most persons have some experience of the kind, the fulfilment of the prediction can hardly be regarded as very wonderful. Epileptic attacks, which, as less common, might have saved the credit of the astrologers, have not visited 'this royal native.' The position of Saturn in Capricorn betokened loss or disaster in one or other of the places ruled over by Capricorn—which, as we have seen, are India, Macedonia, Thrace, Greece, Mexico, Saxony, Wilna, Mecklenburgh, Brandenburgh, and Oxford. Professor Miller expresses the hope that Oxford was the place indicated, and the disaster nothing more serious than some slight scrape with the authorities of Christchurch. But princes never get into scrapes with college dons. Probably some one or other of the 'hair-breadth 'scapes' chronicled by the reporters of his travels in India was the event indicated by the ominous position of Saturn in Capricorn.

A remarkable list of characteristics were derived by Zadkiel from the positions of the various planets and signs in the twelve houses of the 'royal native.' Some, of course, were indicated in more ways than one, which will explain the parenthetical notes in the following alphabetical table which Professor Miller has been at the pains to draw up from Zadkiel's predictions. The prince was to be 'acute, affectionate, amiable, amorous, austere, avaricious, beneficent, benevolent, brave, brilliant, calculated for government' (a quality which may be understood two ways), 'candid, careful of his person, careless, compassionate, courteous (twice over), delighting in eloquence, discreet, envious, fond of glory, fond of learning, fond of music, fond of poetry, fond of sports, fond of the arts and sciences, frank, full of expedients, generous (three times), gracious, honourable, hostile to crime, impervious, ingenious, inoffensive, joyous, just (twice), laborious, liberal, lofty, magnanimous, modest, noble, not easy to be understood (!), parsimonious, pious (twice), profound in opinion, prone to regret his acts, prudent, rash, religious, reverent, self-confident, sincere, singular in mode of thinking, strong, temperate, unreserved, unsteady, valuable in friendship, variable, versatile, violent, volatile, wily, and worthy.' Zadkiel concludes thus:— 'The square of Saturn to the moon will add to the gloomy side of the picture, and give a tinge of melancholy at times to the native's character, and also a disposition to look at the dark side of things, and lead him to despondency; nor will he be at all of a sanguine character, but cool and calculating, though occasionally rash. Yet, all things considered, though firm and sometimes positive in opinion, this royal native, if he live to mount the throne, will sway the sceptre of these realms in moderation and justice, and be a pious and benevolent man, and a merciful sovereign.' Fortunately, the time has long since passed when swaying the sceptre of these realms had any but a figurative meaning, or when Englishmen who obeyed their country's laws depended on the mercy of any man, or when even bad citizens were judged by princes. But we still prefer that princes should be well-mannered gentlemen, and therefore it is sincerely to be hoped that Zadkiel's prediction, so far as it relates to piety and benevolence, may be fulfilled, should this 'royal native' live to mount the throne. As for mercy, it is a goodly quality even in these days and in this country; for if the law no longer tolerates cruelty to men, even on the part of princes, who once had prescribed rights in that direction, there are still some cruel, nay brutal sports in which 'royal natives' might sometimes be tempted to take part. Wherefore let us hope that, even in regard to mercy, the predictions of astrologers respecting this 'royal native' may be fulfilled.

Passing however, from trivialities, let us consider the lessons which the history of astrology teaches us respecting the human mind, its powers and weaknesses. It has been well remarked by Whewell that for many ages 'mysticism in its various forms was a leading character both of the common mind and the speculations of the most intelligent and profound reasoners.' Thus mysticism was the opposite of that habit of thought which science requires, 'namely, clear ideas, distinctly employed to connect well-ascertained facts; inasmuch as the ideas in which it dealt were vague and unstable, and the temper in which they were contemplated was an urgent and aspiring enthusiasm, which could not submit to a calm conference with experience upon even terms.' We have seen what has been the history of one particular form of the mysticism of ancient and mediæval ages. If we had followed the history of alchemy, magic, and other forms of mysticism, we should have seen similar results. True science has gradually dispossessed science falsely so called, until now none but the weaker minds hold by the tenets formerly almost universally adopted. In mere numbers, believers in the ancient superstitions may be by no means insignificant; but they no longer have any influence. It has become a matter of shame to pay any attention to what those few say or do who not merely hold but proclaim the ancient faith in these matters. We can also see why this has been. In old times enthusiasm usurped the place of reason in these cases; but opinions so formed and so retained could not maintain their ground in the presence of reasoning and experience. So soon as intelligent and thoughtful men perceived that facts were against the supposed mysterious influences of the stars, the asserted powers of magicians, the pretended knowledge of alchemists, the false teachings of magic, alchemy, and astrology, were rejected. The lesson thus learned respecting erroneous doctrines which were once widely prevalent has its application in our time, when, though the influence of those teachings has passed away, other doctrines formerly associated with them still hold their ground. Men in old times, influenced by erroneous teachings, wasted their time and energies in idle questionings of the stars, vain efforts to find Arcana of mysterious power, and to acquire magical authority over the elements. Is it altogether clear that in these our times men are not hampered, prevented to some degree from doing all the good they might do in the short life-time allotted to them, by doctrines of another kind? Is there in our day no undue sacrifice of present good in idle questionings? is there no tendency to trust in a vain fetishism to prevent or remove evils which energy could avert or remedy? The time will come, in my belief, when the waste of those energies which in these days are devoted (not merely with the sanction, but the high approval, of some of the best among us) to idle aims, will be deplored as regretfully—but, alas, as idly—as the wasted speculations and labours of those whom Whewell has justly called the most intelligent and profound reasoners of the 'stationary age' of science. The words with which Whewell closes his chapter on the 'Mysticism of the Middle Ages' have their application to the mysticism of the nineteenth century:—'Experience collects her stores in vain, or ceases to collect them, when she can only pour them into the flimsy folds of the lap of Mysticism, who is, in truth, so much absorbed in looking for the treasures which are to fall from the skies, that she heeds little how scantily she obtains, or how loosely she holds, such riches as she might find beside her.'

II.

THE RELIGION OF THE GREAT PYRAMID.

DURING the last few years a new sect has appeared which, though as yet small in numbers, is full of zeal and fervour. The faith professed by this sect may be called the religion of the Great Pyramid, the chief article of their creed being the doctrine that that remarkable edifice was built for the purpose of revealing—in the fulness of time, now nearly accomplished—certain noteworthy truths to the human race. The founder of the pyramid religion is described by one of the present leaders of the sect as 'the late worthy John Taylor, of Gower Street, London;' but hitherto the chief prophets of the new faith have been in this country Professor Smyth, Astronomer Royal for Scotland, and in France the Abbé Moigno. I propose to examine here some of the facts most confidently urged by pyramidalists in support of their views.

But it will be well first to indicate briefly the doctrines of the new faith. They may be thus presented:

The great pyramid was erected, it would seem, under the instructions of a certain Semitic king, probably no other than Melchizedek. By supernatural means, the architects were instructed to place the pyramid in latitude 30° north; to select for its figure that of a square pyramid, carefully oriented; to employ for their unit of length the sacred cubit corresponding to the 20,000,000th part of the earth's polar axis; and to make the side of the square base equal to just so many of these sacred cubits as there are days and parts of a day in a year. They were further, by supernatural help, enabled to square the circle, and symbolised their victory over this problem by making the pyramid's height bear to the perimeter of the base the ratio which the radius of a circle bears to the circumference. Moreover, the great precessional period, in which the earth's axis gyrates like that of some mighty top around the perpendicular to the ecliptic, was communicated to the builders with a degree of accuracy far exceeding that of the best modern determinations, and they were instructed to symbolise that relation in the dimensions of the pyramid's base. A value of the sun's distance more accurate by far than modern astronomers have obtained (even since the recent transit) was imparted to them, and they embodied that dimension in the height of the pyramid. Other results which modern science has achieved, but which by merely human means the architects of the pyramid could not have obtained, were also supernaturally communicated to them; so that the true mean density of the earth, her true shape, the configuration of land and water, the mean temperature of the earth's surface, and so forth, were either symbolised in the great pyramid's position, or in the shape and dimensions of its exterior and interior. In the pyramid also were preserved the true, because supernaturally communicated, standards of length, area, capacity, weight, density, heat, time, and money. The pyramid also indicated, by certain features of its interior structure, that when it was built the holy influences of the Pleiades were exerted from a most effective position—the meridian, through the points where the ecliptic and equator intersect. And as the pyramid thus significantly refers to the past, so also it indicates the future history of the earth, especially in showing when and where the millennium is to begin. Lastly, the apex or crowning stone of the pyramid was no other than the antitype of that stone of stumbling and rock of offence, rejected by builders who knew not its true use, until it was finally placed as the chief stone of the corner. Whence naturally, 'whosoever shall fall upon it'—that is, upon the pyramid religion—'shall be broken; but on whomsoever it shall fall it will grind him to powder.'

If we examine the relations actually presented by the great pyramid—its geographical position, dimensions, shape, and internal structure—without hampering ourselves with the tenets of the new faith on the one hand, or on the other with any serious anxiety to disprove them, we shall find much to suggest that the builders of the pyramid were ingenious mathematicians, who had made some progress in astronomy, though not so much as they had made in the mastery of mechanical and scientific difficulties.

The first point to be noticed is the geographical position of the great pyramid, so far, at least, as this position affects the aspect of the heavens, viewed from the pyramid as from an observatory. Little importance, I conceive, can be attached to purely geographical relations in considering the pyramid's position. Professor Smyth notes that the pyra mid is peculiarly placed with respect to the mouth of the Nile, standing 'at the southern apex of the Delta-land of Egypt.' This region being shaped like a fan, the pyramid, set at the part corresponding to the handle, was, he considers, 'that monument pure and undefiled in its religion through an idolatrous land, alluded to by Isaiah; the monument which was both "an altar to the Lord in the midst of the land of Egypt, and a pillar at the border thereof," and destined withal to become a witness in the latter days, and before the consummation of all things, to the same Lord, and to what He hath purposed upon mankind.' Still more fanciful are some other notes upon the pyramid's geographical position: as (i.) that there is more land along the meridian of the pyramid than on any other all the world round; (ii.) that there is more land in the latitude of the pyramid than in any other; and (iii.) that the pyramid territory of Lower Egypt is at the centre of the dry land habitable by man all the world over.

It does not seem to be noticed by those who call our attention to these points that such coincidences prove too much. It might be regarded as not a mere accident that the great pyramid stands at the centre of the arc of shore-line along which lie the outlets of the Nile; or it might be regarded as not a mere coincidence that the great pyramid stands at the central point of all the habitable land-surface of the globe; or, again, any one of the other relations above mentioned might be regarded as something more than a mere coincidence. But if, instead of taking only one or other of these four relations, we take all four of them, or even any two of them, together, we must regard peculiarities of the earth's configuration as the result of special design which certainly have not hitherto been so regarded by geographers. For instance, if it was by a special design that the pyramid was placed at the centre of the Nile delta, and also by special design that the pyramid was placed at the centre of the land-surface of the earth, if these two relations are each so exactly fulfilled as to render the idea of mere accidental coincidence inadmissible, then it follows, of necessity, that it is through no merely accidental coincidence that the centre of the Nile delta lies at the centre of the land-surface of the earth; in other words, the shore-line along which lie the mouths of the Nile has been designedly curved so as to have its centre so placed. And so of the other relations. The very fact that the four conditions *can* be fulfilled simultaneously is evidence that a coincidence of the sort may result from mere accident.[1] Indeed, the peculiarity of geographical position which really seems to have been in the thoughts of the pyramid architects, introduces yet a fifth condition which by accident could be fulfilled along with the four others.

It would seem that the builders of the pyramid were anxious to place it in latitude 30°, as closely as their means of observation permitted. Let us consider what result they achieved, and the evidence thus afforded respecting their skill and scientific attainments. In our own time, of course, the astronomer has no difficulty in determining with great exactness the position of any given latitude-parallel. But at the time when the great pyramid was built it must have been a matter of very serious difficulty to determine the position of any required latitude-parallel with a great degree of exactitude. The most obvious way of dealing with the difficulty would have been by observing the length of shadows thrown by upright posts at noon in spring and autumn. In latitude 30° north, the sun at noon in spring (or, to speak precisely, on the day of the vernal equinox) is just twice as far from the horizon as he is from the point vertically overhead; and if a pointed post were set exactly upright at true noon (supposed to occur at the moment of the vernal or autumnal equinox), the shadow of the post would be exactly half as long as a line drawn from the top of the pole to the end of the shadow. But observations based on this principle would have presented many difficulties to the

[1] Of course it may be argued that nothing in the world is the result of *mere* accident, and some may assert that even matters which are commonly regarded as entirely casual have been specially designed. It would not be easy to draw the precise line dividing events which all men would regard as to all intents and purposes accidental from those which some men would regard as results of special providence. But common sense draws a sufficient distinction, at least for our present purpose.

architects of the pyramid. The sun not being a point of light, but a globe, the shadow of a pointed rod does not end in a well-defined point. The moment of true noon, which is not the same as ordinary or civil noon, never does agree exactly with the time of the vernal or autumnal equinox, and may be removed from it by any interval of time not exceeding twelve hours. And there are many other circumstances which would lead astronomers, like those who doubtless presided over the scientific preparations for building the great pyramid, to prefer a means of determining the latitude depending on another principle. The stellar heavens would afford practically unchanging indications for their purpose. The stars being all carried round the pole of the heavens, as if they were fixed points in the interior of a hollow revolving sphere, it becomes possible to determine the position of the pole of the star sphere, even though no bright conspicuous star actually occupies that point. Any bright star close by the pole is seen to revolve in a very small circle, whose centre is the pole itself. Such a star is our present so-called pole-star; and, though in the days when the great pyramid was built, that star was not near the pole, another, and probably a brighter star lay near enough to the pole[1] to serve as a pole-star, and to indicate by its circling motion the position of the actual pole of the heavens. This was at that time, and for many sub-

[1] This star, called *Thuban* from the Arabian *al-Thuban*, the Dragon, is now not very bright, being rated at barely above the fourth magnitude, but it was formerly the brightest star of the constellation, as its name indicates. Bayer also assigned to it the first letter of the Greek alphabet; though this is not absolutely decisive evidence that so late as his day it retained its superiority over the second magnitude stars to which Bayer assigned the second and third Greek letters. In the year 2790 B.C., or thereabouts, the star was at its nearest to the true north pole of the heavens, the diameter of the little circle in which it then moved being considerably less than one-fourth the apparent

equent centuries, the leading star of the great constellation :alled the Dragon.

The pole of the heavens, we know, varies in position .according to the latitude of the observer. At the north ›ole it is exactly overhead ; at the equator the poles of the ıeavens are both on the horizon ; and, as the observer :ravels from the equator towards the north or south pole of the earth, the corresponding pole of the heavens rises ıigher and higher above the horizon. In latitude 30° north, or one-third of the way from the equator to the pole, the pole of the heavens is raised one-third of the way from the horizon to the point vertically overhead ; and when this is the case the observer knows that he is in latitude 30°. The builders of the great pyramid, with the almost constantly clear skies of Egypt, may reasonably be supposed to have adopted this means of determining the true position of that thirtieth parallel on which they appear to have designed to place the great building they were about to erect.

It so happens that we have the means of forming an opinion on the question whether they used one method or the other ; whether they employed the sun or the stars to guide them to the geographical position they required. In fact, were it not for this circumstance, I should not have thought it worth while to discuss the qualities of either method. It will presently be seen that the discussion bears importantly on the opinion we are to form of the skill and attainments of the pyramid architects. Every celestial

diameter of the moon. At that time the star must have seemed to all ordinary observation an absolutely fixed centre, round which all the other stars revolved. At the time when the pyramid was built this star was about sixty times farther removed from the true pole, revolving in a circle whose apparent diameter was about seven times as great as the moon's. Yet it would still be regarded as a very useful pole-star, especially as there are very few conspicuous stars in the neighbourhood.

object is apparently raised somewhat above its true position by the refractive power of our atmosphere, being most raised when nearest the horizon and least when nearest the point vertically overhead. This effect is, indeed, so marked on bodies close to the horizon that if the astronomers of the pyramid times had observed the sun, moon, and stars attentively when so placed, they could not have failed to discover the peculiarity. Probably, however, though they noted the time of rising and setting of the celestial bodies, they only made instrumental observations upon them when these bodies were high in the heavens. Thus they remained ignorant of the refractive powers of the air.[1] Now, if they had determined the position of the thirtieth parallel of latitude by observations of the noonday sun (in spring or autumn), then since, owing to refraction, they would have judged the sun to be higher than he really was, it follows that they would have supposed the latitude of any station from which they observed to be lower than it really was. For the lower the latitude the higher is the noonday sun at any given season. Thus, when really in latitude 30° they would have supposed themselves in a latitude lower than 30°, and would have travelled a little farther north to find the proper place, as they would have supposed, for erecting the great pyramid. On the other hand, if they determined the place from observations of the movements of stars near the pole of the heavens, they would make an error of a precisely opposite nature. For the higher the latitude the higher is the pole of the heavens; and refraction, therefore, which apparently raises the pole of the heavens, gives to a station the appearance of being in a higher latitude than it really is, so that the observer

[1] Even that skilful astronomer Hipparchus, who may be justly called the father of observational astronomy, overlooked this peculiarity, which Ptolemy would seem to have been the first to recognise.

would consider he was in latitude 30 north when in reality somewhat south of that latitude. We have only then to inquire whether the great pyramid was set north or south of latitude 30°, to ascertain whether the pyramid architects observed the noonday sun or circumpolar stars to determine their latitude; always assuming (as we reasonably may) that those architects did propose to set the pyramid in that particular latitude, and that they were able to make very accurate observations of the apparent positions of the celestial bodies, but that they were not acquainted with the refractive effects of the atmosphere. The answer comes in no doubtful terms. The centre of the great pyramid's base lies about one mile and a third *south* of the thirtieth parallel of latitude; and from this position the pole of the heavens, as raised by refraction, would appear to be very near indeed to the required position. In fact, if the pyramid had been set about half a mile still farther south the pole would have *seemed* just right.

Of course, such an explanation as I have here suggested appears altogether heretical to the pyramidalists. According to them the pyramid architects knew perfectly well where the true thirtieth parallel lay, and knew also all that modern science has discovered about refraction; but set the pyramid south of the true parallel and north of the position where refraction would just have made the apparent elevation of the pole correct, simply in order that the pyramid might correspond as nearly as possible to each of two conditions, whereof both could not be fulfilled at once. The pyramid would indeed, they say, have been set even more closely midway between the true and the apparent parallels of 30° north, but that the Jeezeh hill on which it is set does not afford a rock foundation any farther north. 'So very close,' says Professor Smyth, 'was the great pyramid placed to the northern brink of its hill, that the edges of the cliff might have broken off under the terrible pressure had not the builders banked up there most firmly the immense mounds of rubbish which came from their work, and which Strabo looked so particularly for 1800 years ago, but could not find. Here they were, however, and still are, utilised in enabling the great pyramid to stand on the very utmost verge of its commanding hill, within the limits of the *two* required latitudes, as well as over the centre of the land's physical and radial formation, and at the same time on the sure and proverbially wise foundation of rock.'

The next circumstance to be noted in the position of the great pyramid (as of all the pyramids) is that the sides are carefully oriented. This, like the approximation to a particular latitude, must be regarded as an astronomical rather than a geographical relation. The accuracy with which the orientation has been effected will serve to show how far the builders had mastered the methods of astronomical observation by which orientation was to be secured. The problem was not so simple as might be supposed by those who are not acquainted with the way in which the cardinal points are correctly determined. By solar observations, or rather by the observations of shadows cast by vertical shafts before and after noon, the direction of the meridian, or north and south line, can theoretically be ascertained. But probably in this case, as in determining the latitude, the builders took the stars for their guide. The pole of the heavens would mark the true north; and equally the pole-star, when below or above the pole, would give the true north, but, of course, most conveniently when below the pole. Nor is it difficult to see how the builders would make use of the pole-star for this purpose. From the middle of the northern side of the intended base they would bore a slant passage tending always from the posision of the pole-star at its lower meridional passage, that star at each successive return to that position serving to direct their progress; while its small range, east and west of the pole, would enable them most accurately to determine the star's true mid-point below the pole; that is, the true north. When they had thus obtained a slant tunnel pointing truly to the meridian, and had carried it down to a point nearly below the middle of the proposed square base, they could, from the middle of the base, bore vertically downwards, until by rough calculation they were near the lower end of the slant tunnel; or both tunnels could be made at the same time. Then a subterranean chamber would be opened out from the slant tunnel. The vertical boring, which need not be wider than necessary to allow a plumb-line to be suspended down it, would enable the architects to determine the point vertically below the point of suspension. The slant tunnel would give the direction of the true north, either from that point or from a point at some known small distance east or west of that point.[1] Thus, a line from some ascertained point near the mouth of the vertical boring to the mouth of the slant tunnel would lie due north and south, and serve as the required guide for the orientation of the pyramid's base. If this base extended beyond the opening of the slant tunnel, then, by continuing this tunnelling through the base tiers of the pyramid, the means would be obtained of correcting the orientation.

This, I say, would be the course naturally suggested to

[1] It would only be by a lucky accident, of course, that the direction of the slant tunnel's axis and that of the vertical from the selected central point would lie in the same vertical plane. The object of the tunnelling would, in fact, be to determine how far apart the vertical planes through these points lay, and the odds would be great against the result proving to be zero.

astronomical architects who had determined the latitude in the manner described above. It may even be described as the only very accurate method available before the telescope had been invented. So that if the accuracy of the orientation appears to be greater than could be obtained by the shadow method, the natural inference, even in the absence of corroborative evidence, would be that the stellar method, and no other, had been employed. Now, in 1779, Nouet, by refined observations, found the error of orientation measured by less than 20 minutes of arc, corresponding roughly to a displacement of the corners by about 37½ inches from their true position, as supposed to be determined from the centre; or to a displacement of a southern corner by 53 inches on an east and west line from a point due south of the corresponding northern corner. This error, for a base length of 9140 inches, would not be serious, being only one inch in about five yards (when estimated in the second way). Yet the result is not quite worthy of the praise given to it by Professor Smyth. He himself, however, by much more exact observations, with an excellent altazimuth, reduced the alleged error from 20 minutes to only 4½, or to 9-40ths of its formerly supposed value. This made the total displacement of a southern corner from the true meridian through the corresponding northern corner, almost exactly one foot, or one inch in about twenty-one yards—a degree of accuracy rendering it practically certain that some stellar method was used in orienting the base.

Now there *is* a slanting tunnel occupying precisely the position of the tunnel which should, according to this view, have been formed in order accurately to orient the pyramid's base, assuming that the time of the building of the pyramid corresponded with one of the epochs when the star Alpha Draconis was distant 3° 42′ from the pole of the heavens. In other words, there is a slant tunnel directed northwards nd upwards from a point deep down below the middle of the pyramid's base, and inclined 26° 17′ to the horizon, the elevation of Alpha Draconis at its lower culmination when 3° 42′ from the pole. The last epoch when the star was thus placed was *circiter* 2160 B.C.; the epoch next before that was 3440 B.C. Between these two we should have to choose, on the hypothesis that the slant tunnel was really directed to that star when the foundations of the pyramid were laid. For the next epoch before the earlier of the two named was about 28,000 B.C., and the pyramid's date cannot have been more remote than 4000 B.C.

The slant tunnel, while admirably fulfilling the requirements suggested, seems altogether unsuited for any other. Its transverse height (that is, its width in a direction perpendicular to its upper and lower faces) did not amount to quite four feet; its breadth was not quite three feet and a half. It was, therefore, not well fitted for an entrance passage to the subterranean chamber immediately under the apex of the pyramid (with which chamber it communicates in the manner suggested by the above theory). It could not have been intended to be used for observing meridian transits of the stars in order to determine sidereal time; for close circumpolar stars, by reason of their slow motion, are the least suited of all for such a purpose. As Professor Smyth says, in arguing against this suggested use of the star, 'no observer in his senses, in any existing observatory, when seeking to obtain the time, would observe the transit of a circumpolar star for anything else than *to get the direction of the meridian to adjust his instrument by.*' (The italics are his.) It is precisely such a purpose (the adjustment, however, not of an instrument, but of the entire structure of the pyramid itself), that I have suggested for this remarkable passage—this 'cream-white, stone-lined, long tube,' where it traverses the masonry of the pyramid, and below that dug through the solid rock to a distance of more than 350 feet.

Let us next consider the dimensions of the square base thus carefully placed in latitude 30° north to the best of the builders' power, with sides carefully oriented.

It seems highly probable that, whatever special purpose the pyramid was intended to fulfil, a subordinate idea of the builders would have been to represent symbolically in the proportions of the building such mathematical and astronomical relations as they were acquainted with. From what we know by tradition of the men of the remote time when the pyramid was built, and what we can infer from the ideas of those who inherited, however remotely, the modes of thought of the earliest astronomers and mathematicians, we can well believe that they would look with superstitious reverence on special figures, proportions, numbers, and so forth. Apart from this, they may have had a quasi-scientific desire to make a lasting record of their discoveries, and of the collected knowledge of their time.

It seems altogether probable, then, that the smaller unit of measurement used by the builders of the great Pyramid was intended, as Professor Smyth thinks, to be equal to the 500,000,000th part of the earth's diameter, determined from their geodetical observations. It was perfectly within the power of mechanicians and mathematicians so experienced as they undoubtedly were—the pyramid attests so much—to measure with considerable accuracy the length of a degree of latitude. They could not possibly (always setting aside the theory of divine inspiration) have known anything about the compression of the earth's globe, and therefore could not have intended, as Professor Smyth supposes, to have had the 500,000,000th part of the earth's polar axis, as distinguished from any other, for their unit of length. But if they made observations in or near latitude 30° north on the supposition that the earth is a globe, their probable error would exceed the difference even between the earth's polar and equatorial diameters. Both differences are largely exceeded by the range of difference among the estimates of the actual length of the sacred cubit, supposed to have contained twenty-five of these smaller units. And, again, the length of the pyramid base-side, on which Smyth bases his own estimate of the sacred cubit, has been variously estimated, the largest measure being 9168 inches, and the lowest 9110 inches. The fundamental theory of the pyramidalists, that the sacred cubit was exactly one 20,000,000th part of the earth's polar diameter, and that the side of the base contained as many cubits and parts of a cubit as there are days and parts of a day in the tropical year (or year of seasons), requires that the length of the side should be 9140 inches, lying between the limits indicated, but still so widely removed from either that it would appear very unsafe to base a theory on the supposition that the exact length is or was 9140 inches. If the measures 9168 inches and 9110 inches were inferior, and several excellent measures made by practised observers ranged around the length 9140 inches, the case would be different. But the best recent measures gave respectively 9110 and 9130 inches; and Smyth exclaims against the unfairness of Sir H. James in taking 9120 as 'therefore the [probable] true length of the side of the great pyramid when perfect,' calling this 'a dishonourable shelving of the honourable older observers with their larger results.' The only other measures, besides these two, are two by Colonel Howard Vyse and by the French *savants*, giving respectively 9168 and 9163·44 inches. The pyramidalists consider 9140 inches a fair mean value from these four. The natural inference, however, is, that the pyramid base is not now in a condition to be satisfactorily measured; and assuredly no such reliance can be placed on the mean value 9140 inches that, on the strength of it, we should believe what otherwise would be utterly incredible, viz. that the builders of the great pyramid knew 'both the size and shape of the earth exactly.' 'Humanly, or by human science, finding it out in that age was, of course, utterly impossible,' says Professor Smyth. But he is so confident of the average value derived from widely conflicting base measures as to assume that this value, not being humanly discoverable, was of necessity 'attributable to God and to His Divine inspiration.' We may agree, in fine, with Smyth, that the builders of the pyramid knew the earth to be a globe; that they took for their measure of length the sacred cubit, which, by their earth measures, they made very fairly approximate to the 20,000,000th part of the earth's mean diameter; but there seems no reason whatever for supposing (even if the supposition were not antecedently of its very nature inadmissible) that they knew anything about the compression of the earth, or that they had measured a degree of latitude in their own place with very wonderful accuracy.[1]

[1] It may, perhaps, occur to the reader to inquire what diameter of the earth, supposed to be a perfect sphere, would be derived from a degree of latitude measured with absolute accuracy near latitude 30°. A degree of latitude measured in polar regions would indicate a diameter greater even than the equatorial; one measured in equatorial regions would indicate a diameter less even than the polar. Near latitude 30° the measurement of a degree of latitude would indicate a diameter very nearly equal to the true polar diameter of the earth. In fact, if it could be proved that the builders of the pyramid used for their unit of length an exact subdivision of the polar diameter, the inference would be that, while the coincidence itself was merely accidental, their measurement of a degree of latitude in their own country had been singularly accurate. By an approximate calculation I find that, taking the earth's compression at 1-300, the diameter of the earth, estimated from the accurate measurement of a degree of latitude in the neighbourhood of the great pyramid, would have made the

But here a very singular coincidence may be noticed, or, rather, is forced upon our notice by the pyramidalists, who strangely enough recognise in it fresh evidence of design, while the unbeliever finds in it proof that coincidences are no sure evidence of design. The side of the pyramid containing 365¼ times the sacred cubit of 25 pyramid inches, it follows that the diagonal of the base contains 12,912 such inches, and the two diagonals together contain 25,824 pyramid inches, or almost exactly as many inches as there are years in the great precessional period. 'No one whatever amongst men,' says Professor Smyth after recording various estimates of the precessional period, 'from his own or school knowledge, knew anything about such a phenomenon, until Hipparchus, some 1900 years after the great pyramid's foundation, had a glimpse of the fact; and yet it had been ruling the heavens for ages, and was recorded in Jeezeh's ancient structure.' To minds not moved to most energetic forgetfulness by the spirit of faith, it would appear that when a square base had been decided upon, and its dimensions fixed, with reference to the earth's diameter and the year, the diagonals of the square base were determined also; and, if it so chanced that they corresponded with some other perfectly independent relation, the fact was not to be credited to the architects. Moreover it is manifest that the closeness of such a coincidence suggests grave doubts how far other coincidences can be relied upon as evidence of design. It seems, for instance, altogether likely that the architects of the pyramid took the sacred cubit equal to one 20,000,000th part of the earth's diameter for their chief unit of length, and intentionally assigned to the side of the pyramid's square base a length

sacred cubit—taken at one 20,000,000th of the diameter—equal to 24·98 British inches; a closer approximation than Professor Smyth's to the estimated mean probable value of the sacred cubit.

of just so many cubits as there are days in the year; and the closeness of the coincidence between the measured length and that indicated by this theory strengthens the idea that this was the builder's purpose. But when we find that an even closer coincidence immediately presents itself, which manifestly is a coincidence *only*, the force of the evidence before derived from mere coincidence is *pro tanto* shaken. For consider what this new coincidence really means. Its nature may be thus indicated: Take the number of days in the year, multiply that number by 50, and increase the result in the same degree that the diagonal of a square exceeds the side—then the resulting number represents very approximately the number of years in the great precessional period. The error, according to the best modern estimates, is about one 575th part of the true period. This is, of course, a merely accidental coincidence, for there is no connection whatever in nature between the earth's period of rotation, the shape of a square, and the earth's period of gyration. Yet this merely accidental coincidence is very much closer than the other supposed to be designed could be proved to be. It is clear, then, that mere coincidence is a very unsafe evidence of design.

Of course the pyramidalists find a ready reply to such reasoning. They argue that, in the first place, it may have been by express design that the period of the earth's rotation was made to bear this particular relation to the period of gyration in the mighty precessional movement: which is much as though one should say that by express design the height of Monte Rosa contains as many feet as there are miles in the 6000th part of the sun's distance.[1] Then,

[1] It is, however, almost impossible to mark any limits to what may be regarded as evidence of design by a coincidence-hunter. I quote the following from the late Professor De Morgan's *Budget of Paradoxes*. Having mentioned that 7 occurs less frequently than any other digit

they urge, the architects were not bound to have a square base for the pyramid; they might have had an oblong or a triangular base, and so forth—all which accords very ill with the enthusiastic language in which the selection of a square base had on other accounts been applauded.

Next let us consider the height of the pyramid. According to the best modern measurements, it would seem that the height when (if ever) the pyramid terminated above in a pointed apex, must have been about 486 feet. And from the comparison of the best estimates of the base side with the best estimates of the height, it seems very likely indeed that the intention of the builders was to make the height bear to the perimeter of the base the same ratio which the radius of a circle bears to the circumference. Remembering the range of difference in the base measures it might be supposed that the exactness of the approximation to this ratio could not be determined very satisfactorily. But as certain casing stones have been discovered which indicate with considerable exactness the slope of the original plane-surfaces of the pyramid, the ratio of the height to the side of the base may be regarded as much more satisfactorily determined than the actual value of either dimension. Of

in the number expressing the ratio of circumference to diameter of a circle, he proceeds: 'A correspondent of my friend Piazzi Smyth notices that 3 is the number of most frequency, and that $3\frac{1}{7}$ is the nearest approximation to it in simple digits. Professor Smyth, whose work on Egypt is paradox of a very high order, backed by a great quantity of useful labour, the results of which will be made available by those who do not receive the paradoxes, is inclined to see confirmation for some of his theory in these phenomena.' In passing, I may mention as the most singular of these accidental digit relations which I have yet noticed, that in the first 110 digits of the square root of 2, the number 7 occurs more than twice as often as either 5 or 9, which each occur eight times, 1 and 2 occurring each nine times, and 7 occurring no less than eighteen times.

course the pyramidalists claim a degree of precision indicating a most accurate knowledge of the ratio between the diameter and the circumference of a circle; and the angle of the only casing stone measured being diversely estimated at 51° 50′ and 51° 52¼′, they consider 50° 51′ 14·3″ the true value, and infer that the builders regarded the ratio as 3·14159 to 1. The real fact is, that the modern estimates of the dimensions of the casing stones (which, by the way, ought to agree better if these stones are as well made as stated) indicate the values 3·1439228 and 3·1396740 for the ratio; and all we can say is, that the ratio really used lay *probably* between these limits, though it may have been outside either. Now the approximation of either is not remarkably close. It requires no mathematical knowledge at all to determine the circumference of a circle much more exactly. 'I thought it very strange,' wrote a circle-squarer once to De Morgan (*Budget of Paradoxes*, p. 389), 'that so many great scholars in all ages should have failed in finding the true ratio, and have been determined to try myself.' 'I have been informed,' proceeds De Morgan, 'that this trial makes the diameter to the circumference as 64 to 201, giving the ratio equal to 3·1410625 exactly. The result was obtained by the discoverer in three weeks after he first heard of the existence of the difficulty. This quadrator has since published a little slip and entered it at Stationers' Hall. He says he has done it by actual measurement; and I hear from a private source that he uses a disc of twelve inches diameter which he rolls upon a straight rail.' The 'rolling is a very creditable one; it is as much below the mark as Archimedes was above it. Its performer is a joiner who evidently knows well what he is about when he measures; he is not wrong by 1 in 3000.' Such skilful mechanicians as the builders of the pyramid could have obtained a closer approximation still by mere measurement. Besides, as they were manifestly mathematicians, such an approximation as was obtained by Archimedes must have been well within their power; and that approximation lies well within the limits above indicated. Professor Smyth remarks that the ratio was 'a quantity which men in general, and all human science too, did not begin to trouble themselves about until long, long ages, languages, and nations had passed away after the building of the great pyramid; and after the sealing up, too, of that grand primeval and prehistoric monument of the patriarchal age of the earth according to Scripture.' I do not know where the Scripture records the sealing up of the great pyramid; but it is all but certain that during the very time when the pyramid was being built astronomical observations were in progress which, for their interpretation, involved of necessity a continual reference to the ratio in question. No one who considers the wonderful accuracy with which, nearly two thousand years before the Christian era, the Chaldæans had determined the famous cycle of the Saros, can doubt that they must have observed the heavenly bodies for several centuries before they could have achieved such a success; and the study of the motions of the celestial bodies compels 'men to trouble themselves' about the famous ratio of the circumference to the diameter.

We now come upon a new relation (contained in the dimensions of the pyramid as thus determined) which, by a strange coincidence, causes the height of the pyramid to appear to symbolise the distance of the sun. There were 5813 pyramid inches, or 5819 British inches, in the height of the pyramid according to the relations already indicated. Now, in the sun's distance, according to an estimate recently adopted and freely used,[1] there are 91,400,000 miles or

[1] I have substituted this value in the article 'Astronomy,' of the *British Encyclopædia*, for the estimate formerly used, viz. 95,233,055

5791 thousand millions of inches—that is, there are approximately as many thousand millions of inches in the sun's distance as there are inches in the height of the pyramid. If we take the relation as exact we should infer for the sun's distance 5819 thousand millions of inches, or 91,840,000 miles—an immense improvement on the estimate which for so many years occupied a place of honour in our books of astronomy. Besides, there is strong reason for believing that, when the results of recent observations are worked out, the estimated sun distance will be much nearer this pyramid value than even to the value 91,400,000 recently adopted. This result, which one would have thought so damaging to faith in the evidence from coincidence—nay, quite fatal after the other case in which a close coincidence had appeared by merest accident—is regarded by the pyramidalist as a perfect triumph for their faith.

They connect it with another coincidence, viz. that, assuming the height determined in the way already indicated, then it so happens that the height bears to half a diagonal of the base the ratio 9 to 10. Seeing that the perimeter of the base symbolises the annual motion of the earth round the sun, while the height represents the radius of a circle with that perimeter, it follows that the height should symbolise the sun's distance. 'That line, further,' says Professor Smyth (speaking on behalf of Mr. W. Petrie, the discoverer of this relation), 'must represent' this radius 'in the proportion of 1 to 1,000,000,000' (or *ten* raised to power *nine*), 'because amongst other reasons 10 to 9 is practically the shape of the great pyramid.' For this building 'has such an angle at the corners, that for every ten units its structure advances inwards on the diagonal of the base, it practically

miles. But there is good reason for believing that the actual distance is nearly 92,000,000 miles.

rises upwards, or points to sunshine' (*sic*) 'by *nine*. Nine, too, out of the ten characteristic parts (viz. five angles and five sides) being the number of those parts which the sun shines on in such a shaped pyramid, in such a latitude near the equator, out of a high sky, or, as the Peruvians say, when the sun sets on the pyramid with all its rays.' The coincidence itself on which this perverse reasoning rests is a singular one—singular, that is, as showing how close an accidental coincidence may run. It amounts to this, that if the number of days in the year be multiplied by 100, and a circle be drawn with a circumference containing 100 times as many inches as there are days in the year, the radius of the circle will be very nearly one 1,000,000,000th part of the sun's distance. Remembering that the pyramid inch is assumed to be one 500,000,000th part of the earth's diameter, we shall not be far from the truth in saying that, as a matter of fact, the earth by her orbital motion traverses each day a distance equal to two hundred times her own diameter. But, of course, this relation is altogether accidental. It has no real cause in nature.[1]

Such relations show that mere numerical coincidences, however close, have little weight as evidence, except where

[1] It may be matched by other coincidences as remarkable and as little the result of the operation of any natural law. For instance, the following strange relation, introducing the dimensions of the sun himself, nowhere, so far as I have yet seen, introduced among pyramid relations, even by pyramidalists: 'If the plane of the ecliptic were a true surface, and the sun were to commence rolling along that surface towards the part of the earth's orbit where she is at her mean distance, while the earth commenced rolling upon the sun (round one of his great circles), each globe turning round in the same time,—then, by the time the earth had rolled its way once round the sun, the sun would have almost exactly reached the earth's orbit. This is only another way of saying that the sun's diameter exceeds the earth's in almost exactly the same degree that the sun's distance exceeds the sun's diameter.'

they occur in series. Even then they require to be very cautiously regarded, seeing that the history of science records many instances where the apparent law of a series has been found to be falsified when the theory has been extended. Of course this reason is not quoted in order to throw doubt on the supposition that the height of the pyramid was intended to symbolise the sun's distance. That supposition is simply inadmissible if the hypothesis, according to which the height was already independently determined in another way, is admitted. Either hypothesis might be admitted were we not certain that the sun's distance could not possibly have been known to the builders of the pyramid; or both hypotheses may be rejected: but to admit both is out of the question.

Considering the multitude of dimensions of length, surface, capacity, and position, the great number of shapes, and the variety of material existing within the pyramid, and considering, further, the enormous number of relations (presented by modern science) from among which to choose, can it be wondered at if fresh coincidences are being continually recognised? If a dimension will not serve in one way, use can be found for it in another; for instance, if some measure of length does not correspond closely with any known dimension of the earth or of the solar system (an unlikely supposition), then it can be understood to typify an interval of time. If, even after trying all possible changes of that kind, no coincidence shows itself (which is all but impossible), then all that is needed to secure a coincidence is that the dimensions should be manipulated a little.

Let a single instance suffice to show how the pyramidalists (with perfect honesty of purpose) hunt down a coincidence. The slant tunnel already described has a transverse height, once no doubt uniform, now giving various measures from 47·14 pyramid inches to 47·32 inches, so that the vertical height from the known inclination of the tunnel would be estimated at somewhere between 52.64 inches and 52·85. Neither dimension corresponds very obviously with any measured distance in the earth or solar system. Nor when we try periods, areas, etc., does any very satisfactory coincidence present itself. But the difficulty is easily turned into a new proof of design. Putting all the observations together (says Professor Smyth), 'I deduced 47·24 pyramid inches to be the transverse height of the entrance passage; and computing from thence with the observed angle of inclination the vertical height, that came out 52·76 of the same inches. But the sum of those two heights, or the height taken up and down, equals 100 inches, which length, as elsewhere shown, is the general pyramid linear representation of a day of twenty-four hours. And the mean of the two heights, or the height taken one way only, and impartially to the middle point between them, equals fifty inches; which quantity is, therefore, the general pyramid linear representation of only half a day. In which case, let us ask what the entrance passage has to do with half rather than a whole day?'

On relations such as these, which, if really intended by the architect, would imply an utterly fatuous habit of concealing elaborately what he desired to symbolise, the pyramidalists base their belief that 'a Mighty Intelligence did both think out the plans for it, and compel unwilling and ignorant idolators, in a primal age of the world, to work mightily both for the future glory of the one true God of Revelation, and to establish lasting prophetic testimony touching a further development, still to take place, of the absolutely Divine Christian dispensation.'

III.

THE MYSTERY OF THE PYRAMIDS.

Few subjects of inquiry have proved more perplexing than the question of the purpose for which the pyramids of Egypt were built. Even in the remotest ages of which we have historical record, nothing seems to have been known certainly on this point. For some reason or other, the builders of the pyramids concealed the object of these structures, and this so successfully that not even a tradition has reached us which purports to have been handed down from the epoch of the pyramids' construction. We find, indeed, some explanations given by the earliest historians; but they were professedly only hypothetical, like those advanced in more recent times. Including ancient and modern theories, we find a wide range of choice. Some have thought that these buildings were associated with the religion of the early Egyptians; others have suggested that they were tombs; others, that they combined the purposes of tombs and temples, that they were astronomical observatories, defences against the sands of the Great Desert, granaries like those made under Joseph's direction, places of resort during excessive overflows of the Nile; and many other uses have been suggested for them. But none of these ideas are found on close examination to be tenable as representing the sole purpose of the pyramids, and few of them have strong claims to be regarded as presenting even a chief object of these remarkable structures. The significant and perplexing history of the three oldest pyramids—the Great Pyramid of Cheops, Shofo, or Suphis, the pyramid of Chephren, and the pyramid of Mycerinus; and the most remarkable of all the facts known respecting the pyramids generally, viz., the circumstance that one pyramid after another was built as though each had become useless soon after it was finished, are left entirely unexplained by all the theories above mentioned, save one only, the tomb theory, and that does not afford by any means a satisfactory explanation of the circumstances.

I propose to give here a brief account of some of the most suggestive facts known respecting the pyramids, and, after considering the difficulties which beset the theories heretofore advanced, to indicate a theory (new so far as I know) which seems to me to correspond better with the facts than any heretofore advanced; I suggest it, however, rather for consideration than because I regard it as very convincingly supported by the evidence. In fact, to advance any theory at present with confident assurance of its correctness, would be simply to indicate a very limited acquaintance with the difficulties surrounding the subject.

Let us first consider a few of the more striking facts recorded by history or tradition, noting, as we proceed, whatever ideas they may suggest as to the intended character of these structures.

It is hardly necessary to say, perhaps, that the history of the Great Pyramid is of paramount importance in this inquiry. Whatever purpose pyramids were originally intended to subserve, must have been conceived by the builders of *that* pyramid. New ideas may have been superadded by the builders of later pyramids, but it is unlikely that the original purpose can have been entirely abandoned. Some great purpose there was, which the rulers of ancient Egypt proposed to fulfil by building very massive pyramidal structures on a particular plan. It is by inquiring into the history of the first and most massive of these structures, and by examining its construction, that we shall have the best chance of finding out what that great purpose was.

According to Herodotus, the kings who built the pyramids reigned not more than twenty-eight centuries ago; but there can be little doubt that Herodotus misunderstood the Egyptian priests from whom he derived his information, and that the real antiquity of the pyramid-kings was far greater. He tells us that, according to the Egyptian priests, Cheops 'on ascending the throne plunged into all manner of wickedness. He closed the temples, and forbade the Egyptians to offer sacrifice, compelling them instead to labour one and all in his service, viz., in building the Great Pyramid.' Still following his interpretation of the Egyptian account, we learn that one hundred thousand men were employed for twenty years in building the Great Pyramid, and that ten years were occupied in constructing a causeway by which to convey the stones to the place and in conveying them there. 'Cheops reigned fifty years; and was succeeded by his brother Chephren, who imitated the conduct of his predecessor, built a pyramid—but smaller than his brother's—and reigned fifty-six years. Thus during one hundred and six years, the temples were shut and never opened.' Moreover, Herodotus tells us that 'the Egyptians so detested the memory of these kings, that they do not much like even to mention their names. Hence they commonly call the pyramids after Philition, a shepherd who at that time fed his flocks about the place.' 'After Chephren, Mycerinus, son of Cheops, ascended the throne, he reopened the temples, and allowed the people to resume the practice of sacrifice. He, too, left a pyramid, but much inferior in size to his father's. It is built, for half of its height, of the stone of Ethiopia,' or, as Professor Smyth (whose extracts from Rawlinson's translation I have here followed) adds 'expensive red granite.' 'After Mycerinus, Asychis ascended the throne. He built the eastern gateway of the Temple of Vulcan (Phtha); and, being desirous of eclipsing all his predecessors on the throne, left as a monument of his reign a pyramid of brick.'

This account is so suggestive, as will presently be shown, that it may be well to inquire whether it can be relied on. Now, although there can be no doubt that Herodotus misunderstood the Egyptians in some matters, and in particular as to the chronological order of the dynasties, placing the pyramid kings far too late, yet in other respects he seems not only to have understood them correctly, but also to have received a correct account from them. The order of the kings above named corresponds with the sequence given by Manetho, and also found in monumental and hieroglyphic records. Manetho gives the names Suphis I., Suphis II., and Mencheres, instead of Cheops, Chephren, and Mycerinus; while, according to the modern Egyptologists, Herodotus's Cheops was Shofo, Shufu, or Koufou; Chephren was Shafre, while he was also called Nou-Shofo or Noum-Shufu as the brother of Shofo; and Mycerinus was Menhere or Menkerre. But the identity of these kings is not questioned. As to the true dates there is much doubt, and it is probable that the question will long continue open; but the determination of the exact epochs when the several pyramids were built is not very important in connection with our present inquiry. We may, on the whole, fairly take the points quoted above from Herodotus, and proceed to consider the significance of the narrative, with sufficient confidence that in all essential respects it is trustworthy.

There are several very strange features in the account.

In the first place, it is manifest that Cheops (to call the first king by the name most familiar to the general reader) attached great importance to the building of his pyramid. It has been said, and perhaps justly, that it would be more interesting to know the plan of the architect who devised the pyramid than the purpose of the king who built it. But the two things are closely connected. The architect must have satisfied the king that some highly important purpose in which the king himself was interested, would be subserved by the structure. Whether the king was persuaded to undertake the work as a matter of duty, or only to advance his own interests, may not be so clear. But that the king was most thoroughly in earnest about the work is certain. A monarch in those times would assuredly not have devoted an enormous amount of labour and material to such a scheme unless he was thoroughly convinced of its great importance. That the welfare of his people was not considered by Cheops in building the Great Pyramid is almost equally certain. He might, indeed, have had a scheme for their good which either he did not care to explain to them or which they could not understand. But the most natural inference from the narrative is that his purpose had no reference whatever to their welfare. For though one could understand his own subjects hating him while he was all the time working for their good, it is obvious that his memory would not have been hated if some important good had eventually been gained from his scheme. Many a far-seeing ruler has been hated while living on account of the very work for which his memory has been revered. But the memory of Cheops and his successors was held in detestation.

May we, however, suppose that, though Cheops had not the welfare of his own people in his thoughts, his purpose was nevertheless not selfish, but intended in some way to promote the welfare of the human race? I say his purpose, because, whoever originated the scheme, Cheops carried it out; it was by means of his wealth and through his power that the pyramid was built. This is the view adopted by Professor Piazzi Smyth and others, in our own time, and first suggested by John Taylor. 'Whereas other writers, says Smyth, 'have generally esteemed that the mysterious persons who directed the building of the Great Pyramid (and to whom the Egyptians, in their traditions, and for ages afterwards, gave an immoral and even abominable character) must therefore have been very bad indeed, so that the world at large has always been fond of standing on, kicking, and insulting that dead lion, whom they really knew not; he, Mr. John Taylor, seeing how religiously bad the Egyptians themselves were, was led to conclude, on the contrary, that those *they* hated (and could never sufficiently abuse) might, perhaps, have been pre-eminently good; or were, at all events, of *different religious faith* from themselves.' 'Combining this with certain unmistakable historical facts,' Mr. Taylor deduced reasons for believing that the directors of the building designed to record in its proportions, and in its interior features, certain important religious and scientific truths, not for the people then living, but for men who were to come 4000 years or so after.

I have already considered at length (see the preceding Essay) the evidence on which this strange theory rests. But there are certain matters connecting it with the above narrative which must here be noticed. The mention of the shepherd Philition, who fed his flocks about the place where the Great Pyramid was built, is a singular feature of Herodotus's narrative. It reads like some strange misinterpretation of the story related to him by the Egyptian priests. It is obvious that if the word Philition did not represent a people, but a person, this person must have been very eminent and distinguished—a shepherd-king, not a mere shepherd. Rawlinson, in a note on this portion of the narrative of Herodotus, suggests that Philitis was probably a shepherd-prince from Palestine, perhaps of Philistine descent, 'but so powerful and domineering, that it may be traditions of his oppressions in that earlier age which, mixed up afterwards in the minds of later Egyptians with the evils inflicted on their country by the subsequent shepherds of better known dynasties, lent so much fear to their religious hate of Shepherd times and that name.' Smyth, somewhat modifying this view, and considering certain remarks of Manetho respecting an alleged invasion of Egypt by shepherd-kings, 'men of an ignoble race (from the Egyptian point of view) who had the confidence to invade our country, and easily subdued it to their power without a battle,' comes to the conclusion that some Shemite prince, 'a contemporary of, but rather older than, the Patriarch Abraham,' visited Egypt at this time, and obtained such influence over the mind of Cheops as to persuade him to erect the pyramid. According to Smyth, the prince was no other than Melchizedek, king of Salem, and the influence he exerted was supernatural. With such developments of the theory we need not trouble ourselves. It seems tolerably clear that certain shepherd-chiefs who came to Egypt during Cheops' reign were connected in some way with the designing of the Great Pyramid. It is clear also that they were men of a different religion from the Egyptians, and persuaded Cheops to abandon the religion of his people. Taylor, Smyth, and the Pyramidalists generally, consider this sufficient to prove that the pyramid was erected for some purpose connected with religion. 'The pyramid,' in fine, says Smyth, 'was charged by God's inspired shepherd-prince, in the beginning of human time, to keep a certain message secret and inviolable for 4000 years, and it has done so; and in the next thousand years it was to enunciate that message to all men, with more than traditional force, more than all the authenticity of copied manuscripts or reputed history; and that part of the pyramid's usefulness is now beginning.'

There are many very obvious difficulties surrounding this theory; as, for example (i.) the absurd waste of power in setting supernatural machinery at work 4000 years ago with cumbrous devices to record its object, when the same machinery, much more simply employed now, would effect the alleged purpose far more thoroughly; (ii.) the enormous amount of human misery and its attendant hatreds brought about by this alleged divine scheme; and (iii.) the futility of an arrangement by which the pyramid was only to subserve its purpose when it had lost that perfection of shape on which its entire significance depended, according to the theory itself. But, apart from these, there is a difficulty, nowhere noticed by Smyth or his followers, which is fatal, I conceive, to this theory of the pyramid's purpose. The second pyramid, though slightly inferior to the first in size, and probably far inferior in quality of masonry, is still a structure of enormous dimensions, which must have required many years of labour from tens of thousands of workmen. Now, it seems impossible to explain why Chephren built this second pyramid, if we adopt Smyth's theory respecting the first pyramid. For either Chephren knew the purpose for which the Great Pyramid was built, or he did not know it. If he knew that purpose, and it was that indicated by Smyth, then he also knew that no second pyramid was wanted. On that hypothesis, all the labour bestowed on the second pyramid was wittingly and wilfully wasted. This, of course is incredible. But, on the other hand, if Chephren did not know what was the purpose for which the Great

Pyramid was built, what reason could Chephren have had for building a pyramid at all? The only answer to this question seems to be that Chephren built the second pyramid in hopes of finding out why his brother had built the first, and this answer is simply absurd. It is clear enough that whatever purpose Cheops had in building the first pyramid, Chephren must have had a similar purpose in building the second; and we require a theory which shall at least explain why the first pyramid did not subserve for Chephren the purpose which it subserved or was meant to subserve for Cheops. The same reasoning may be extended to the third pyramid, to the fourth, and in fine to all the pyramids, forty or so in number, included under the general designation of the Pyramids of Ghizeh or Jeezeh. The extension of the principle to pyramids later than the second is especially important as showing that the difference of religion insisted on by Smyth has no direct bearing on the question of the purpose for which the Great Pyramid itself was constructed. For Mycerinus either never left or else returned to the religion of the Egyptians. Yet he also built a pyramid, which, though far inferior in size to the pyramids built by his father and uncle, was still a massive structure, and relatively more costly even than theirs, because built of expensive granite. The pyramid built by Asychis, though smaller still, was remarkable as built of brick; in fact, we are expressly told that Asychis desired to eclipse all his predecessors in such labours, and accordingly left this brick pyramid as a monument of his reign.

We are forced, in fact, to believe that there was some special relation between the pyramid and its builder, seeing that each one of these kings wanted a pyramid of his own. This applies to the Great Pyramid quite as much as to the others, despite the superior excellence of that structure. Or rather, the argument derives its chief force from the superiority of the Great Pyramid. If Chephren, no longer perhaps having the assistance of the shepherd-architects in planning and superintending the work, was unable to construct a pyramid so perfect and so stately as his brother's, the very fact that he nevertheless built a pyramid shows that the Great Pyramid did not fulfil for Chephren the purpose which it fulfilled for Cheops. But, if Smyth's theory were true, the Great Pyramid would have fulfilled finally and for all men the purpose for which it was built. Since this was manifestly not the case, that theory is, I submit, demonstrably erroneous.

It was probably the consideration of this point, viz. that each king had a pyramid constructed for himself, which led to the theory that the pyramids were intended to serve as tombs. This theory was once very generally entertained. Thus we find Humboldt, in his remarks on American pyramids, referring to the tomb theory of the Egyptian pyramids as though it were open to no question. 'When we consider,' he says, 'the pyramidical monuments of Egypt, of Asia, and of the New Continent, from the same point of view, we see that, though their form is alike, their destination was altogether different. The group of pyramids of Ghizeh and at Sakhara in Egypt; the triangular pyramid of the Queen of the Scythians, Zarina, which was a stadium high and three in circumference, and which was decorated with a colossal figure; the fourteen Etruscan pyramids, which are said to have been enclosed in the labyrinth of the king Porsenna, at Clusium—were reared to serve as the sepulchres of the illustrious dead. Nothing is more natural to men than to commemorate the spot where rest the ashes of those whose memory they cherish whether it be, as in the infancy of the race, by simple mounds of earth, or, in later periods, by the towering height of the tumulus. Those of the Chinese and of Thibet have only a few metres of elevation. Farther to the west the dimensions increase; the tumulus of the king Alyattes, father of Crœsus, in Lydia, was six stadia, and that of Ninus was more than ten stadia in diameter. In the north of Europe the sepulchre of the Scandinavian king Gormus and the queen Daneboda, covered with mounds of earth, are three hundred metres broad, and more than thirty high.'

But while we have abundant reason for believing that in Egypt, even in the days of Cheops and Chephren, extreme importance was attached to the character of the place of burial for distinguished persons, there is nothing in what is known respecting earlier Egyptian ideas to suggest the probability that any monarch would have devoted many years of his subjects' labour, and vast stores of material, to erect a mass of masonry like the Great Pyramid, solely to receive his own body after death. Far less have we any reason for supposing that many monarchs in succession would do this, each having a separate tomb built for him. It might have been conceivable, had only the Great Pyramid been erected, that the structure had been raised as a mausoleum for all the kings and princes of the dynasty. But it seems utterly incredible that such a building as the Great Pyramid should have been erected for one king's body only—and that, not in the way described by Humboldt, when he speaks of men commemorating the spot where rest the remains of those whose memory they cherish, but at the expense of the king himself whose body was to be there deposited. Besides, the first pyramid, the one whose history must be regarded as most significant of the true purpose of these buildings, was not built by an Egyptian holding in great favour the special religious ideas of his people, but by one who had adopted other views and those not belonging, so far as can be seen, to a people among whom sepulchral rites were held in exceptional regard.

A still stronger objection against the exclusively tombic theory resides in the fact that this theory gives no account whatever of the characteristic features of the pyramids themselves. These buildings are all, without exception, built on special astronomical principles. Their square bases are so placed as to have two sides lying east and west, and two lying north and south, or, in other words, so that their four faces front the four cardinal points. One can imagine no reason why a tomb should have such a position. It is not, indeed, easy to understand why any building at all, except an astronomical observatory, should have such a position. A temple perhaps devoted to sun-worship, and generally to the worship of the heavenly bodies, might be built in that way. For it is to be noticed that the peculiar figure and position of the pyramids would bring about the following relations :—When the sun rose and set south of the east and west points, or (speaking generally) between the autumn and the spring equinoxes, the rays of the rising and setting sun illuminated the southern face of the pyramid; whereas during the rest of the year, that is, during the six months between the spring and autumn equinoxes, the rays of the rising and setting sun illuminated the northern face. Again, all the year round the sun's rays passed from the eastern to the western face at solar noon. And lastly, during seven months and a half of each year, namely, for three months and three quarters before and after mid-summer, the noon rays of the sun fell on all four faces of the pyramid, or, according to a Peruvian expression (so Smyth avers), the sun shone on the pyramid 'with all his rays.' Such conditions as these might have been regarded as very suitable for a temple devoted to sun-worship. Yet the temple theory is as untenable as the tomb theory. For, in the first place, the pyramid form—as the pyramids were originally built, with perfectly smooth slant-faces, not terraced into steps as now through the loss of the casing-stones—was entirely unsuited for all the ordinary requirements of a temple of worship. And further, this theory gives no explanation of the fact that each king built a pyramid, and each king only one. Similar difficulties oppose the theory that the pyramids were intended to serve as astronomical observatories. For while their original figure, however manifestly astronomical in its relations, was quite unsuited for observatory work, it is manifest that if such had been the purpose of pyramid-building, so soon as the Great Pyramid had once been built, no other would be needed. Certainly none of the pyramids built afterwards could have subserved any astronomical purpose which the first did not subserve, or have subserved nearly so well as the Great Pyramid those purposes (and they are but few) which that building may be supposed to have fulfilled as an astronomical observatory.

Of the other theories mentioned at the beginning of this paper none seem to merit special notice, except perhaps the theory that the pyramids were made to receive the royal treasures, and this theory rather because of the attention it received from Arabian literati, during the ninth and tenth centuries, than because of any strong reasons which can be suggested in its favour. 'Emulating,' says Professor Smyth, 'the enchanted tales of Bagdad,' the court poets of Al Mamoun (son of the far-famed Haroun al Raschid) 'drew gorgeous pictures of the contents of the pyramid's interior. . . . All the treasures of Sheddad Ben Ad the great Antediluvian king of the earth, with all his medicines and all his sciences, they declared were there, told over and over again. Others, though, were positive that the founder-king was no other than Saurid Ibn Salhouk, a far greater one than the other; and these last gave many more minute particulars, some of which are at least interesting to us in the present day, as proving that, amongst the Egypto-

Arabians of more than a thousand years ago, the Jeezeh pyramids, headed by the grand one, enjoyed a pre-eminence of fame vastly before all the other pyramids of Egypt put together; and that if any other is alluded to after the Great Pyramid (which has always been the notable and favourite one, and chiefly was known then as the East pyramid), it is either the second one at Jeezeh, under the name of the West pyramid; or the third one, distinguished as the Coloured pyramid, in allusion to its red granite, compared with the white limestone casings of the other two (which, moreover, from their more near, but by no means exact, equality of size, went frequently under the affectionate designation of "the pair").'

The report of Ibn Abd Alkohm, as to what was to be found in each of these three pyramids, or rather of what, according to him, was put into them originally by King Saurid, runs as follows: 'In the Western pyramid, thirty treasuries filled with store of riches and utensils, and with signatures made of precious stones, and with instruments of iron and vessels of earth, and with arms which rust not, and with glass which might be bended and yet not broken, and with strange spells, and with several kinds of *alakakirs* (magical precious stones) single and double, and with deadly poisons, and with other things besides. He made also in the East' (the Great Pyramid) 'divers celestial spheres and stars, and what they severally operate in their aspects, and the perfumes which are to be used to them, and the books which treat of these matters. He put also into the coloured pyramid the commentaries of the priests in chests of black marble, and with every priest a book, in which the wonders of his profession and of his actions and of his nature were written, and what was done in his time, and what is and what shall be from the beginning of time to the end of it.' The rest of this worthy's report relates to certain treasurers placed within these three pyramids to guard their contents, and (like all or most of what I have already quoted) was a work of imagination. Ibn Abd Alkohm, in fact, was a romancist of the first water.

Perhaps the strongest argument against the theory that the pyramids were intended as strongholds for the concealment of treasure, resides in the fact that, search being made, no treasure has been discovered. When the workmen employed by Caliph Al Mamoun, after encountering manifold difficulties, at length broke their way into the great ascending passage leading to the so-called King's Chamber, they found 'a right noble apartment, thirty-four feet long, seventeen broad, and nineteen high, of polished red granite throughout, walls, floor, and ceiling, in blocks squared and true, and put together with such exquisite skill that the joints are barely discernible to the closest inspection. But where is the treasure—the silver and the gold, the jewels, medicines, and arms?—These fanatics look wildly around them, but can see nothing, not a single *dirhem* anywhere. They trim their torches, and carry them again and again to every part of that red-walled, flinty hall, but without any better success. Nought but pure polished red granite, in mighty slabs, looks upon them from every side. The room is clean, garnished too, as it were, and, according to the ideas of its founders, complete and perfectly ready for its visitors so long expected, so long delayed. But the gross minds who occupy it now, find it all barren, and declare that there is nothing whatever for them in the whole extent of the apartment from one end to another; nothing except an empty stone chest without a lid.'

It is, however, to be noted that we have no means of learning what had happened between the time when the pyramid was built and when Caliph Al Mamoun's workmen broke their way into the King's Chamber. The place may, after all, have contained treasures of some kind; nor, indeed, is it incompatible with other theories of the pyramid to suppose that it was used as a safe receptacle for treasures. It is certain, however, that this cannot have been the special purpose for which the pyramids were designed. We should find in such a purpose no explanation whatever of any of the most stringent difficulties encountered in dealing with other theories. There could be no reason why strangers from the East should be at special pains to instruct an Egyptian monarch how to hide and guard his treasures. Nor, if the Great Pyramid had been intended to receive the treasures of Cheops, would Chephren have built another for his own treasures, which must have included those gathered by Cheops. But, apart from this, how inconceivably vast must a treasure-hoard be supposed to be, the safe guarding of which would have repaid the enormous cost of the great Pyramid in labour and material! And then, why should a mere treasure-house have the characteristics of an astronomical observatory? Manifestly, if the pyramids were used at all to receive treasures, it can only have been as an entirely subordinate though perhaps convenient means of utilising these gigantic structures.

Having thus gone through all the suggested purposes of the pyramids save two or three which clearly do not possess any claim to serious consideration, and having found none which appear to give any sufficient account of the history and principal features of these buildings, we must either abandon the inquiry or seek for some explanation quite different from any yet suggested. Let us consider what are the principal points of which the true theory of the pyramids should give an account.

In the first place, the history of the pyramids shows that the erection of the first great pyramid was in all probability either suggested to Cheops by wise men who visited

Egypt from the East, or else some important information conveyed to him by such visitors caused him to conceive the idea of building the pyramid. In either case we may suppose, as the history indeed suggests, that these learned men, whoever they may have been, remained in Egypt to superintend the erection of the structure. It may be that the architectural work was not under their supervision; in fact, it seems altogether unlikely that shepherd-rulers would have much to teach the Egyptians in the matter of architecture. But the astronomical peculiarities which form so significant a feature of the Great Pyramid were probably provided for entirely under the instructions of the shepherd chiefs who had exerted so strange an influence upon the mind of King Cheops.

Next, it seems clear that self-interest must have been the predominant reason in the mind of the Egyptian king for undertaking this stupendous work. It is true that his change of religion implies that some higher cause influenced him. But a ruler who could inflict such grievous burdens on his people in carrying out his purpose that for ages afterwards his name was held in utter detestation, cannot have been solely or even chiefly influenced by religious motives. It affords an ample explanation of the behaviour of Cheops, in closing the temples and forsaking the religion of his country, to suppose that the advantages which he hoped to secure by building the pyramid depended in some way on his adopting this course. The visitors from the East may have refused to give their assistance on any other terms, or may have assured him that the expected benefit could not be obtained if the pyramid were erected by idolaters. It is certain, in any case, that they were opposed to idolatry; and we have thus some means of inferring who they were and whence they came. We know that one particular branch of one particular race in the East was characterised by a most marked hatred of idolatry in all its forms. Terah and his family, or, probably, a sect or division of the Chaldæan people, went forth from Ur of the Chaldees, to go into the land of Canaan—and the reason why they went forth we learn from a book of considerable historical interest (the book of Judith) to have been because 'they would not worship the gods of their fathers who were in the land of the Chaldæans.' The Bible record shows that members of this branch of the Chaldæan people visited Egypt from time to time. They were shepherds, too, which accords well with the account of Herodotus above quoted. We can well understand that persons of this family would have resisted all endeavours to secure their acquiescence in any scheme associated with idolatrous rites. Neither promises nor threats would have had much influence on them. It was a distinguished member of the family, the patriarch Abraham, who said: 'I have lift up mine hand unto the Lord, the most high God, the possessor of heaven and earth, that I will not take from a thread even to a shoe-latchet, and that I will not take anything that is thine, lest thou shouldest say, I have made Abram rich.' Vain would all the promises and all the threats of Cheops have been to men of this spirit. Such men might help him in his plans, suggested, as the history shows, by teachings of their own, but it must be on their own conditions, and those conditions would most certainly include the utter rejection of idolatrous worship by the king in whose behalf they worked, as well as by all who shared in their labours. It seems probable that they convinced both Cheops and Chephren, that unless these kings gave up idolatry, the purpose, whatever it was, which the pyramid was erected to promote, would not be fulfilled. The mere fact that the Great Pyramid was built either directly at the suggestion of these visitors, or because they had persuaded Cheops of the truth of some important doctrine, shows that they must have gained great influence over his mind. Rather we may say that he must have been so convinced of their knowledge and power as to have accepted with unquestioning confidence all that they told him respecting the particular subject over which they seemed to possess so perfect a mastery.

But having formed the opinion, on grounds sufficiently assured, that the strangers who visited Egypt and superintended the building of the Great Pyramid were kinsmen of the patriarch Abraham, it is not very difficult to decide what was the subject respecting which they had such exact information. They or their parents had come from the land of the Chaldæans, and they were doubtless learned in all the wisdom of their Chaldæan kinsmen. They were masters, in fact, of the astronomy of their day, a science for which the Chaldæans had shown from the earliest ages the most remarkable aptitude. What the actual extent of their astronomical knowledge may have been it would be difficult to say. But it is certain, from the exact knowledge which later Chaldæans possessed respecting long astronomical cycles, that astronomical observations must have been carried on continuously by that people for many hundreds of years. It is highly probable that the astronomical knowledge of the Chaldæans in the days of Terah and Abraham was much more accurate than that possessed by the Greeks even after the time of Hipparchus.[1] We see

[1] It has been remarked that, though Hipparchus had the enormous advantage of being able to compare his own observations with those recorded by the Chaldæans, he estimated the length of the year less correctly than the Chaldæans. It has been thought by some that the Chaldæans were acquainted with the true system of the universe, but I do not know that there are sufficient grounds for this supposition.

indeed, in the accurate astronomical adjustment of the Great Pyramid, that the architects must have been skilful astronomers and mathematicians; and I may note here, in passing, how strongly this circumstance confirms the opinion that the visitors were kinsmen of Terah and Abraham. All we know from Herodotus and Manetho, all the evidence from the circumstances connected with the religion of the pyramid-kings, and the astronomical evidence given by the pyramids themselves, tends to assure us that members of that particular branch of the Chaldæan family which went out from Ur of the Chaldees because they would not worship the gods of the Chaldæans, extended their wanderings to Egypt, and eventually superintended the erection of the Great Pyramid so far as astronomical and mathematical relations were concerned.

But not only have we already decided that the pyramids were not intended solely or chiefly to subserve the purpose of astronomical observatories, but it is certain that Cheops would not have been personally much interested in any astronomical information which these visitors might be able to communicate. Unless he saw clearly that something was to be gained from the lore of his visitors, he would not have undertaken to erect any astronomical buildings at their suggestion, even if he had cared enough for their knowledge to pay any attention to them whatever. Most probably the reply Cheops would have made to any communications respecting mere astronomy, would have run much in the style of the reply made by the Turkish Cadi, Imaum Ali Zadè to a friend of Layard's who had apparently bored him about double stars and comets: 'Oh my

Diodorus Siculus and Apollonius Myndius mention, however, that they were able to predict the return of comets, and this implies that their observations had been continued for many centuries with great care and exactness.

soul! oh my lamb!' said Ali Zadè, 'seek not after the things which concern thee not. Thou camest unto us, and we welcomed thee: go in peace. Of a truth thou hast spoken many words; and there is no harm done, for the speaker is one and the listener is another. After the fashion of thy people thou hast wandered from one place to another until thou art happy and content in none. Listen, oh my son! There is no wisdom equal unto the belief in God! He created the world, and shall we liken ourselves unto Him in seeking to penetrate into the mysteries of His creation? Shall we say, Behold this star spinneth round that star, and this other star with a tail goeth and cometh in so many years! Let it go! He from whose hand it came will guide and direct it. But thou wilt say unto me, Stand aside, oh man, for I am more learned than thou art, and have seen more things. If thou thinkest that thou art in this respect better than I am, thou art welcome. I praise God that I seek not that which I require not. Thou art learned in the things I care not for; and as for that which thou hast seen, I defile it. Will much knowledge create thee a double belly, or wilt thou seek paradise with thine eyes?' Such, omitting the references to the Creator, would probably have been the reply of Cheops to his visitors, had they only had astronomical facts to present him with. Or, in the plenitude of his kingly power, he might have more decisively rejected their teaching by removing their heads.

But the shepherd-astronomers had knowledge more attractive to offer than a mere series of astronomical discoveries. Their ancestors had

> Watched from the centres of their sleeping flocks
> Those radiant Mercuries, that seemed to move
> Carrying through æther in perpetual round
> Decrees and resolutions of the gods;

and though the visitors of King Cheops had themselves rejected the Sabaistic polytheism of their kinsmen, they had not rejected the doctrine that the stars in their courses affect the fortunes of men. We know that among the Jews, probably the direct descendants of the shepherd-chiefs who visited Cheops, and certainly close kinsmen of theirs, and akin to them also in their monotheism, the belief in astrology was never regarded as a superstition. In fact, we can trace very clearly in the books relating to this people that they believed confidently in the influences of the heavenly bodies. Doubtless the visitors of King Cheops shared the belief of their Chaldæan kinsmen that astrology is a true science, 'founded' indeed (as Bacon expresses their views) 'not in reason and physical contemplations, but in the direct experience and observation of past ages.' Josephus records the Jewish tradition (though not as a tradition but as a fact) that 'our first father, Adam, was instructed in astrology by divine inspiration,' and that Seth so excelled in the science, that, 'foreseeing the Flood and the destruction of the world thereby, he engraved the fundamental principles of his art (astrology) in hieroglyphical emblems, for the benefit of after ages, on two pillars of brick and stone.' He says farther on that the Patriarch Abraham, 'having learned the art in Chaldæa, when he journeyed into Egypt taught the Egyptians the sciences of arithmetic and astrology.' Indeed, the stranger called Philitis by Herodotus may, for aught that appears, have been Abraham himself; for it is generally agreed that the word Philitis indicated the race and country of the visitors, regarded by the Egyptians as of Philistine descent and arriving from Palestine. However, I am in no way concerned to show that the shepherd-astronomers who induced Cheops to build the Great Pyramid were even contemporaries of Abraham and Melchizedek. What seems sufficiently obvious is all that I care to maintain, namely, that these shepherd-astronomers were of Chaldæan birth and training, and therefore astrologers, though, unlike their Chaldæan kinsmen, they rejected Sabaism or star-worship, and taught the belief in one only Deity.

Now, if these visitors were astrologers, who persuaded Cheops, and were honestly convinced themselves, that they could predict the events of any man's life by the Chaldæan method of casting nativities, we can readily understand many circumstances connected with the pyramids which have hitherto seemed inexplicable. The pyramid built by a king would no longer be regarded as having reference to his death and burial, but to his birth and life, though after his death it might receive his body. Each king would require to have his own nativity-pyramid, built with due symbolical reference to the special celestial influences affecting his fortunes. Every portion of the work would have to be carried out under special conditions, determined according to the mysterious influences ascribed to the different planets and their varying positions—

> now high, now low, then hid.
> Progressive, retrograde, or standing still.

If the work had been intended only to afford the means of predicting the king's future, the labour would have been regarded by the monarch as well bestowed. But astrology involved much more than the mere prediction of future events. Astrologers claimed the power of ruling the planets—that is, of course, not of ruling the motions of those bodies, but of providing against evil influences or strengthening good influences which they supposed the celestial orbs to exert in particular aspects. Thus we can understand that while the mere basement layers of the pyramid would have served for the process of casting the royal nativity, with due mystic observances, the further progress of building the pyramid would supply the necessary means and indications for ruling the planets most potent in their influence upon the royal career.

Remembering the mysterious influence which astrologers ascribed to special numbers, figures, positions, and so forth, the care with which the Great Pyramid was so proportioned as to indicate particular astronomical and mathematical relations is at once explained. The four sides of the square base were carefully placed with reference to the cardinal points, precisely like the four sides of the ordinary square scheme of nativity.[1] The eastern side faced the Ascendant, the southern faced the Mid-heaven, the western faced the Descendant, and the northern faced the Imum Cœli. Again, we can understand that the architects would

[1] The language of the modern Zadkiels and Raphaëls, though meaningless and absurd in itself, yet, as assuredly derived from the astrology of the oldest times, may here be quoted. (It certainly was not invented to give support to the theory I am at present advocating.) Thus runs the jargon of the tribe: 'In order to illustrate plainly to the reader what astrologers mean by the "houses of heaven," it is proper for him to bear in mind the four cardinal points. The eastern, facing the rising sun, has at its centre the first grand angle or first house, termed the Horoscope or ascendant. The northern, opposite the region where the sun is at midnight, or the *cusp* of the lower heaven or nadir, is the Imum Cœli, and has at its centre the fourth house. The western, facing the setting sun, has at its centre the third grand angle or seventh house or descendant. And lastly, the southern, facing the noonday sun, has at its centre the astrologer's tenth house, or Mid-heaven, the most powerful angle or house of honour.' 'And although,' proceeds the modern astrologer, 'we cannot in the ethereal blue discern these lines or terminating divisions, both reason and experience assure us that they certainly exist; therefore the astrologer has certain grounds for the choice of his four angular houses' (out of twelve in all) 'which, resembling the palpable demonstration they afford, are in the astral science esteemed the most powerful of the whole.'—Raphaël's *Manual of Astrology*.

have made a circuit of the base correspond in length with the number of days in the year—a relation which, according to Prof. P. Smyth, is fulfilled in this manner, that the four sides contain one hundred times as many pyramid inches as there are days in the year. The pyramid inch, again, is itself mystically connected with astronomical relations, for its length is equal to the five hundred millionth part of the earth's diameter, to a degree of exactness corresponding well with what we might expect Chaldæan astronomers to attain. Prof. Smyth, indeed, believes that it was exactly equal to that proportion of the earth's polar diameter—a view which would correspond with his theory that the architects of the Great Pyramid were assisted by divine inspiration; but what is certainly known about the sacred cubit, which contained twenty-five of these inches, corresponds better with the diameter which the Chaldæan astronomers, if they worked very carefully, would have deduced from observations made in their own country, on the supposition which they would naturally have made that the earth is a perfect globe, not compressed at the poles. It is not indeed at all certain that the sacred cubit bore any reference to the earth's dimensions; but this seems tolerably well made out—that the sacred cubit was about 25 inches in length, and that the circuit of the pyramid's base contained a hundred inches for every day of the year. Relations such as these are precisely what we might expect to find in buildings having an astrological significance. Similarly, it would correspond well with the mysticism of astrology that the pyramid should be so proportioned as to make the height be the radius of a circle whose circumference would equal the circuit of the pyramid's base. Again, that long slant tunnel, leading downwards from the pyramid's northern face, would at once find a meaning in this astrological theory. The slant tunnel pointed to the pole-star of Cheops' time, when due north below the true pole of the heavens. This circumstance had no observational utility. it could afford no indication of time, because a pole-star moves very slowly, and the pole-star of Cheops' day must have been in view through that tunnel for more than an hour at a time. But, apart from the mystical significance which an astrologer would attribute to such a relation, it may be shown that this slant tunnel is precisely what the astrologer would require in order to get the horoscope correctly.

Another consideration remains to be mentioned which, while strengthening the astrological theory of the pyramids, may bring us even nearer to the true aim of those who planned and built these structures.

It is known also that the Chaldæans from the earliest times pursued the study of alchemy in connection with astrology, not hoping to discover the philosopher's stone by chemical investigations alone, but by carrying out such investigations under special celestial influence. The hope of achieving this discovery, by which he would at once have had the means of acquiring illimitable wealth, would of itself account for the fact that Cheops expended so much labour and material in the erection of the Great Pyramid, seeing that, of necessity, success in the search for the philosopher's stone would be a main feature of his fortunes, and would therefore be astrologically indicated in his nativity-pyramid, or perhaps even be secured by following mystical observances proper for ruling his planets.

The elixir of life may also have been among the objects which the builders of the pyramids hoped to discover.

It may be noticed, as a somewhat significant circumstance, that, in the account given by Ibn Abd Alkohm of the contents of the various pyramids, those assigned to the Great Pyramid relate entirely to astrology and associated mysteries. It is, of course, clear that Abd Alkohm drew largely on his imagination. Yet it seems probable that there was also some basis of tradition for his ideas. And certainly one would suppose that, as he assigned a treasurer to the East pyramid ('a statue of black agate, his eyes open and shining, sitting on a throne with a lance'), he would have credited the building with treasure also, had not some tradition taught otherwise. But he says that King Saurid placed in the East pyramid, not treasures, but 'divers celestial spheres and stars, and what they severally operate in their aspects, and the perfumes which are to be used to them, and the books which treat of these matters.'[1]

But, after all, it must be admitted that the strongest evidence in favour of the astrological (and alchemical) theory of the pyramids is to be found in the circumstance that all other theories seem untenable. The pyramids were undoubtedly erected for some purpose which was regarded by their builders as most important. This purpose certainly related to the personal fortunes of the kingly builders. It was worth an enormous outlay of money, labour, and material. This purpose was such, furthermore,

[1] Arabian writers give the following account of Egyptian progress in astrology and the mystical arts: Nacrawasch, the progenitor of Misraim, was the first Egyptian prince, and the first of the magicians who excelled in astrology and enchantment. Retiring into Egypt with his family of eighty persons, he built Essous, the most ancient city of Egypt, and commenced the first dynasty of Misraimitish princes, who excelled as cabalists, diviners, and in the mystic arts generally. The most celebrated of the race were Naerasch, who first represented by images the twelve signs of the zodiac; Gharnak, who openly described the arts before kept secret; Hersall, who first worshipped idols; Sehlouk, who worshipped the sun; Saurid (King Saurid of Ibn Abd Alkohm's account), who erected the first pyramids and invented the magic mirror; and Pharaoh, the last king of the dynasty, whose name was afterwards taken as a kingly title, as Cæsar later became a general imperial title.

that each king required to have his own pyramid. It was in some way associated with astronomy, for the pyramids are built with most accurate reference to celestial aspects. It also had its mathematical and mystical bearings, seeing that the pyramids exhibit mathematical and symbolical peculiarities not belonging to their essentially structural requirements. And lastly, the erection of the pyramids was in some way connected with the arrival of certain learned persons from Palestine, and presumably of Chaldæan origin. All these circumstances accord well with the theory I have advanced; while only some of them, and these not the most characteristic, accord with any of the other theories. Moreover, no fact known respecting the pyramids or their builders is inconsistent with the astrological (and alchemical) theory. On the whole, then, if it cannot be regarded as demonstrated (in its general bearing, of course, for we cannot expect any theory about the pyramids to be established in minute details), the astrological theory may fairly be described as having a greater degree of probability in its favour than any hitherto advanced.

IV.

SWEDENBORG'S VISIONS OF OTHER WORLDS.

IF it were permitted to men to select a sign whereby they should know that a message came from the Supreme Being, probably the man of science would select for the sign the communication of some scientific fact beyond the knowledge of the day, but admitting of being readily put to the test. The evidence thus obtained in favour of a revelation would correspond in some sense to that depending on prophecies; but it would be more satisfactory to men having that particular mental bent which is called the scientific. Whether this turn of mind is inherent or the result of training, it certainly leads men of science to be more exacting in considering the value of evidence than any men, except perhaps lawyers. In the case of the student of science, St. Paul's statement that 'prophecies' 'shall fail' has been fulfilled, whereas it may be doubted whether evidence from 'knowledge' would in like manner 'vanish away.' On the contrary, it would grow stronger and stronger, as knowledge from observation, from experiment, and from calculation continually increased. It can scarcely be said that this has happened with such quasi-scientific statements as have actually been associated with revelation. If we regard St. Paul's reference to knowledge as relating to such statements as these, then nothing could be more complete than the fulfilment of his own prediction, 'Whether there be prophecies, they shall fail; whether there be tongues, they shall cease; whether there be knowledge, it shall vanish away.' The evidence from prophecies fails for the exact inquirer, who perceives the doubts which exist (among the most earnest believers) as to the exact meaning of the prophetic words, and even in some cases as to whether prophecies have been long since fulfilled or relate to events still to come. The evidence from 'tongues' has ceased, and those are dust who are said to have spoken in strange tongues. The knowledge which was once thought supernatural has utterly vanished away. But if, in the ages of faith, some of the results of modern scientific research had been revealed, as the laws of the solar system, the great principle of the conservation of energy, or the wave theory of light, or if some of the questions which still remain for men of science to solve had been answered in those times, the evidence for the student of science would have been irresistible. Of course he will be told that even then he would have hardened his heart; that the inquiry after truth tending naturally to depravity of mind, he would reject even evidence based on his beloved laws of probability; that his 'wicked and adulterous generation seeketh "in vain" after a sign,' and that if he will not accept Moses and the prophets, neither would he believe though one rose from the dead. Still the desire of the student of science to base his faith on convincing evidence (in a matter as important to him as to those who abuse him) does seem to have something reasonable in it after all. The mental qualities which cause him to be less easily satisfied than others, came to him in the same way as his bodily qualities; and even if the result to which his mental training leads him is as unfortunate as some suppose, that training is not strictly speaking so heinously sinful that nothing short of the eternal reprobation meted out to him by earthly judges can satisfy divine justice. So that it may be thought not a wholly unpardonable sin to speak of a sign which, had it been accorded, would have satisfied even the most exacting student of science. Apart, too, from all question of faith, the mere scientific interest of divinely inspired communications respecting natural laws and processes would justify a student of science in regarding them as most desirable messages from a being of superior wisdom and benevolence. If prophecies and tongues, why not knowledge, as evidence of a divine mission?

Such thoughts are suggested by the claim of some religious teachers to the possession of knowledge other than that which they could have gained by natural means. The claim has usually been quite honest. The teacher of religion tests the reality of his mission in simple *à priori* confidence that he has such a mission, and that therefore some one or other of the tests he applies will afford the required evidence. To one, says St. Paul, is given the word of wisdom; to another, the word of knowledge; to another, faith; to another, the gift of healing; to another, the working of miracles; to another prophecy; to another, the discerning of spirits; to another, divers kinds of tongues: and so forth. If a man like Mahomet, who believes in his mission to teach, finds that he cannot satisfactorily work miracles—that mountains will not be removed at his bidding—then some other evidence satisfies him of the reality of his mission. Swedenborg, than whom, perhaps, no more honest man ever lived, said and believed that to him had been granted the discerning of spirits. 'It is to be observed,' he said, 'that a man may be instructed by spirits and angels if his interiors be so open as to enable him to speak and be in company with them, for man in his essence is a spirit, and is with spirits as to his interiors; so that he whose interiors are opened by the Lord may converse with them, as man with man. *This privilege I have enjoyed daily now for twelve years.*'

It indicates the fulness of Swedenborg's belief in this privilege that he did not hesitate to describe what the spirits taught him respecting matters which belong rather to science than to faith; though it must be admitted that probably he supposed there was small reason for believing that his statements could ever be tested by the results of scientific research. The objects to which his spiritual communications related were conveniently remote. I do not say this as desiring for one moment to suggest that he purposely selected those objects, and not others which might be more readily examined. He certainly believed in the reality of the communications he described. But possibly there is some law in things visionary, corresponding to the law of mental operation with regard to scientific theories; and as the mind theorises freely about a subject little understood, but cautiously where many facts have been ascertained, so probably exact knowledge of a subject prevents the operation of those illusions which are regarded as supernatural communications. It is in a dim light only that the active imagination pictures objects which do not really exist; in the clear light of day they can no longer be imagined. So it is with mental processes.

Probably there is no subject more suitable in this sense for the visionary than that of life in other worlds. It has always had an attraction for imaginative minds, simply because it is enwrapped in so profound a mystery; and there has been little to restrain the fancy, because so little is certainly known of the physical condition of other worlds. Recently, indeed, a somewhat sudden and severe check has been placed on the liveliness of imagination which had enabled men formerly to picture to themselves the inhabitants of other orbs in space. Spectroscopic analysis and exact telescopic scrutiny will not permit some speculations to be entertained which formerly met with favour. Yet even now there has been but a slight change of scene and time. If men can no longer imagine inhabitants of one planet because it is too hot, or of another because it is too cold, of one body because it is too deeply immersed in vaporous masses, or of another because it has neither atmosphere nor water, we have only to speculate about the unseen worlds which circle round those other suns, the stars; or, instead of changing the region of space where we imagine worlds, we can look backward to the time when planets now cold and dead were warm with life, or forward to the distant future when planets now glowing with fiery heat shall have cooled down to a habitable condition.

Swedenborg's imaginative mind seems to have fully felt the charm of this interesting subject. It was, indeed, because of the charm which he found in it, that he was readily persuaded into the belief that knowledge had been supernaturally communicated to him respecting it. 'Because I had a desire,' he says, 'to know if there are other earths, and to learn their nature and the character of their inhabitants, it was granted me by the Lord to converse and have intercourse with spirits and angels who had come from other earths, with some for a day, with some for a week, and with some for months. From them I have received information respecting the earths from and near which they are, the modes of life, customs and worship of their inhabitants, besides various other particulars of interest, all which, having come to my knowledge in this way, I can describe as things which I have seen and heard.'

It is interesting (psychologically) to notice how the reasoning which had convinced Swedenborg of the existence of other inhabited worlds is attributed by him to the spirits.

'It is well known in the other life,' he says, 'that there are many earths with men upon them; for there (that is, in the spiritual life) every one who, from a love of truth and consequent use, desires it, is allowed to converse with the spirits of other earths, so as to be assured that there is a plurality of worlds, and be informed that the human race is not confined to one earth only, but extends to numberless earths. . . . I have occasionally conversed on this subject with the spirits of our earth, and the result of our conversation was that a man of enlarged understanding may conclude from various considerations that there are many earths with human inhabitants upon them. For it is an inference of reason that masses so great as the planets are, some of which exceed this earth in magnitude, are not empty bodies, created only to be carried in their motion round the sun, and to shine with their scanty light for the benefit of one earth only; but that they must have a nobler use. He who believes, as every one ought to believe, that the Deity created the universe for no other end than the existence of the human race, and of heaven from it (for the human race is the seminary of heaven), must also believe that wherever there is an earth there are human inhabitants. That the planets which are visible to us, being within the boundary of our solar system, are earths, may appear from various considerations. They are bodies of earthy matter, because they reflect the sun's light, and when seen through the telescope appear, not as stars shining with a flaming lustre, but as earths, variegated with obscure spots. Like our earth, they are carried round the sun by a progressive motion, through the path of the Zodiac, whence they have years and seasons of the year, which are spring, summer, autumn, and winter; and they rotate upon their axes, which makes days, and times of the day, as morning, midday, evening, and night. Some of them also have satellites, which perform their revolutions about their globes, as the moon does about ours. The planet Saturn, as being farthest from the sun, has besides an immense luminous ring, which supplies that earth with much, though reflected, light. How is it possible for any one acquainted with these facts, and who thinks from reason, to assert that such bodies are uninhabited?'

Remembering that this reasoning was urged by the spirits, and that during twelve years Swedenborg's interiors had been opened in such sort that he could converse with spirits from other worlds, it is surprising that he should have heard nothing about Uranus or Neptune, to say nothing of the zone of asteroids, or again, of planets as yet unknown which may exist outside the path of Neptune. He definitely commits himself, it will be observed, to the statement that Saturn is the planet farthest from the sun. And elsewhere, in stating where in these spiritual communications the 'idea' of each planet was conceived to be situated, he leaves no room whatever for Uranus and Neptune, and makes no mention of other bodies in the solar system than those known in his day. This cannot have been because the spirits from then unknown planets did not feel themselves called upon to communicate with the spirit of one who knew nothing of their home, for he received visitors from worlds in the starry heavens far beyond human ken. It would almost seem, though to the faithful Swedenborgian the thought will doubtless appear very wicked, that the system of Swedenborg gave no place to Uranus and Neptune, simply because he knew nothing about those planets. Otherwise, what a noble opportunity there would have been for establishing the truth of Swedenborgian doctrines by revealing to the world the existence of planets hitherto unknown. Before the reader pronounces this a task beneath the dignity of the spirits and angels who taught Swedenborg it will be well for him to examine the news which they actually imparted.

I may as well premise, however, that it does not seem to me worth while to enter here at any length into Swedenborg's descriptions of the inhabitants of other worlds, because what he has to say on this subject is entirely imaginative. There is a real interest for us in his ideas respecting the condition of the planets, because those ideas were based (though unconsciously) upon the science of his day, in which he was no mean proficient. And even where his mysticism went beyond what his scientific attainments suggested, a psychological interest attaches to the workings of his imagination. It is as curious a problem to trace his ideas to their origin as it sometimes is to account for the various phases of a fantastic dream, such a dream, for instance, as that which Armadale, the doctor, and Midwinter, in 'Armadale,' endeavour to connect with preceding events. But Swedenborg's visions of the behaviour and appearance of the inhabitants of other earths have little interest, because it is hopeless to attempt to account for even their leading features. For instance, what can we make of such a passage as the following, relating to the spirits who came from Mercury?—'Some of them are desirous to appear, not like the spirits of other earths as men, but as crystalline globes. Their desire to appear so, although they do not, arises from the circumstance that the knowledges of things immaterial are in the other life represented by crystals.'

Yet some even of these more fanciful visions significantly indicate the nature of Swedenborg's philosophy. One can recognise his disciples and his opponents among the inhabitants of various favoured and unhappy worlds, and one perceives how the wiser and more dignified of his spiritual visitors are made to advocate his own views, and to deride those of his adversaries. Some of the teachings thus circuitously advanced are excellent.

For instance, Swedenborg's description of the inhabitants of Mercury and their love of abstract knowledge contains an instructive lesson. 'The spirits of Mercury imagine,' he says, 'that they know so much, that it is almost impossible to know more. But it has been told them by the spirits of our earth, that they do not know many things, but few, and that the things which they know not are comparatively infinite, and in relation to those they do know are as the waters of the largest ocean to those of the smallest fountain; and further, that the first advance to wisdom is to know, acknowledge, and perceive that what we do know, compared with what we do not know, is so little as hardly to amount to anything.'[1] So far we may suppose that Swedenborg presents his own ideas, seeing

[1] It is noteworthy how Swedenborg here anticipates a saying of Laplace, the greatest mathematician the world has known, save Newton alone. Newton's remark that he seemed but as a child who had gathered a few shells on the shores of ocean, is well known. Laplace's words, '*Ce que nous connaissons est peu de chose; ce que nous ignorons est immense*,' were not, as is commonly stated, his last. De Morgan gives the following account of Laplace's last moments, on the authority of Laplace's friend and pupil, the well-known mathematician Poisson: 'After the publication (in 1825) of the fifth volume of the Mécanique Céleste, Laplace became gradually weaker, and with it musing and abstracted. He thought much on the great problems of existence, and often muttered to himself, "*Qu'est-ce que c'est que tout cela!*" After many alternations he appeared at last so permanently prostrated that his family applied to his favourite pupil, M. Poisson, to try to get a word from him. Poisson paid a visit, and after a few words of salutation, said, "J'ai une bonne nouvelle à vous annoncer: on a reçu au Bureau des Longitudes une lettre d'Allemagne annonçant que M. Bessel a vérifié par l'observation vos découvertes théoriques sur les satellites de Jupiter." Laplace opened his eyes and answered with deep gravity. "*L'homme ne poursuit que des chimères.*" He never spoke again. His death took place March 5, 1827.'

that he is describing what has been told the Mercurial spirits by the spirits of our earth, of whom (during these spiritual conversations) he was one. But he proceeds to describe how angels were allowed to converse with the Mercurial spirits in order to convince them of their error. 'I saw another angel,' says he, after describing one such conversation, 'conversing with them; he appeared at some altitude to the right; he was from our earth, and he enumerated very many things of which they were ignorant. . . . As they had been proud on account of their knowledges, on hearing this they began to humble themselves. Their humiliation was represented by the sinking of the company which they formed, for that company then appeared as a volume or roll, . . . as if hollowed in the middle and raised at the sides. . . . They were told what that signified, that is, what they thought in their humiliation, and that those who appeared elevated at the sides were not as yet in any humiliation. Then I saw that the volume was separated, and that those who were not in humiliation were remanded back towards their earth, the rest remaining.'

Little being known to Swedenborg, as indeed little is known to the astronomers of our own time, about Mercury, we find little in the visions relating to that planet which possesses any scientific interest. He asked the inhabitants who were brought to him in visions about the sun of the system, and they replied that it looks larger from Mercury than as seen from other worlds. This of course was no news to Swedenborg. They explained further, that the inhabitants enjoy a moderate temperature, without extremes of heat or cold. 'It was given to me,' proceeds Swedenborg, 'to tell them that it was so provided by the Lord, that they might not be exposed to excessive heat from their greater proximity to the sun, since heat does not arise from the sun's nearness, but from the height and density of the atmosphere, as appears from the cold on high mountains even in hot climates; also that heat is varied according to the direct or oblique incidence of the sun's rays, as is plain from the seasons of winter and summer in every region.' It is curious to find thus advanced, in a sort of lecture addressed to visionary Mercurials, a theory which crops up repeatedly in the present day, because the difficulty which suggests it is dealt with so unsatisfactorily for the most part in our text-books of science. Continually we hear of some new paradoxist who propounds as a novel doctrine the teaching that the atmosphere, and not the sun, is the cause of heat. The mistake was excusable in Swedenborg's time. In fact it so chanced that, apart from the obvious fact on which the mistake is usually based—the continued presence, namely, of snow on the summits of high mountains even in the torrid zone—it had been shown shortly before by Newton, that the light fleecy clouds seen sometimes even in the hottest weather above the wool-pack or cumulus clouds are composed of minute crystals of ice. Seeing that these tiny crystals can exist under the direct rays of the sun in hot summer weather, many find it difficult to understand how those rays can of themselves have any heating power. Yet in reality the reasoning addressed by Swedenborg to his Mercurial friends was entirely erroneous. If he could have adventured as far forth into time as he did into space, and could have attended in the spirit the lectures of one John Tyndall, a spirit of our earth, he would have had this matter rightly explained to him. In reality the sun's heat is as effective directly at the summit of the highest mountain as at the sea-level. A thermometer exposed to the sun in the former position indicates indeed a slightly higher temperature than one similarly exposed to the sun (when at the same altitude) at the sea-level. But the air does not get warmed to the same degree, simply because, owing to its rarity and relative dryness, it fails to retain any portion of the heat which passes through it.

It is interesting to notice how Swedenborg's scientific conceptions of the result of the (relatively) airless condition of our moon suggested peculiar fancies respecting the lunar inhabitants. Interesting, I mean, psychologically: for it is curious to see scientific and fanciful conceptions thus unconsciously intermingled. Of the conscious intermingling of such conceptions instances are common enough. The effects of the moon's airless condition have been often made the subject of fanciful speculations. The reader will remember how Scheherazade, in 'The Poet at the Breakfast Table,' runs on about the moon. 'Her delight was unbounded, and her curiosity insatiable. If there were any living creatures there, what odd things they must be. They couldn't have any lungs nor any hearts. What a pity! Did they ever die? How could they expire if they didn't breathe? Burn up? No air to burn in. Tumble into some of those horrid pits, perhaps, and break all to bits. She wondered how the young people there liked it, or whether there were any young people there. Perhaps nobody was young and nobody was old, but they were like mummies all of them—what an idea!—two mummies making love to each other! So she went on in a rattling, giddy kind of way, for she was excited by the strange scene in which she found herself, and quite astonished the young astronomer with her vivacity.' But Swedenborg's firm belief that the fancies engendered in his mind were scientific realities is very different from the conscious play of fancy in the passage just quoted. It must be remembered that Swedenborg regarded his visions with as much confidence as though they were revelations made by means of scientific instruments; nay, with even more confidence, for he knew that scientific observations may be misunderstood, whereas he was fully persuaded that his visions were miraculously provided for his enlightenment, and that therefore he would not be allowed to misunderstand aught that was thus revealed to him.

'It is well known to spirits and angels,' he says, 'that there are inhabitants in the moon, and in the moons or satellites which revolve about Jupiter and Saturn. Even those who have not seen and conversed with spirits who are from them entertain no doubt of their being inhabited, for they, too, are earths, and where there is an earth there is man; man being the end for which every earth exists, and without an end nothing was made by the Great Creator. Every one who thinks from reason in any degree enlightened, must see that the human race is the final cause of creation.'

The moon being inhabited then by human beings, but being very insufficiently supplied with air, it necessarily follows that these human beings must be provided in some way with the means of existing in that rare and tenuous atmosphere. Tremendous powers of inspiration and expiration would be required to make that air support the life of the human body. Although Swedenborg could have had no knowledge of the exact way in which breathing supports life (for Priestley was his junior by nearly half a century), yet he must clearly have perceived that the quantity of air inspired has much to do with the vitalising power of the indraught. No ordinary human lungs could draw in an adequate supply of air from such an atmosphere as the moon's; but by some great increase of breathing power it might be possible to live there: at least, in Swedenborg's time there was no reason for supposing otherwise. Reason, then, having convinced him that the lunar inhabitants must possess extraordinary breathing apparatus, and presumably most powerful voices, imagination presented them to him accordingly. 'Some spirits appeared overhead,' he says, 'and thence were heard voices like thunder; for their voices sounded precisely like thunder from the clouds after lightning. I supposed it was a great multitude of spirits who had the art of giving voices with such a sound. The more simple spirits who were with me derided them, which greatly surprised me. But the cause of their derision was soon discovered, which was, that the spirits who thundered were not many, but few, and were as little as children, and that on former occasions they (the thunderers) had terrified them by such sounds, and yet were unable to do them the least harm. That I might know their character, some of them descended from on high, where they thundered; and, what surprised me, one carried another on his back, and the two thus approached me. Their faces appeared not unhandsome, but longer than those of other spirits. In stature they were like children of seven years old, but the frame was more robust, so that they were like men. It was told me by the angels that they were from the moon. He who was carried by the other came to me, applying himself to my left side under the elbow, and thence spoke. He said, that when they utter their voices they thunder in this way,'—and it seems likely enough that if there are any living speaking beings in the moon, their voice, could they visit the earth, would be found to differ very markedly from the ordinary human voice. 'In the spiritual world their thunderous voices have their use. For by their thundering the spirits from the moon terrify spirits who are inclined to injure them, so that the lunar spirits go in safety where they will. To convince me the sound they make was of this kind, he (the spirit who was carried by the other) retired, but not out of sight, and thundered in like manner. They showed, moreover, that the voice was thundered by being uttered from the abdomen like an eructation. It was perceived that this arose from the circumstance that the inhabitants of the moon do not, like the inhabitants of other earths, speak from the lungs, but from the abdomen, and thus from air collected there, the reason of which is that the atmosphere with which the moon is surrounded is not like that of other earths.'

In his intercourse with spirits from Jupiter, Swedenborg heard of animals larger than those that live on the earth. It has been a favourite idea of many believers in other worlds than ours, that though in each world the same races of animals exist, they would be differently proportioned; and there has been much speculation as to the probable size of men and other animals in worlds much larger or much smaller than the earth. When as yet ideas about other worlds were crude, the idea prevailed that giants exist in the larger orbs, and pygmies in the smaller. Whether this idea had its origin in conceptions as to the eternal fitness of things or not, does not clearly appear. It seems certainly at first view natural enough to suppose that the larger beings would want more room and so inhabit the larger dwelling-places. It was a pleasing thought that, if we could visit Jupiter or Saturn, we should find the human inhabitants there

> In bigness to surpass earth's giant sons;

but that if we could visit our moon or Mercury, or whatever smaller worlds there are, we should find men

> Now less than smallest dwarfs, in narrow room
> Throng numberless, like that pygmæan race
> Beyond the Indian mount; or fairy elves,
> Whose midnight revels, by a forest side
> Or fountain, some belated peasant sees,
> Or dreams he sees.

Later the theory was started that the size of beings in various worlds depends on the amount of light received from the central sun. Thus Wolfius asserted that the inhabitants of Jupiter are nearly fourteen feet high, which he proved by comparing the quantity of sunlight which reaches the Jovians with that which we Terrenes receive. Recently, however, it has been noted that the larger the planet, the smaller in all probability must be the inhabitants, if any. For if there are two planets of the same density but unequal size, gravity must be greater at the surface of the larger planet, and where gravity is great large animals are cumbered by their weight. It is easy to see this by comparing the muscular strength of two men similarly proportioned, but unequal in height. Suppose one man five feet in height, the other six; then the cross section of any given muscle will be less for the former than for the latter in the proportion of twenty-five (five times five) to thirty-six (six times six). Roughly, the muscular strength of the bigger man will be half as great again as that of the smaller. But the weights of the men will be proportioned as 125 (five times five times five) to 216 (six times six times six), so that the weight of the bigger man exceeds that of the smaller nearly as seven exceeds four, or by three-fourths. The taller man exceeds the smaller, then, much more in weight than he does in strength; he is accordingly less active in proportion to his size. Within certain limits, of course, size increases a man's effective as well as his real strength. For instance, our tall man in the preceding illustration cannot lift his own weight as readily as the small man can lift his; but he can lift a weight of three hundred pounds as easily as the small man can lift a weight of two hundred pounds. When we get beyond certain limits of height, however, we get absolute weakness as the result of the increase of weight. Swift's Brobdingnags, for instance, would have been unable to stand upright; for they were six times as tall as men, and therefore each Brobdingnag would have weighed 216 times as much as a man, but would have possessed only thirty-six times the muscular power. Their weight would have been greater, then, in a sixfold greater degree than their strength, and, so far as their mere weight was concerned, their condition would have resembled that of an ordinary man under a load five times exceeding his own weight. As no man could walk or stand upright under such a load, so the Brobdingnags would have been powerless to move, despite, or rather because of, their enormous stature. Applying the general considerations here enunciated to the question of the probable size of creatures like ourselves in other planets, we see that men in Jupiter should be much smaller, men in Mercury much larger, than men on the earth. So also with other animals.

But Swedenborg's spirit visitors from these planets taught differently. 'The horses of our earth,' he says, 'when seen by the spirits of Jupiter, appeared to me smaller than usual, though rather robust; which arose from the idea those spirits had respecting them. They informed me that among them there are animals similar, though much larger; but that they are wild, and in the woods, and that when they come in sight they cause terror though they are harmless; they added that their terror of them is natural or innate.'[1] On the other hand the inhabitants of Mercury, who might be thirteen feet high yet as active as our men, appeared slenderer than Terrene men. 'I was desirous to know,' says Swedenborg, 'what kind of face and person the people in Mercury have, compared with those of the

[1] The reason assigned by Swedenborg is fanciful enough. 'In the spiritual sense,' he says, 'a horse signifies the intellectual principle formed from scientifics, and as they are afraid of cultivating the intellectual faculties by worldly sciences, from this comes an influx of fear. They care nothing for scientifics which are of human erudition.'

people on our earth. There therefore stood before me a female exactly resembling the women on that earth. Her face was beautiful, but it was smaller than that of a woman of our earth; she was more slender, but of equal height; she wore a linen head-dress, not artfully yet gracefully disposed. A man also was presented. He, too, was more slender than the men of our earth; he wore a garment of deep blue, closely fitted to his body without folds or flowing skirts. Such, I learn, were the personal form and costume of the humans of that earth. Afterwards there was shown me a species of the oxen and cows, which did not indeed differ much from those on our earth, except that they were smaller, and made some approach to the stag and hind species.' We have seen, too, that the lunar spirits were no larger than children seven years old.

One passage of Swedenborg's description of Jupiter is curious. 'Although on that earth,' he says, 'spirits speak with men' (*i.e.* with Jovian men) 'man in his turn does not speak with spirits, except to say, when instructed, *that he will do so no more*,'—which we should regard as a bull if it were not news from the Jovian spirit world. 'Nor is man allowed to tell any one that a spirit has spoken to him; if he does so, he is punished. Those spirits of Jupiter when they were with me, at first supposed they were with a man of their own earth; but when in my turn I spoke with them, and thought of publishing what passed between us and so relating it to others, then, because they were not allowed to chastise me, they discovered they were with a stranger.'

It has been a favourite idea with those who delight in the argument from design, that the moons of the remoter planets have been provided for the express purpose of making up for the small amount of sunlight which reaches those planets. Jupiter receives only about one twenty-seventh part of the light which we receive from the sun; but then, has he not four moons to make his nights glorious? Saturn is yet farther away from the sun, and receives only the ninetieth part of the light we get from the sun; but then he has eight moons and his rings, and the nocturnal glory of his skies must go far to compensate the Saturnians for the small quantity of sunlight they receive. The Saturnian spirits who visited Swedenborg were manifestly indoctrinated with these ideas. For they informed him that the nocturnal light of Saturn is so great that some Saturnians worship it, calling it the Lord. These wicked spirits are separated from the rest, and are not tolerated by them. 'The nocturnal light,' say the spirits, 'comes from the immense ring which at a distance encircles that earth, and from the moons which are called the satellites of Saturn.' And again, being questioned further 'concerning the great ring which appears from our earth to rise above the horizon of that planet, and to vary its situations, they said that it does not appear to them as a ring, but only as a snow-white substance in heaven in various directions.' Unfortunately for our faith in the veracity of these spirits, it is certain that the moons of Saturn cannot give nearly so much light as ours, while the rings are much more effective as darkeners than as illuminators. One can readily calculate the apparent size of each of the moons as seen from Saturn, and thence show that the eight discs of the moons together are larger than our moon's disc in about the proportion of forty-five to eight. So that if they were all shining as brightly as our full moon and all full at the same time, their combined light would exceed hers in that degree. But they are not illuminated as our moon is. They are illuminated by the same remote sun which illuminates Saturn, while our moon is illuminated by a sun giving her as much light as we ourselves receive. Our moon then is illuminated ninety times more brightly than the moons of Saturn, and as her disc is less than all theirs together, not as one to ninety, but as sixteen to ninety, it follows that all the Saturnian moons, if full at the same time, would reflect to Saturn one-sixteenth part of the light which we receive from the full moon.[1] As regards the rings of Saturn, nothing can be more certain than that they tend much more to deprive Saturn of light then to make up by reflection for

[1] Similar reasoning applies to the moons of Jupiter, and it so chances that the result in their case comes out exactly the same as in the case of Saturn; all the Jovian moons, if full together, would reflect only the sixteenth part of the light which we receive from the full moon. It is strange that scientific men of considerable mathematical power have used the argument from design apparently supplied by the satellites, without being at the pains to test its validity by the simple mathematical calculations necessary to determine the quantity of light which these bodies can reflect to the planets round which they travel. Brewster and Whewell, though they took opposite sides in the controversy about other inhabited worlds, agreed in this. Brewster, of course, holding the theory that all the planets are inhabited, very naturally accepted the argument from design in this case. Whewell, in opposing that theory, did not dwell at all upon the subjects of the satellites. But in his 'Bridgewater Treatise on Astronomy and General Physics,' he says, 'Taking only the ascertained cases of Venus, the Earth, Jupiter, and Saturn, we conceive that a person of common understanding will be strongly impressed with the persuasion that the satellites are placed in the system with a view to compensate for the diminished light of the sun at greater distances. Mars is an exception; some persons might conjecture from this case that the arrangement itself, like other useful arrangements, has been brought about by some wider law which we have not yet detected. But whether or not we entertain such a guess (it can be nothing more), we see in other parts of creation so many examples of apparent exceptions to rules, which are afterwards found to be capable of explanation, or to be provided for by particular contrivances, that no one familiar with such contemplations will, by one anomaly, be driven from the persuasion that the end which the arrangements of the satellites seem suited to answer is really one of the ends of their creation.'

the small amount of light which Saturn receives directly from the sun. The part of the ring which lies between the planet and the sun casts a black shadow upon Saturn, this shadow sometimes covering an extent of surface many times exceeding the entire surface of our earth. The shadow thus thrown upon the planet creeps slowly, first one way, then another, northwards and southwards over the illuminated hemisphere of the planet (as pictured in the 13th plate of my treatise on Saturn), requiring for its passage from the arctic to the antarctic regions and back again to the arctic regions of the planet, a period nearly equal to that of a generation of terrestrial men. Nearly thirty of our years the process lasts, during half of which time the northern hemisphere suffers, and during the other half the southern. The shadow band, which be it remembered stretches right athwart the planet from the extreme eastern to the extreme western side of the illuminated hemisphere, is so broad during the greater part of the time that in some regions (those corresponding to our temperate zones) the shadow takes two years in passing, during which time the sun cannot be seen at all, unless for a few moments through some chinks in the rings, which are known to be not solid bodies, but made up of closely crowded small moons. And the slow passage of this fearful shadow, which advances at the average rate of some twenty miles a day, but yet hangs for years over the regions athwart which it sweeps, occurs in the very season when the sun's small direct supply of heat would require to be most freely compensated by nocturnal light—in the winter season, namely, of the planet. Moreover, not only during the time of the shadow's passage, but during the entire winter half of the Saturnian year, the ring reflects no light during the night time, the sun being on the other or summer side of the ring's plane.[1] The only noc-

[1] The reader who cares enough about such subjects to take the

turnal effect which would be observable would be the obliteration of the stars covered by the ring system. It is strange that, this being so, the spirits from Saturn should have made

necessary trouble, can easily make a little model of Saturn and his ring system, which will very prettily illustrate the effect of the rings both in reflecting light to the planet's darkened hemisphere and in cutting off light from the planet's illuminated hemisphere. Take a ball, say an ordinary hand-ball, and pierce it through the centre with a fine knitting-needle. Cut out a flat ring of card, proportioned to the ball as the ring system of Saturn to his ball. (If the ball is two inches in diameter, strike out on a sheet of cardboard two concentric circles, one of them with a radius of a little more than an inch and a half, the other with a radius of about two inches and three-eights, and cut out the ring between these two circles.) Thrust the knitting-needle through this ring in such a way that the ball shall lie in the middle of the ring, as the globe of Saturn hangs (without knitting-needle connections) in the middle of his ring system. Thrust another knitting-needle centrally through the ball square to the plane of the ring, and use this second needle, which we may call the polar one, as a handle. Now take the ball and ring into sunlight, or the light of a lamp or candle, holding them so that the shadow of the ring is as thin as possible. This represents the position of the shadow at the time of Saturnian spring or autumn. Cause the shadow slowly to shift until it surrounds the part of the ball through which the polar needle passes on one side. This will represent the position of the shadow at the time of mid-winter for the hemisphere corresponding to that side of the ball. Notice that while the shadow is traversing this half of the ball, the side of the ring which lies towards that half is in shadow, so that a fly or other small insect on that half of the ball would see the darkened side of the ring. A Saturnian correspondingly placed would get no reflected sunlight from the ring system. Move the ball and ring so that the shadow slowly returns to its first position. You will then have illustrated the changes taking place during one half of a Saturnian year. Continue the motion so that the shadow passes to the other half of the ball, and finally surrounds the other point through which the polar needle passes. The polar point which the shadow before surrounded will now be seen to be in the light, and this half of the ball will illustrate the hemisphere of Saturn where it is midsummer. It will also be seen that the side of the ring towards this half of the no mention of the circumstance; and even more strange that these spirits and others should have asserted that the moons and rings of Saturn compensate for the small amount of light directly received from the sun. Most certainly a Swedenborg of our own time would find the spirits from Saturn more veracious and more communicative about these matters, though even what *he* would hear from the spirits would doubtless appear to sceptics of the twenty-first century to be no more than he could have inferred from the known facts of the science of his day.

But Swedenborg was not content merely to receive visits from the inhabitants of other planets in the solar system. He was visited also by the spirits of earths in the starry heaven; nay, he was enabled to visit those earths himself. For man, even while living in the world, 'is a spirit as to his interiors, the body which he carries about in the world only serving him for performing functions in this natural or terrestrial sphere, which is the lowest.' And to certain men it is granted not only to converse as a spirit with angels and spirits, but to traverse in a spiritual way the vast distances which separate world from world and system from system, all the while remaining in the body. Swedenborg was one of these. 'The interiors of my spirit,' he says, 'are opened by the Lord, so that while I am in the body I can at the same time be with angels in heaven, and not only converse with them, but behold the wonderful things which are there and describe them, that henceforth it may no more be said, "Who ever came from heaven to

ball is now in the light, so that a small insect on this half of the ball would see the bright side of the ring. A Saturnian correspondingly placed would get reflected sunlight from the ring system *both by day and by night.* Moving the ball and ring so that the shadow returns to its first position, an entire Saturnian year will have been illustrated. These changes can be still better shown with a Saturnian orrery (see plate viii. of my Saturn), which can be very easily constructed.

assure us it exists and tell us what is there?" He who is unacquainted with the arcana of heaven cannot believe that man can see earths so remote, and give any account of them from sensible experience. But let him know that spaces and distances, and consequently progressions, existing in the natural world, in their origin and first causes are changes of the state of the interiors; that with angels and spirits progressions appear according to changes of state; and that by changes of state they may be apparently translated from one place to another, and from one earth to another, even to earths at the boundaries of the universe; so likewise may man as to his spirit, his body still remaining in its place. This has been the case with me.'

Before describing his visits to earths in the starry heavens, Swedenborg is careful to indicate the probability that such earths exist. 'It is well known to the learned world,' he says, 'that every star is a sun in its place, remaining fixed like the sun of our earth.' The proper motions of the stars had, alas! not been discovered in Swedenborg's day, nor does he seem to have been aware what a wild chase he was really entering upon in his spiritual progressions. Conceive the pursuit of Sirius or Vega as either sun rushed through space with a velocity of thirty or forty miles in every second of time! To resume, however, the account which Swedenborg gives of the ideas of the learned world of his day. 'It is the distance which makes a star appear in a small form; consequently' (the logical necessity is not manifest, however) 'each star, like the sun of our system, has around it planets which are earths; and the reason these are not visible to us is because of their immense distance and their having no light but from their own star, which light cannot be reflected so far as to reach us.' 'To what other end,' proceeds this most convincing reasoning, 'can be so immense a heaven with such a multitude of stars? For man is the end for which the universe was created. It has been ascertained by calculation that supposing there were in the universe a million earths, and on every earth three hundred millions of men and two hundred generations within six thousand years, and that to every man or spirit was allotted a space of three cubic ells, the collective number of men or spirits could not occupy a space equal to a thousandth part of this earth, thus not more than that occupied by one of the satellites of Jupiter or Saturn; a space on the universe almost undiscernible, for a satellite is hardly visible to the naked eye. What would this be for the Creator of the universe, to whom the whole universe filled with earths could not be enough' (for what?), 'seeing that he is infinite.' However, it is not on this reasoning alone that Swedenborg relies. He tells us, honestly beyond all doubt, that he knows the truth of what he relates. 'The information I am about to give,' he says, 'respecting the earths in the starry heaven is from experimental testimony; from which it will likewise appear how I was translated thither as to my spirit, the body remaining in its place.'

His progress in his first star-hunt was to the right, and continued for about two hours. He found the boundary of our solar system marked first by a white but thick cloud, next by a fiery smoke ascending from a great chasm. Here some guards appeared, who stopped some of the company, because these had not, like Swedenborg and the rest, received permission to pass. They not only stopped those unfortunates, but tortured them, conduct for which terrestrial analogues might possibly be discovered.

Having reached another system, he asked the spirits of one of the earths there how large their sun was and how it appeared. They said it was less than the sun of our earth, and has a flaming appearance. Our sun, in fact, is larger than other suns in space, for from that earth starry heavens are seen, and a star larger than the rest appears, which, say those spirits, 'was declared from heaven' to be the sun of Swedenborg's earthly home.

What Swedenborg saw upon that earth has no special interest. The men there, though haughty, are loved by their respective wives because they, the men, are good. But their goodness does not appear very manifest from anything in the narrative. The only man seen by Swedenborg took from his wife 'the garment which she wore, and threw it over his own shoulders; loosening the lower part, which flowed down to his feet like a robe (much as a man of our earth might be expected to loosen the tie-back of the period, if he borrowed it in like manner) he thus walked about clad.'

He next visited an earth circling round a star, which he learned was one of the smaller sort, not far from the equator. Its greater distance was plain from the circumstance that Swedenborg was two days in reaching it. In this earth he very nearly fell into a quarrel with the spirits. For hearing that they possess remarkable keenness of vision, he 'compared them with eagles which fly aloft, and enjoy a clear and extensive view of objects beneath.' At this they were indignant, supposing,' poor spirits, 'that he compared them to eagles as to their rapacity, and consequently thought them wicked.' He hastened to explain, however, that he 'did not liken them to eagles as to their rapacity, but as to sharpsightedness.'

Swedenborg's account of a third earth in the star-depths contains a very pretty idea for temples and churches. The temples in that earth 'are constructed,' he says, of trees, not cut down, but growing in the place where they were first planted. On that earth, it seems, there are trees of an extraordinary size and height; these they set in rows when young, and arrange in such an order that they may serve when they grow up to form porticoes and colonnades. In the meanwhile, by cutting and pruning, they fit and prepare the tender shoots to entwine one with another, and join together so as to form the groundwork and floor of the temple to be constructed, and to rise at the sides as walls, and above to bend into arches to form the roof. In this manner they construct the temple with admirable art, elevating it high above the ground. They prepare also an ascent into it, by continuous branches of the trees, extended from the trunk and firmly connected together. Moreover, they adorn the temple without and within in various ways, by disposing the foliage into particular forms; thus they build entire groves. But it was not permitted me to see the nature of these temples, only I was informed that the light of their sun is let in by apertures amongst the branches, and is everywhere transmitted through crystals; whereby the light falling on the walls is refracted in colours like those of the rainbow, particularly blue and orange, of which they are fondest. Such is their architecture, which they prefer to the most magnificent palaces of our earth.'

Other earths in the starry heavens were visited by Swedenborg, but the above will serve sufficiently to illustrate the nature of his observations. One statement, by the way, was made to him which must have seemed unlikely ever to be contravened, but which has been shown in our time to be altogether erroneous. In the fourth star-world he visited, he was told that that earth, which travels round its sun in 200 days of fifteen hours each, is one of the least in the universe, being scarcely 500 German miles, say 2000 English miles, in circumference. This would make its diameter about 640 English miles. But there is not one of the whole family of planetoids which has a diameter so great as this, and many of these earths must be less than fifty miles in diameter. Now Swedenborg remarks that he had his information from the angels, 'who made a comparison in all these particulars with things of a like nature on our earth, according to what they saw in me or in my memory. Their conclusions were formed by angelic ideas, whereby are instantly known the measure of space and time in a just proportion with respect to space and time elsewhere. Angelic ideas, which are spiritual, in such calculations infinitely excel human ideas, which are natural.' He must therefore have met, unfortunately, with untruthful angels.

The real source of Swedenborg's inspirations will be tolerably obvious—to all, at least, who are not Swedenborgians. But our account of his visions would not be complete in a psychological sense without a brief reference to the personal allusions which the spirits and angels made during their visits or his wanderings. His distinguished rival, Christian Wolf, was encountered as a spirit by spirits from Mercury, who 'perceived that what he said did not rise above the sensual things of the natural man, because in speaking he thought of honour, and was desirous, as in the world (for in the other world every one is like his former self), to connect various things into series, and from these again continually to deduce others, and so form several chains of such, which they did not see or acknowledge to be true, and which, therefore, they declared to be chains which neither cohered in themselves nor with the conclusions, calling them the obscurity of authority;' so they ceased to question him further, and presently left him. Similarly, a spirit who in this world had been a 'prelate and a preacher,' and 'very pathetic, so that he could deeply move his hearers,' got no hearing among the spirits of a certain earth in the starry heavens; for they said they could tell 'from the tone of the voice whether a discourse came from the heart or not;' and as his discourse came not from the heart, 'he was unable to teach them, whereupon he was silent.' Convenient thus to have spirits and angels tc confirm our impressions of other men, living or dead.

Apart from the psychological interest attaching tc Swedenborg's strange vision, one cannot but be strongly impressed by the idea pervading them, that to beings suitably constituted all that takes place in other worlds might be known. Modern science recognises a truth here; for in that mysterious ether which occupies all space, messages are at all times travelling by which the history of every orb is constantly recorded. No world, however remote or insignificant; no period, however distant—but has its history thus continually proclaimed in ever widening waves. Nay, by these waves also (to beings who could read their teachings aright) the future is constantly indicated. For, as the waves which permeate the ether could only be situated as they actually are, at any moment, through past processes, each one of which is consequently indicated by those ethereal waves, so also there can be·but one series of events in the future, as the sequel of the relations actually indicated by the ethereal undulations. These, therefore, speak as definitely and distinctly of the future as of the past. Could we but rid us of the gross habiliments of flesh, and by some new senses be enabled to feel each order of ethereal undulations, even of those only which reach our earth, all knowledge of the past and future would be within our power. The consciousness of this underlies the fancies of Swedenborg, just as it underlies the thought of him who sang—

> There's not an orb which thou behold'st
> But in his motion like an angel sings,
> Still quiring to the young-eyed cherubim.
> But while this muddy vesture of decay
> Doth grossly close us in, we cannot hear it.

V.

OTHER WORLDS AND OTHER UNIVERSES.

If any one shall gravely tell me that I have spent my time idly in a vain and fruitless inquiry after what I can never become sure of, the answer is that at this rate he would put down all natural philosophy, as far as it concerns itself in searching into the nature of such things. In such noble and sublime studies as these, 'tis a glory to arrive at probability, and the search itself rewards the pains. But there are many degrees of probable, some nearer to the truth than others, in the determining of which lies the chief exercise of our judgment. And besides the nobleness and pleasure of the studies, may we not be so bold as to say that they are no small help to the advancement of wisdom and morality?—HUYGHENS, *Conjectures concerning the Planetary Worlds.*

THE interest with which astronomy is studied by many who care little or nothing for other sciences is due chiefly to the thoughts which the celestial bodies suggest respecting life in other worlds than ours. There is no feeling more deeply seated in the human heart—not the belief in higher than human powers, not the hope of immortality, not even the fear of death—than the faith in realms of life where other conditions are experienced than those we are acquainted with here. It is not vulgar curiosity or idle fancy that suggests the possibilities of life in other worlds. It has been the conviction of the profoundest thinkers, of men of highest imagination. The mystery of the star-depths has had its charm for the mathematician as well as for the poet; for the exact observer as for the most fruitful theoriser; nay, for the man of business as for him whose life is passed in communing with nature. If we analyse the interest with which the generality of men inquire into astronomical matters apparently not connected with the question of life in other worlds, we find in every case that it has been out of this question alone or chiefly that that interest has sprung. The great discoveries made during the last few years respecting the sun for example, might seem remote from the subject of life in other worlds. It is true that Sir William Herschel thought the sun might be the abode of living creatures; and Sir John Herschel even suggested the possibility that the vast streaks of light called the solar willow-leaves, objects varying from two hundred to a thousand miles in length, might be living creatures whose intense lustre was the measure of their intense vitality. But modern discoveries had rendered all such theories untenable. The sun is presented to us as a mighty furnace, in whose fires the most stubborn elements are not merely melted but vaporised. The material of the sun has been analysed, the motions and changes taking place on his surface examined, the laws of his being determined. How, it might be asked, is the question of life in other worlds involved in these researches? The faith of Sir David Brewster in the sun as the abode of life being dispelled, how could discoveries respecting the sun interest those who care about the subject of the plurality of worlds? The answer to these questions is easily found. The real interest which solar researches have possessed for those who are not astronomers has resided in the evidence afforded respecting the sun's position as the fire, light, and life of the system of worlds whereof our world is one. The mere facts discovered respecting the sun would be regarded as so much dry detail were they not brought directly into relation with our earth and its wants, and therefore with the wants of the other earths which circle round the sun; but when thus dealt with they immediately excite attention and interest. I do not speak at random in asserting this, but describe the result of widely ranging observation. I have addressed hundreds of audiences in Great Britain and America on the subject of recent solar discoveries, and I have conversed with many hundreds of persons of various capacity and education, from men almost uncultured to men of the highest intellectual power; and my invariable experience has been that solar research derives its chief interest when viewed in relation to the sun's position as the mighty ruler, the steadfast sustainer, the beneficent almoner of the system of worlds to which our earth belongs. It is the same with other astronomical subjects. Few care for the record of lunar observations, save in relation to the question whether the moon is or has been the abode of living creatures. The movements of comets and meteors, and the discoveries recently made respecting their condition, have no interest except in relation to the position of these bodies in the economy of solar systems, or to the possible part which they may at one time have performed in building up worlds and suns. None save astronomers, and few only of these, care for researches into the star-depths, except in connection with the thought that every star is a sun and therefore probably the light and fire of a system of worlds like those which circle around our own sun.

It is singular how variously this question of life in other worlds has been viewed at various stages of astronomical progress. From the time of Pythagoras, who first, so far as is known, propounded the general theory of the plurality of worlds, down to our own time, when Brewster and Chalmers on the one hand, and Whewell on the other, have advocated rival theories probably to be both set aside for a theory at once intermediate to and more widely ranging in time and space than either, the aspect of the subject has constantly varied, as new lights have been thrown upon it from different directions. It may be interesting briefly to consider what has been thought in the past on this strangely attractive question, and then to indicate the view towards which modern discoveries seem manifestly to point—a view not likely to undergo other change than that resulting from clearer vision and closer approach. In other words, I shall endeavour to show that the theory to which we are now led by all the known facts is correct in general, though, as fresh knowledge is obtained, it may undergo modification in details. We now see the subject from the right point of view, though as science progresses we may come to see it more clearly and definedly.

When men believed the earth to be a flat surface above which the heavens were arched as a tent or canopy, they were not likely to entertain the belief in other worlds than ours. During the earlier ages of mankind ideas such as these prevailed. The earth had been fashioned into its present form and condition, the heavens had been spread over it, the sun, and moon, and stars had been set in the heavens for its use and adornment, and there was no thought of any other world.

But while this was the general belief, there was already a school of philosophy where another doctrine had been taught. Pythagoras had adopted the belief of Apollonius Pergæus that the sun is the centre of the planetary paths, the earth one among the planets—a belief inseparable from the doctrine of the plurality of worlds. Much argument has been advanced to show that this belief never was adopted before the time of Copernicus, and unquestionably it must be admitted that the theory was not presented in the clear and simple form to which we have become accustomed. But it is not necessary to weigh the conflicting arguments for and against the opinion that Pythagoras and others regarded the earth as not the fixed centre of the universe. The certain fact that the doctrine of the plurality of worlds was entertained (I do not say adopted) by them, proves sufficiently that they cannot have believed the earth to be fixed and central. The idea of other worlds like our earth is manifestly inconsistent with the belief that the earth is the central body around which the whole universe revolves.

That this is so is well illustrated by the fate of the unfortunate Giordano Bruno. He was one of the first disciples of Copernicus, and, having accepted the doctrine that the earth travels round the sun as one among his family of planets, was led very naturally to the belief that the other planets are inhabited. He went farther, and maintained that as the earth is not the only inhabited world in the solar system, so the sun is not the only centre of a system of inhabited worlds, but each star a sun like him, about which many planets revolve. This was one of the many heresies for which Bruno was burned at the stake. It is easy, also, to recognise in the doctrine of many worlds as the natural sequel of the Copernican theory, rather than in the features of this theory itself, the cause of the hostility with which theologians regarded it, until, finding it proved, they discovered that it is directly taught in the books which they interpret for us so variously. The Copernican theory was not rejected—nay, it was even countenanced—until this particular consequence of the theory was recognised. But within a few years from the persecution of Bruno, Galileo was imprisoned, and the last years of his life made miserable, because it had become clear that in setting the earth adrift from its position as centre of the universe, he and his brother Copernicans were sanctioning the belief in other worlds than ours. Again and again, in the attacks made by clericals and theologians upon the Copernican theory, this lamentable consequence was insisted upon. Unconscious that they were advancing the most damaging argument which could be conceived for the cause they had at heart, they maintained, honestly but unfortunately, that with the new theory came the manifest inference that our earth is not the only and by no means the most important world in the universe—a doctrine manifestly inconsistent (so they said) with the teachings of the Scriptures.

It was naturally only by a slow progression that men were able to advance into the domain spread before them by the Copernican theory, and to recognise the real minuteness of the earth both in space and time. They more quickly recognised the earth's insignificance in space, because the new theory absolutely forced this fact upon them. If the earth, whose globe they knew to be minute compared with her distance from the sun, is really circling around the sun in a mighty orbit many millions of miles in diameter, it follows of necessity that the fixed stars must lie so far away that even the span of the earth's orbit is reduced to nothing by comparison with the vast depths beyond which lie even the nearest of those suns. This was Tycho Brahe's famous and perfectly sound argument against the Copernican theory. 'The stars remain fixed in apparent position all the time, yet the Copernicans tell us that the earth from which we view the stars is circling once a year in an orbit many millions of miles in diameter; how is it that from so widely ranging a point of view we do not see widely different celestial scenery? Who can believe that the stars are so remote that by comparison the span of the earth's path is a mere point?' Tycho's argument was of course valid.[1] Of two things one. Either the earth does not travel round the sun, or the stars are much farther away than men had conceived possible in Tycho's time. His mistake lay in rejecting the correct conclusion because simply it made the visible universe seem many millions of times vaster than he had supposed. Yet the universe, even as thus enlarged, was but a point to the universe visible in our day, which in turn will dwindle to a point compared with the universe as men will see it a few centuries hence; while that or the utmost range of space over which men can ever extend their survey is doubtless as nothing to the real universe of occupied space.

Such has been the progression of our ideas as to the position of the earth in space. Forced by the discoveries of Copernicus to regard our earth as a mere point compared with the distances of the nearest fixed stars, men gradually learned to recognise those distances which at first had seemed infinite as in their turn evanescent even by comparison with that mere point of space over which man is able by instrumental means to extend his survey.

Though there has been a similar progression in men's ideas as to the earth's position in time, that progression has not been carried to a corresponding extent. Men have not been so bold in widening their conceptions of time as in widening their conceptions of space. It is here and thus that, in my judgment, the subject of life in other worlds has been hitherto incorrectly dealt with. Men have given up as utterly idle the idea that the existence of worlds is to be

[1] Not 'of course' because Tycho used it, for, like other able students of science, he made mistakes from time to time. Thus he argued that the earth cannot rotate on her axis, because if she did bodies raised above her surface would be left behind—an argument which even the mechanical knowledge of his own time should have sufficed to invalidate, though it is still used from time to time by paradoxers of our own day.

limited to the special domain of space to which our earth belongs; but they are content to retain the conception that the domain of time to which our earth's history belongs, 'this bank and shoal of time' on which the life of the earth is cast, is the period to which the existence of other worlds than ours should be referred.

This, which is to be noticed in nearly all our ordinary treatises on astronomy, appears as a characteristic peculiarity of works advocating the theory of the plurality of worlds. Brewster and Dick and Chalmers, all in fact who have taken that doctrine under their special protection, reason respecting other worlds as though, if they failed to prove that other orbs are inhabited *now*, or are at least *now* supporting life in some way or other, they failed of their purpose altogether. The idea does not seem to have occurred to them that there is room and verge enough in eternity of time not only for activity but for rest. They must have all the orbs of space busy at once in the one work which they seem able to conceive as the possible purpose of those bodies—the support of life. The argument from analogy, which they had found effective in establishing the general theory of the plurality of worlds, is forgotten when its application to details would suggest that not *all* orbs are *at all times* either the abode of life or in some way subserving the purposes of life.

We find, in all the forms of life with which we are acquainted, three characteristic periods—first the time of preparation for the purposes of life; next, the time of fitness for those purposes; and thirdly, the time of decadence tending gradually to death. We see among all objects which exist in numbers, examples of all these stages existing at the same time. In every race of living creatures there are the young as yet unfit for work, the workers, and those past work; in every forest there are saplings, seed-bearing trees, and trees long past the seed-bearing period. We know that planets, or rather, speaking more generally, the orbs which people space, pass through various stages of development, during some only of which they can reasonably be regarded as the abode of life or supporting life; yet the eager champion of the theory of many worlds will have them all in these life-bearing or life-supporting stages, none in any of the stages of preparation, none in any of the stages of decrepitude or death.

This has probably had its origin in no small degree from the disfavour with which in former years the theory of the growth and development of planets and systems of planets was regarded. Until the evidence became too strong to be resisted, the doctrine that our earth was once a baby world, with many millions of years to pass through before it could be the abode of life, was one which only the professed atheist (so said too many divines) could for a moment entertain; while the doctrine that not the earth alone, but the whole of the solar system, had developed from a condition utterly unlike that through which it is now passing, could have had its origin only in the suggestions of the Evil One. Both doctrines were pronounced to be so manifestly opposed to the teachings of Moses, and not only so, but so manifestly inconsistent with the belief in a Supreme Being, that—that further argument was unnecessary, and denunciation only was required. So confident were divines on these points, that it would not have been very wonderful if some few students of science had mistaken assertion for proof, and so concluded that the doctrines towards which science was unmistakably leading them really were inconsistent with what they had been taught to regard as the Word of God. Whether multiplied experiences taught men of science to wait before thus deciding, or however matters fell out, it certainly befell before very long that the terrible doctrine of cosmical development was supported by such powerful evidence, astronomical and terrestrial, as to appear wholly irresistible. Then, not only was the doctrine accepted by divines, but shown to be manifestly implied in the sacred narrative of the formation of the earth and heavens, sun, and moon, and stars; while upon those unfortunate students of science who had not changed front in good time, and were found still arguing on the mistaken assumption that the development of our system was not accordant with that ancient narrative, freshly forged bolts were flung from the Olympus of orthodoxy.

So far as the other argument—from the inconsistency of the development theory with belief in a Supreme Being—was concerned, the student of science was independent of the interpretations which divines claim the sole right of assigning to the ancient books. Science has done so much more than divinity (which in fact has done nothing) to widen our conceptions of space and time, that she may justly claim full right to deal with any difficulties arising from such enlargement of our ideas. With the theological difficulty science would not care to deal at all, were she not urged to do so by the denunciations of divines; and when, so urged, she touches that difficulty, she is quickly told that the difficulty is insuperable, and not long after that it has no existence, and (on both accounts) that it should have been left alone. But with the difficulty arising from the widening of our ideas respecting space and time, science may claim good, almost sole, right to deal. The path to a solution of the problem is not difficult to find. At a first view, it does seem to those whose vision had been limited to a contracted field, that the wide domain of time and space in which processes of development are found to take place is the universe itself, that to deny the formation of our earth by a special creative act is to deny the existence of a Creator, that to regard the beginning of our earth as a process of development is to assert that development has been in operation from the beginning of all things. But when we recognise clearly that vastness and minuteness, prolonged and brief duration, are merely relative, we perceive that in considering our earth's history we have to deal only with small parts of space and brief periods of time, by comparison with all space and all time. Our earth is very large compared with a tree or an animal, but very small compared with the solar system, a mere point compared with the system of stars to which the sun belongs, and absolutely as nothing compared with the universe of space; and in like manner, while the periods of her growth and development occupy periods very long-lasting compared with those required for the growth and development of a tree or an animal, they are doubtless but brief compared with the eras of the development of our solar system, a mere instant compared with the eras of the development of star-systems, and absolutely evanescent compared with eternity. We have no more reason for rejecting the belief in a Creator because our earth or the solar system is found to have developed to its present condition from an embryonic primordial state, than we have had ever since men first found that animals and trees are developed from the germ. The region of development is larger, the period of development lasts longer, but neither the one nor the other is infinite; and being finite, both one and the other are simply nothing by comparison with infinity. It is a startling thought, doubtless, that periods of time compared with which the life of a man, the existence of a nation, nay, the duration of the human race itself, sink into insignificance, should themselves in turn be dwarfed into nothingness by comparison with periods of a still higher order. But the thought is not more startling than that other thought which we have been compelled to admit—the thought that the earth on which we live, and the solar system to which it belongs, though each so vast that all known material objects are as nothing by comparison, are in turn as nothing compared with the depths of space separating us from even the nearest among the fixed stars. One thought, as I have said, we have been compelled to admit, the other has not as yet been absolutely forced upon us. Though men have long since given up the idea that the earth and heavens have endured but a few thousand years, it is still possible to believe that the birth of our solar system, whether by creative act or by the beginning of processes of development, belongs to the beginning of all time. But this view cannot be regarded as even probable. Although it has never been proved that any definite relation must subsist between time (occupied by events) and space (occupied by matter), the mind naturally accepts the belief that such a relation exists. As we find the universe enlarging under the survey of science, our conceptions of the duration of the universe enlarge also. When the earth was supposed to be the most important object in creation, men might reasonably assign to time itself (regarded as the interval between the beginning of the earth and the consummation of all things when the earth should perish) a moderate duration; but it is equally reasonable that, as the insignificance of the earth's domain in space is recognised, men should recognise also the presumable insignificance of the earth's existence in time.

In this respect, although we have nothing like the direct evidence afforded by the measurement of space, we yet have evidence which can scarcely be called in question. We find in the structure of our earth the signs of its former condition. We see clearly that it was once intensely hot! and we know from experimental researches on the cooling of various earths that many millions of years must have been required by the earth in cooling down from its former igneous condition. We may doubt whether Bischoff's researches can be relied upon in details, and so be unwilling to assign with him a period of 350 millions of years to a single stage of the process of cooling. But that the entire process lasted tens of millions and probably hundreds of millions of years cannot be doubted. Recognising such enormous periods as these in the development of one of the smallest fruits of the great solar tree of life, we cannot but admit at least the reasonableness of believing that the larger fruits (Jupiter, for instance, with 340 times as much matter, and Saturn with 100 times) must require periods still vaster, probably many times larger. Indeed, science shows not only that this view is reasonable, but that no other view is possible. For the mighty root of the tree of life, the great orb of the sun, containing 340 *thousand* times as much matter as the earth, yet mightier periods would be needed. The growth and development of these, the parts of the great system, must of necessity require much shorter time-intervals than the growth and development of the system regarded as a whole. The enormous period when the germs only of the sun and planets existed as yet, when the chaotic substance of the system had not yet blossomed into worlds, the mighty period which is to follow the death of the last surviving member of the system, when the whole scheme will remain as the dead trunk of a tree remains after the last leaf has fallen, after the last movement of sap within the trunk—these periods must be infinite compared with those which measure the duration of even the mightiest separate members of the system.

But all this has been left unnoticed by those who have argued in support of the Brewsterian doctrine of a plurality of worlds. They argue as if it had never been shown that every member of the solar system, as of all other such systems in space, has to pass through an enormously long period of preparation before becoming fit to be the abode of life, and that after being fit for life (for a period very long to our conceptions, but by comparison with the other exceedingly short) it must for countless ages remain as an extinct world. Or else they reason as though it had been proved that the relatively short life-bearing periods in the existence of the several planets must of necessity synchronise, instead of all the probabilities lying overwhelmingly the other way.

While this has been (in my judgment) a defect in what may be called the Brewsterian theory of other worlds, a defect not altogether dissimilar has characterised the opposite or Whewellite theory. Very useful service was rendered to astronomy by Whewell's treatise upon, or rather against, the plurality of worlds, calling attention as it did to the utter feebleness of the arguments on which men had been content to accept the belief that other planets and other systems are inhabited. But some among the most powerfully urged arguments against that belief tacitly relied on the assumption of a similarity of general condition among the members of the solar system. For instance, the small mean density of Jupiter and Saturn had, on the Brewsterian theory, been explained as probably due to vast hollow spaces in those planets' interiors—an explanation which (if it could be admitted) would leave us free to believe that Jupiter and Saturn may be made of the same materials as our own earth. With this was pleasantly intermixed the conception that the inhabitant of these planets may have his 'home in subterranean cities warmed by central fires, or in crystal caves cooled by ocean tides, or may float with the Nereids upon the deep, or mount upon wings as eagles, or rise upon the pinions of the dove, that he may flee away and be at rest,' with much more in the same fanciful vein. We now know that there can be no cavities more than a few miles below the crust of a planet, simply because, under the enormous pressures which would exist, the most solid matter would be perfectly plastic. But while Whewell's general objection to the theory that Jupiter or Saturn is in the same condition as our earth thus acquires new force, the particular explanation which he gave of the planet's small density is open to precisely the same general objection. For he assumes that, because the planet's mean density is little greater than that of water, the planet is probably a world of water and ice with a cindery nucleus, or in fact just such a world as would be formed if a sufficient quantity of water in the same condition as the water of our seas were placed at Jupiter's greater distance from the sun, around a nucleus of earthy or cindery matter large enough to make the density of the entire planet thus formed equal to that of Jupiter, or about one-third greater than the density of water. In this argument there are in reality two assumptions, of precisely the same nature as those which Whewell set himself to combat. It is first assumed that some material existing on a large scale in our earth, and nearly of the same density as Jupiter, must constitute the chief bulk of that planet, and secondly that the temperature of Jupiter's globe must be that which a globe of such material would have if placed where Jupiter is. The possibility that Jupiter may be in an entirely different stage of planetary life—or, in other words, that the youth, middle life, and old age of that planet may belong to quite different eras from the corresponding periods of our earth's life—is entirely overlooked. Rather, indeed, it may be said that the extreme probability of this, on any hypothesis respecting the origin of the solar system, and its absolute certainty on the hypothesis of the development of that system, are entirely overlooked.

A fair illustration of the erroneous nature of the arguments which have been used, not only in advocating rival theories respecting the plurality of worlds, but also in dealing with subordinate points, may be presented as follows:

Imagine a wide extent of country covered with scattered trees of various size, and with plants and shrubs, flowers and herbs, down to the minutest known. Let us suppose a race of tiny creatures to subsist on one of the fruits of a tree of moderate size, their existence as a race depending entirely on the existence of the fruit on which they subsist, while the existence of the individuals of their race lasts but for a few minutes. Furthermore, let there be no regular fruit season either on their tree or in their region of vegetable life, but fruits forming, growing, and decaying all the time.

Let us next conceive these creatures to be possessed of a power of reasoning respecting themselves, their fruit world, the tree on which it hangs, and to some degree even respecting such other trees, plants, flowers, and so forth, as the limited range of their vision might be supposed to include. It would be a natural thought with them, when first they began to exercise this power of reasoning, that their fruit home was the most important object in existence, and themselves the chief and noblest of living beings. It would also be very natural that they should suppose the formation of their world to correspond with the beginning of time, and the formation of their race to have followed the formation of their world by but a few seconds. They would conclude that a Supreme Being had fashioned their world and themselves by special creative acts, and that what they saw outside their fruit world had been also specially created, doubtless to subserve their wants.

Let us now imagine that gradually, by becoming more closely observant than they had been, by combining together to make more complete observations, and above all by preserving the records of observations made by successive generations, these creatures began to obtain clearer ideas respecting their world and the surrounding regions of space. They would find evidence that the fruit on which they lived had not been formed precisely as they knew it, but had undergone processes of development. The distressing discovery would be made that this development could not possibly have taken place in a few seconds, but must have required many hours, nay, even several of those enormous periods called by us days.

This, however, would only be the beginning of their troubles. Gradually the more advanced thinkers and the closest observers would perceive that not only had their world undergone processes of development, but that its entire mass had been formed by such processes—that in fact it had not been created at all, in the sense in which they had understood the word, but had *grown.* This would be very dreadful to these creatures, because they would not readily be able to dispossess their minds of the notion that they were the most important beings in the universe, their domain of space coextensive with the universe, the duration of their world coextensive with time.

But passing over the difficulties thus arising, and the persecution and abuse to which those would be subjected who maintained the dangerous doctrine that their fruit home had been developed, not created, let us consider how these creatures would regard the question of other worlds than their own. At first they would naturally be unwilling to admit the possibility that other worlds as important as their own could exist. But if after a time they found reason to believe that their world was only one of several belonging to a certain tree system, the idea would occur to them, and would gradually come to be regarded as something more than probable, that those other fruit worlds. like their own, might be the abode of living creatures. And probably at first, while as yet the development of their own world was little understood, they would conceive the notion that all the fruits, large or small, upon their tree system were in the same condition as their own, and either inhabited by similar races or at least in the same full vigour of life-bearing existence. But so soon as they recognised the law of development of their own world, and the relation between such development and their own requirements, they would form a different opinion, if they found that only during certain stages of their world's existence life could exist upon it. If, for instance, they perceived that their fruit world must once have been so bitter and harsh in texture that no creatures in the least degree like themselves could have lived upon it, and that it was passing slowly but surely through processes by which it would become one day dry and shrivelled and unable to support living creatures, they would be apt, if their reasoning powers were fairly developed, to inquire whether other fruits which they saw around them on their tree system were either in the former or in the latter condition. If they found reason to believe certain fruits were in one or other of these stages, they would regard such fruits as not yet the abode of life or as past the life-supporting era. It seems probable even that another idea would suggest itself to some among their bolder thinkers. Recognising in their own world in several instances what to their ideas resembled absolute waste of material or of force, it might appear to them quite possible that some, perhaps even a large proportion, of the fruits upon their tree were not only not supporting life at the particular epoch of observation, but never had supported life and never would—that, through some cause or other, life would never appear upon such fruits even when they were excellently fitted for the support of life. They might even conceive that some among the fruits of their tree had failed or would fail to come to the full perfection of fruit life.

Looking beyond their own tree—that is, the tree to which their own fruit world belonged—they would perceive other trees, though their visual powers might not enable them to know whether such trees bore fruit, whether they were in other respects like their own, whether those which seemed larger or smaller were really so, or owed their apparent largeness to nearness, or their apparent smallness to great distance. They would be apt perhaps to generalise a little too daringly respecting these remote tree systems, concluding too confidently that a shrub or a flower was a tree system like their own, or that a great tree, every branch of which was far larger than their entire tree system, belonged to the same order and bore similar fruit. They might mistake, also, in forgetting the probable fact that as every fruit in their own tree system had its own period of life, very brief compared with the entire existence of the fruit, so every tree might have its own fruit-bearing season. Thus, contemplating a tree which they supposed to be like their own in its nature, they might say, 'Yonder is a tree system crowded with fruits, each the abode of many myriads of creatures like ourselves:' whereas in reality the tree might be utterly unlike their own, might not yet have reached or might long since have passed the fruit-bearing stage, might when in that stage bear fruit utterly unlike any they could even imagine, and each such fruit during its brief life-bearing condition might be inhabited by living beings utterly unlike any creatures they could conceive.

Yet again, we can very well imagine that the inhabitants of our fruit world, though they might daringly overleap the narrow limits of space and time within which their actual life or the life of their race was cast, though they might learn to recognise the development of their own world and of others like it, even from the very blossom, would be utterly unable to conceive the possibility that the tree itself to which their world belonged had developed by slow processes of growth from a time when it was less even than their own relatively minute home.

Still less would it seem credible to them, or even conceivable, that the whole forest region to which they belonged, containing many orders of trees differing altogether from their own tree system, besides plants and shrubs, and flowers and herbs (forms of vegetation of whose use they could form no just conception whatever), had itself grown; that once the entire forest domain had been under vast masses of water—the substance which occasionally visited their world in the form of small drops; that such changes were but minute local phenomena of a world infinitely higher in order than their own; that that world in turn was but one of the least of the worlds forming a yet higher system; and so on *ad infinitum*. Such ideas would seem to them not merely inconceivable, but many degrees beyond the widest conceptions of space and time which they could regard as admissible.

Our position differs only in degree, not in kind, from that of these imagined creatures, and the reasoning which we perceive (though they could not) to be just for such creatures is just for us also. It was perfectly natural that before men recognised the evidences of development in the structure of our earth they should regard the earth and all things upon the earth and visible from the earth as formed by special creative acts precisely as we see them now. But so soon as they perceived that the earth is undergoing processes of development and has undergone such processes in the past, it was reasonable, though at first painful, to conclude that on this point they had been mistaken. Yet as we recognise the absurdity of the supposition that, because fruits and trees grow, and were not made in a single instant as we know them, therefore there is no Supreme Being, so may we justly reject as absurd the same argument, enlarged in scale, employed to induce the conclusion that because planets and solar systems have been developed to their present condition, and were not created in their present form, therefore there is no Creator, no God. I do not know that the argument ever has been used in this form; but it has been used to show that those who believe in the development of worlds and systems must of necessity be atheists, an even more mischievous conclusion than the other; for none who had not examined the subject would be likely to adopt the former conclusion, but many might be willing to believe that a number of their fellow-men hold obnoxious tenets, without inquiring closely or at all into the reasoning on which the assertion had been based.

But it is more important to notice how our views respecting other worlds should be affected by those circumstances in the evidence *we* have, which correspond with the features of the evidence on which the imagined inhabitants of the fruit world would form their opinion. It was natural that when men first began to reason about themselves and their home they should reject the idea of other worlds like ours, and perhaps it was equally natural that when first the idea was entertained that the planets may be worlds like ours, men should conceive that all those worlds are in the same condition as ours. But it would be, or rather it *is*, as unreasonable for men to maintain such an opinion now, when the laws of planetary development are understood, when the various dimensions of the planets are known, and when the shortness of the life-supporting period of a planet's existence compared with the entire duration of the planet has been clearly recognised, as it would be for the imagined inhabitants of a small fruit on a tree to suppose that all the other fruits on the tree, though some manifestly far less advanced in development and others far more advanced than their own, were the abode of the same forms of life, though these forms were seen to require those conditions, and no other, corresponding to the stage of development through which their own world was passing.

Viewing the universe of suns and worlds in the manner here suggested, we should adopt a theory of other worlds which would hold a position intermediate between the Brewsterian and the Whewellite theories. (It is not on this account that I advocate it, let me remark in passing, but simply because it accords with the evidence, which is not the case with the others.) Rejecting on the one hand the theory of the plurality of worlds in the sense implying that all existing worlds are inhabited, and on the other hand the theory of but one world, we should accept a theory which might be entitled the Paucity of Worlds, only that relative not absolute paucity must be understood. It is absolutely certain that this theory is the correct one, if we admit two postulates, neither of which can be reasonably questioned—viz., first, that the life-bearing era of any world is short compared with the entire duration of that world; and secondly, that there can have been no cause which set all the worlds in existence, not simultaneously, which would be amazing enough, but (which would be infinitely more surprising) in such a way that after passing each through its time of preparation, longer for the large worlds and shorter for the small worlds, they all reached at the same time the life-bearing era. But quite apart from this antecedent probability, amounting as it does to absolute certainty if these two highly probably postulates are admitted, we have the actual evidence of the planets we can examine—that evidence proving incontestably, as I have shown elsewhere, that such planets as Jupiter and Saturn are still in the state of preparation, still so intensely hot that no form of life could possibly exist upon them, and that such bodies as our moon have long since passed the life-bearing stage, and are to all intents and purposes defunct.

But may we not go farther? Recognising in our own world, in many instances, what to our ideas resembles waste—waste seeds, waste lives, waste races, waste regions, waste forces—recognising superfluity and superabundance in all the processes and in all the works of nature, should it not appear at least possible that some, perhaps even a large proportion, of the worlds in the multitudinous systems peopling space, are not only not now supporting life, but never have supported life and never will? Does this idea differ in kind, however largely to our feeble conceptions it may seem to differ in degree, from the idea of the imagined creatures on a fruit, that some or even many fruits excellently fitted for the support of life might not subserve that purpose? And as those creatures might conceive (as we *know*) that some fruits, even many, fail to come to the full perfection of fruit life, may not we without irreverence conceive (as higher beings than ourselves may *know*) that a planet or a sun may fail in the making? We cannot say that in such a case there would be a waste or loss of material, though we may be unable to conceive how the lost sun or planet could be utilised. Our imagined insect reasoners would be unable to imagine that fruits plucked from their tree system were otherwise than wasted, for they would conceive that their idea of the purpose of fruits was the only true one; yet they would be altogether mistaken, as we may be in supposing the main purpose of planetary existence is the support of life.

In like manner, when we pass in imagination beyond the limits of our own system, we may learn a useful lesson from the imagined creatures' reasoning about other tree systems than that to which their world belonged. Astronomers have been apt to generalise too daringly respecting remote stars and star systems, as though our solar system were a true picture of all solar systems, the system of stars to which our sun belongs a true picture of all star systems. They have been apt to forget that, as every world in our own system has its period of life, short by comparison with the entire duration of the world, so each solar system, each system of such systems, may have its own life-bearing season, infinitely long according to our conceptions, but very short indeed compared with the entire duration of which the life-bearing season would be only a single era.

Lastly, though men may daringly overleap the limits of time and space within which their lives are cast, though they may learn to recognise the development of their own world and of others like it even from the blossom of nebulosity, they seem unable to rise to the conception that the mighty tree which during remote æons bore those nebulous blossoms sprang itself from cosmical germs. We are unable to conceive the nature of such germs; the processes of development affecting them belong to other orders than any processes we know of, and required periods compared with which the inconceivable, nay, the inexpressible periods required for the development of the parts of our universe, are as mere instants. Yet have we every reason which analogy can afford to believe that even the development of a whole universe such as ours should be regarded as but a minute local phenomenon of a universe infinitely higher in order, that universe in turn but a single member of a system of such universes, and so on, even *ad infinitum*. To reject the belief that this is possible is to share the folly of beings such as we have conceived regarding their tiny world as a fit centre whence to measure the universe, while yet, from such a stand-point, this little earth on which we live would be many degrees beyond the limits where for them the inconceivable would begin. To reject the belief that this is not only possible, but real, is to regard the few short steps by which man has advanced towards the unknown as a measurable approach towards limits of space, towards the beginning and the end of all things. Until it can be shown that space is bounded by limits beyond which neither matter nor void exists, that time had a beginning before which it was not and tends to an end after which it will exist no more, we may confidently accept the belief that the history of our earth is as evanescent in time as the earth itself is evanescent in space, and that nothing we can possibly learn about our earth, or about the system it belongs to, or about systems of such systems, can either prove or disprove aught respecting the scheme and mode of government of the universe itself. It is true now as it was in days of yore, and it will remain true as long as the earth and those who dwell on it endure, that what men know is nothing, the unknown infinite.

VI.

SUNS IN FLAMES.

In November 1876 news arrived of a catastrophe the effects of which must in all probability have been disastrous, not to a district, or a country, or a continent, or even a world, but to a whole system of worlds. The catastrophe happened many years ago—probably at least a hundred—yet the messenger who brought the news has not been idle on his way, but has sped along at a rate which would suffice to circle this earth eight times in the course of a second. That messenger has had, however, to traverse millions of millions of miles, and only reached our earth November 1876. The news he brought was that a sun like our own was in conflagration; and on a closer study of his message something was learned as to the nature of the conflagration, and a few facts tending to throw light on the question (somewhat interesting to ourselves) whether our own sun is likely to undergo a similar mishap at any time. What would happen if he did, we know already. The sun which has just met with this disaster—that is, which so suffered a few generations ago—blazed out for a time with several hundred times its former lustre. If our sun were to increase as greatly in light and heat, the creatures on the side of our earth turned towards him at the time would be destroyed in an instant. Those on the dark or night hemisphere would not have to wait for their turn till the earth, by rotating, carried them into view of the destroying sun. In much briefer space the effect of his new fires would be felt all over the earth's surface. The heavens would be dissolved and the elements would melt with fervent heat. In fact no description of such a catastrophe, as affecting the night half of the earth, could possibly be more effective and poetical than St. Peter's account of the day of the Lord, coming 'as a thief in the night; in the which the heavens shall pass away with a great noise, and the elements shall melt with fervent heat, the earth also and the works that are therein being burned up;' though I imagine the apostle would have been scarce prepared to admit that the earth was in danger from a solar conflagration. Indeed, according to another account, the sun was to be turned into darkness and the moon into blood, before that great and notable day of the Lord came—a description corresponding well with solar and lunar eclipses, the most noteworthy 'signs in the heavens,' but agreeing very ill with the outburst of a great solar conflagration.

Before proceeding to inquire into the singular and significant circumstances of the recent outburst, it may be found interesting to examine briefly the records which astronomy has preserved of similar catastrophes in former years. These may be compared to the records of accidents on the various railway lines in a country or continent. Those other suns which we call stars are engines working the mighty mechanism of planetary systems, as our sun maintains the energies of our own system; and it is a matter of some interest to us to inquire in how many cases, among the many suns within the range of vision, destructive explosions occur. We may take the opportunity, later, to inquire into the number of cases in which the machinery of solar systems appears to have broken down.

The first case of a solar conflagration on record is that

of the new star observed by Hipparchus some 2000 years ago. In his time, and indeed until quite recently, an object of this kind was called a new star, or a temporary star. But we now know that when a star makes its appearance where none had before been visible, what has really happened has been that a star too remote to be seen has become visible through some rapid increase of splendour. When the new splendour dies out again, it is not that a star has ceased to exist; but simply that a faint star which had increased greatly in lustre has resumed its original condition. Hipparchus's star must have been a remarkable object, for it was visible in full daylight, whence we may infer that it was many times brighter than the blazing Dog-star. It is interesting in the history of science, as having led Hipparchus to draw up a catalogue of stars, the first on record. Some moderns, being sceptical, rejected this story as a fiction; but Biot examining Chinese Chronicles[1] relating to the times of Hipparchus, finds that in 134 B.C. (about nine years before the date of Hipparchus's catalogue) a new star was recorded as having appeared in the constellation Scorpio.

The next new star (that is, stellar conflagration) on

[1] Chinese chronicles contain other references to new stars. The annals of Ma-touan-lin, which contain the official records of remarkable appearances in the heavens, include some phenomena which manifestly belong to this class. Thus they record that in the year 173 a star appeared between the stars which mark the hind feet of the Centaur. This star remained visible from December in that year until July in the next (about the same time as Tycho Brahe's and Kepler's new stars, presently to be described). Another star, assigned by these annals to the year 1011, seems to be the same as a star referred to by Hepidannus as appearing A.D. 1012. It was of extraordinary brilliancy, and remained visible in the southern part of the heavens during three months. The annals of Ma-touan-lin assign to it a position low down in Sagittarius.

record is still more interesting, as there appears some reason for believing that before long we may see another outburst of the same star. In the years 945, 1264, and 1572, brilliant stars appeared in the region of the heavens between Cepheus and Cassiopeia. Sir J. Herschel remarks, that, 'from the imperfect account we have of the places of the two earlier, as compared with that of the last, which was well determined, as well as from the tolerably near coincidence of the intervals of their appearance, we may suspect them, with Goodricke, to be one and the same star, with a period of 312 or perhaps of 156 years.' The latter period may very reasonably be rejected, as one can perceive no reason why the intermediate returns of the star to visibility should have been overlooked, the star having appeared in a region which never sets. It is to be noted that, the period from 945 to 1264 being 319 years, and that from 1264 to 1572 only 308 years, the period of this star (if Goodricke is correct in supposing the three outbursts to have occurred in the same star) would seem to be diminishing. At any time, then, this star might now blaze out in the region between Cassiopeia and Cepheus, for more than 304 years have already passed since its last outburst.

As the appearance of a new star led Hipparchus to undertake the formation of his famous catalogue, so did the appearance of the star in Cassiopeia, in 1572, lead the Danish astronomer Tycho Brahe to construct a new and enlarged catalogue. (This, be it remembered, was before the invention of the telescope.) Returning one evening (November 11, 1572, old style) from his laboratory to his dwelling-house, he found, says Sir J. Herschel, 'a group of country people gazing at a star, which he was sure did not exist an hour before. This was the star in question.'

The description of the star and its various changes is more interesting at the present time, when the true nature of these phenomena is understood, than it was even in the time when the star was blazing in the firmament. It will be gathered from that description and from what I shall have to say farther on about the results of recent observations on less splendid new stars, that, if this star should reappear in the next few years, our observers will probably be able to obtain very important information from it. The message from it will be much fuller and more distinct than any we have yet received from such stars, though we have learned quite enough to remain in no sort of doubt as to their general nature.

The star remained visible, we learn, about sixteen months, during which time it kept its place in the heavens without the least variation. 'It had all the radiance of the fixed stars, and twinkled like them; and was in all respects like Sirius, except that it surpassed Sirius in brightness and magnitude.' It appeared larger than Jupiter, which was at that time at his brightest, and was scarcely inferior to Venus. *It did not acquire this lustre gradually*, but shone forth at once of its full size and brightness, 'as if,' said the chroniclers of the time, 'it had been of instantaneous creation.' For three weeks it shone with full splendour, during which time it could be seen at noonday 'by those who had good eyes, and knew where to look for it.' But before it had been seen a month, it became visibly smaller, and from the middle of December 1572 till March 1574, when it entirely disappeared, it continually diminished in magnitude. 'As it decreased in size, it varied in colour: at first its light was white and extremely bright; it then became yellowish; afterwards of a ruddy colour like Mars; and finished with a pale livid white resembling the colour of Saturn.' All the details of this account should be very carefully noted. It will presently be seen that they are highly characteristic.

Those who care to look occasionally at the heavens to know whether this star has returned to view may be interested to learn whereabouts it should be looked for. The place may be described as close to the back of the star-gemmed chair in which Cassiopeia is supposed to sit—a little to the left of the seat of the chair, supposing the chair to be looked at in its normal position. But as Cassiopeia's chair is always inverted when the constellation is most conveniently placed for observation, and indeed as nine-tenths of those who know the constellation suppose the chair's legs to be the back, and *vice versâ*, it may be useful to mention that the star was placed somewhat thus with respect to the straggling W formed by the five chief stars of Cassiopeia.

There is a star not very far from the place here indicated, but rather nearer to the middle angle of the W. This, however, is not a bright star; and cannot possibly be mistaken for the expected visitant. (The place of Tycho's star is indicated in my School Star-Atlas and also in my larger Library Atlas. The same remark applies to both the new stars in the Serpent-Bearer, presently to be described.)

In August 1596 the astronomer Fabricius observed a new star in the neck of the Whale, which also after a time disappeared. It was not noticed again till the year 1637, when an observer rejoicing in the name of Phocyllides Holwarda observed it, and, keeping a watch, after it had vanished, upon the place where it had appeared, saw it again come into view nine months after its disappearance. Since then it has been known as a variable star with a period of about 331 days 8 hours. When brightest this star is of the second magnitude. It indicates a somewhat singular remissness on the part of the astronomers of former days, that a star shining so conspicuously for a fortnight, once in each period of $331\frac{1}{3}$ days, should for so many years have remained undetected. It may, perhaps, be thought that, noting this, I should withdraw the objection raised above against Sir J. Herschel's idea that the star in Cassiopeia may return to view once in 156 years, instead of once in 312 years. But there is a great difference between a star which at its brightest shines only as a second-magnitude star, so that it has twenty or thirty companions of equal or greater lustre above the horizon along with it, and a star which surpasses three-fold the splendid Sirius. We have seen that even in Tycho Brahe's day, when probably the stars were not nearly so well known by the community at large, the new star in Cassiopeia had not shone an hour before the country people were gazing at it with wonder. Besides, Cassiopeia and the Whale are constellations very different in position. The familiar stars of Cassiopeia are visible on every clear night, for they never set. The stars of the Whale, at least of the part to which the wonderful variable star belongs, are below the horizon during rather more than half the twenty-four hours; and a new star there would only be noticed, probably (unless of exceeding splendour), if it chanced to appear during that part of the year when the Whale is high above the horizon between eventide and midnight, or in the autumn and early winter.

It is a noteworthy circumstance about the variable star in the Whale, deservedly called Mira, or The Wonderful, that it does not always return to the same degree of brightness. Sometimes it has been a very bright second-magnitude star when at its brightest, at others it has barely exceeded the third magnitude. Hevelius relates that during the four years between October 1672 and December 1676, Mira did not show herself at all! As this star fades out, it changes in colour from white to red.

Towards the end of September 1604, a new star made

its appearance in the constellation Ophiuchus, or the Serpent-Bearer. Its place was near the heel of the right foot of 'Ophiuchus huge.'. Kepler tells us that it had no hair or tail, and was certainly not a comet. Moreover, like the other fixed stars, it kept its place unchanged, showing unmistakably that it belonged to the star-depths, not to nearer regions. 'It was exactly like one of the stars, except that in the vividness of its lustre, and the quickness of its sparkling, it exceeded anything that he had ever seen before. It was every moment changing into some of the colours of the rainbow, as yellow, orange, purple, and red; though it was generally white when it was at some distance from the vapours of the horizon.' In fact, these changes of colour must not be regarded as indicating aught but the star's superior brightness. Every very bright star, when close to the horizon, shows these colours, and so much the more distinctly as the star is the brighter. Sirius, which surpasses the brightest stars of the northern hemisphere full four times in lustre, shows these changes of colour so conspicuously that they were regarded as specially characteristic of this star, insomuch that Homer speaks of Sirius (not by name, but as the 'star of autumn') shining most beautifully 'when laved of ocean's wave'—that is, when close to the horizon. And our own poet, Tennyson, following the older poet, sings how

> the fiery Sirius alters hue,
> And bickers into red and emerald.

The new star was brighter than Sirius, and was about five degrees lower down, when at its highest above the horizon, than Sirius when *he* culminates. Five degrees being equal to nearly ten times the apparent diameter of the moon, it will be seen how much more favourable the conditions were in the case of Kepler's star for those coloured scintillations which characterised that orb. Sirius never rises very high above the horizon. In fact, at his highest (near midnight in winter, and, of course, near midday in summer) he is about as high above the horizon as the sun at midday in the first week in February. Kepler's star's greatest height above the horizon was little more than three-fourths of this, or equal to about the sun's elevation at midday on January 13 or 14 in any year.

Like Tycho Brahe's star, Kepler's was brighter even than Jupiter, and only fell short of Venus in splendour. It preserved its lustre for about three weeks, after which time it gradually grew fainter and fainter until some time between October 1605 and February 1606, when it disappeared. The exact day is unknown, as during that interval the constellation of the Serpent-Bearer is above the horizon in the day-time only. But in February 1606, when it again became possible to look for the new star in the night-time, it had vanished. It probably continued to glow with sufficient lustre to have remained visible, but for the veil of light under which the sun concealed it, for about sixteen months altogether. In fact, it seems very closely to have resembled Tycho's star, not only in appearance and in the degree of its greatest brightness, but in the duration of its visibility.

In the year 1670 a new star appeared in the constellation Cygnus, attaining the third magnitude. It remained visible, but not with this lustre, for nearly two years. After it had faded almost out of view, it flickered up again for awhile, but soon after it died out, so as to be entirely invisible. Whether a powerful telescope would still have shown it is uncertain, but it seems extremely probable. It may be, indeed, that this new star in the Swan is the same which has made its appearance within the last few weeks; but on this point the evidence is uncertain.

On April 20, 1848, Mr. Hind (Superintendent of the Nautical Almanac, and discoverer of ten new members of the solar system) noticed a new star of the fifth magnitude in the Serpent-Bearer, but in quite another part of that large constellation than had been occupied by Kepler's star. A few weeks later, it rose to the fourth magnitude. But afterwards its light diminished until it became invisible to ordinary eyesight. It did not vanish utterly, however. It is still visible with telescopic power, shining as a star of the eleventh magnitude, that is five magnitudes below the faintest star discernible with the unaided eye.

This is the first new star which has been kept in view since its apparent creation. But we are now approaching the time when it was found that as so-called new stars continue in existence long after they have disappeared from view, so also they are not in reality new, but were in existence long before they became visible to the naked eye.

On May 12, 1866, shortly before midnight, Mr. Birmingham, of Tuam, noticed a star of the second magnitude in the Northern Crown, where hitherto no star visible to the naked eye had been known. Dr. Schmidt, of Athens, who had been observing that region of the heavens the same night, was certain that up to 11 P.M., Athens local time, there was no star above the fourth magnitude in the place occupied by the new star. So that, if this negative evidence can be implicitly relied on, the new star must have sprung at least from the fourth, and probably from a much lower magnitude, to the second, in less than three hours—eleven o'clock at Athens corresponding to about nine o'clock by Irish railway time. A Mr. Barker, of London, Canada, put forward a claim to having seen the new star as early as May 4—a claim not in the least worth investigating, so far as the credit of first seeing the new star is concerned, but exceedingly important in its bearing on the nature of the outburst affecting the star in Corona. It is unpleasant to have to throw discredit on any definite assertion of facts; unfortunately, however, Mr. Barker, when his claim was challenged, laid before Mr. Stone, of the Greenwich Observatory, such very definite records of observations made on May 4, 8, 9, and 10, that we have no choice but either to admit these observations, or to infer that he experienced the delusive effects of a very singular trick of memory. He mentions in his letter to Mr. Stone that he had sent full particulars of his observations on those early dates to Professor Watson, of Ann Arbor University, on May 17; but (again unfortunately) instead of leaving that letter to tell its own story in Professor Watson's hands, he asked Professor Watson to return it to him: so that when Mr. Stone very naturally asked Professor Watson to furnish a copy of this important letter, Professor Watson had to reply, 'About a month ago, Mr. Barker applied to me for this letter, and I returned it to him, as requested, without preserving a copy. I can, however,' he proceeded, 'state positively that he did not mention any actual observation earlier than May 14. He said he thought he had noticed a strange star in the Crown about two weeks before the date of his first observation—May 14—but not particularly, and that he did not recognise it until the 14th. He did not give any date, and did not even seem positive as to identity. . . . When I returned the letter of May 17, I made an endorsement across the first page, in regard to its genuineness, and attached my signature. I regret that I did not preserve a copy of the letter in question; but if the original is produced, it will appear that my recollection of its contents is correct.' I think no one can blame Mr. Stone, if, on the receipt of this letter, he stated that he had not the 'slightest hesitation' in regarding Mr.

Barker's earlier observations as 'not entitled to the slightest credit.'[1]

It may be fairly taken for granted that the new star leapt very quickly, if not quite suddenly, to its full splendour. Birmingham, as we have seen, was the first to notice it, on May 12. On the evening of May 13, Schmidt of Athens discovered it independently, and a few hours later it was noticed by a French engineer named Courbebaisse. Afterwards, Baxendell of Manchester, and others independently saw the star. Schmidt, examining Argelander's charts of 324,000 stars (charts which I have had the pleasure of mapping in a single sheet), found that the star was not a new

[1] Still a circumstance must be mentioned which tends to show that the star may have been visible a few hours earlier than Dr. Schmidt supposed. Mr. M. Walter, surgeon of the 4th regiment, then stationed in North India, wrote (oddly enough, on May 12, 1867, the first anniversary of Mr. Birmingham's discovery) as follows to Mr. Stone :—'I am certain that this same conflagration was distinctly perceptible here at least six hours earlier. My knowledge of the fact came about in this wise. The night of the 12th of May last year was exceedingly sultry, and about eight o'clock on that evening I got up from the tea-table and rushed into my garden to seek a cooler atmosphere. As my door opens towards the east, the first object that met my view was the Northern Crown. My attention was at once arrested by the sight of a strange star outside the crown' (that is, outside the circlet of stars forming the diadem, not outside the constellation itself). The new star 'was then certainly quite as bright—I rather thought more so—as its neighbour Alphecca,' the chief gem of the crown. 'I was so much struck with its appearance, that I exclaimed to those indoors, "Why, here is a new comet!"' He made a diagram of the constellation, showing the place of the new star correctly. Unfortunately, Mr. Walter does not state why he is so confident, a year after the event, that it was on the 12th of May, and not on the 13th, that he noticed the new star. If he fixed the date only by the star's appearance as a second-magnitude star, his letter proves nothing; for we know that on the 13th it was still shining as brightly as Alphecca, though on the 14th it was perceptibly fainter.

one, but had been set down by Argelander as between the ninth and tenth magnitudes. Referring to Argelander's list, we find that the star had been twice observed—viz., on May 18, 1855, and on March 31, 1856.

Birmingham wrote at once to Mr. Huggins, who, in conjunction with the late Dr. Miller, had been for some time engaged in observing stars and other celestial objects with the spectroscope. These two observers at once directed their telescope armed with spectroscopic adjuncts—the telespectroscope is the pleasing name of the compound instrument—to the new-comer. The result was rather startling. It may be well, however, before describing it, to indicate in a few words the meaning of various kinds of spectroscopic evidence.

The light of the sun, sifted out by the spectroscope, shows all the colours but not all the tints of the rainbow. It is spread out into a large rainbow-tinted streak, but at various places (a few thousand) along the streak there are missing tints; so that in fact the streak is crossed by a multitude of dark lines. We know that these lines are due to the absorptive action of vapours existing in the atmosphere of the sun, and from the position of the lines we can tell what the vapours are. Thus, hydrogen by its absorptive action produces four of the bright lines. The vapour of iron is there, the vapour of sodium, magnesium, and so on. Again, we know that these same vapours, which, by their absorptive action, cut off rays of certain tints, emit light of just those tints. In fact, if the glowing mass of the sun could be suddenly extinguished, leaving his atmosphere in its present intensely heated condition, the light of the faint sun which would thus be left us would give (under spectroscopic scrutiny) those very rays which now seem wanting. There would be a spectrum of multitudinous bright lines, instead of a rainbow-tinted spectrum crossed by multitudinous dark lines. It is, indeed, only by contrast that the dark lines appear dark, just as it is only by contrast that the solar spots seem dark. Not only the penumbra but the umbra of a sunspot, not only the umbra but the nucleus, not only the nucleus but the deeper black which seems to lie at the core of the nucleus, shine really with a lustre far exceeding that of the electric light, though by contrast with the rest of the sun's surface the penumbra looks dark, the umbra darker still, the nucleus deep black, and the core of the nucleus jet black. So the dark lines across the solar spectrum mark where certain rays are relatively faint, though in reality intensely lustrous. Conceive another change than that just imagined. Conceive the sun's globe to remain as at present, but the atmosphere to be excited to many times its present degree of light and splendour: then would all these dark lines become bright, and the rainbow-tinted background would be dull or even quite dark by contrast. This is not a mere fancy. At times, local disturbances take place in the sun which produce just such a change in certain constituents of the sun's atmosphere, causing the hydrogen, for example, to glow with so intense a heat that, instead of its lines appearing dark, they stand out as bright lines. Occasionally, too, the magnesium in the solar atmosphere (over certain limited regions only, be it remembered) has been known to behave in this manner. It was so during the intensely hot summer of 1872, insomuch that the Italian observer Tacchini, who noticed the phenomenon, attributed to such local overheating of the sun's magnesium vapour the remarkable heat from which we then for a time suffered.

Now, the stars are suns, and the spectrum of a star is simply a miniature of the solar spectrum. Of course, there are characteristic differences. One star has more hydrogen, at least more hydrogen at work absorbing its rays, and thus has the hydrogen lines more strongly marked than they are in the solar spectrum. Another star shows the lines of various metals more conspicuously, indicating that the glowing vapours of such elements, iron, copper, mercury, tin, and so forth, either hang more densely in the star's atmosphere than in our sun's, or, being cooler, absorb their special tints more effectively. But speaking generally, a stellar spectrum is like the solar spectrum. There is the rainbow-tinted streak, which implies that the source of light is glowing solid, liquid, or highly compressed vaporous matter, and athwart the streak there are the multitudinous dark lines which imply that around the glowing heart of the star there are envelopes of relatively cool vapours.

We can understand, then, the meaning of the evidence obtained from the new star in the Northern Crown.

In the first place, the new star showed the rainbow-tinted streak crossed by dark lines, which indicated its sun-like nature. *But, standing out on that rainbow-tinted streak as on a dark background, were four exceedingly bright lines—lines so bright, though fine, that clearly most of the star's light came from the glowing vapours to which these lines belonged.* Three of the lines belonged to hydrogen, the fourth was not identified with any known line.

Let us distinguish between what can certainly be concluded from this remarkable observation, and what can only be inferred with a greater or less degree of probability.

It is absolutely certain that when Messrs. Huggins and Miller made their observation (by which time the new star had faded from the second to the third magnitude), enormous masses of hydrogen around the star were glowing with a heat far more intense than that of the star itself within the hydrogen envelope. It is certain that the increase in the star's light, rendering the star visible which before had been far beyond the range of ordinary eyesight, was due to the abnormal heat of the hydrogen surrounding hat remote sun.

But it is not so clear whether the intense glow of the nydrogen was caused by combustion or by intense heat without combustion. The difference between the two causes of increased light is important; because on the opinion we form on this point must depend our opinion as to the probability that our sun may one day experience a similar catastrophe, and also our opinion as to the state of the sun in the Northern Crown after the outburst. To illustrate the distinction in question, let us take two familiar cases of the emission of light. A burning coal glows with red light, and so does a piece of iron placed in a coal fire. But the coal and the iron are undergoing very different processes. The coal is burning, and will presently be consumed; the iron is not burning (except in the sense that it is burning hot, which means only that it will make any combustible substance burn which is brought into contact with it), and it will not be consumed though the coal fire be maintained around it for days and weeks and months. So with the hydrogen flames which play at all times over the surface of our own sun. They are not burning like the hydrogen flames which are used for the oxy-hydrogen lantern. Were the solar hydrogen so burning, the sun would quickly be extinguished. They are simply aglow with intensity of heat, as a mass of red-hot iron is aglow; and, so long as the sun's energies are maintained, the hydrogen around him will glow in this way without being consumed. As the new fires of the star in the Crown died out rapidly, it is possible that in their case there was actual combustion. On the other hand, it is also possible, and perhaps on the whole more probable, that the hydrogen surrounding the star was simply set glowing with increased lustre owing to some cause not as yet ascertained.

Let us see how these two theories have been actually worded by the students of science themselves who have maintained them.

'The sudden blazing forth of this star,' says Mr. Huggins, 'and then the rapid fading away of its light, suggest the rather bold speculation that in consequence of some great internal convulsion, a large volume of hydrogen and other gases was evolved from it, the hydrogen, by its combination with some other element,' in other words, by *burning*, 'giving out the light represented by the bright lines, and at the same time heating to the point of vivid incandescence the solid matter of the star's surface.' 'As the liberated hydrogen gas became exhausted' (I now quote not Huggins's own words, but words describing his theory in a book which he has edited) 'the flame gradually abated, and, with the consequent cooling, the star's surface became less vivid, and the star returned to its original condition.'

On the other hand, the German physicists, Meyer and Klein, consider the sudden development of hydrogen, in quantities sufficient to explain such an outburst, exceedingly unlikely. They have therefore adopted the opinion, that the sudden blazing out of the star was occasioned by the violent precipitation of some mighty mass, perhaps a planet, upon the globe of that remote sun, 'by which the momentum of the falling mass would be changed into molecular motion, or in other words into heat and light.' It might even be supposed, they urge, that the star in the Crown, by its swift motion, may have come in contact with one of the star clouds which exist in large numbers in the realms of space. 'Such a collision would necessarily set the star in a blaze and occasion the most vehement ignition of its hydrogen.'

Fortunately, our sun is safe for many millions of years to come from contact from any one of its planets. The reader must not, however, run away with the idea that the danger consists only in the gradual contraction of planetary orbits sometimes spoken of. That contraction, if it is taking place at all, of which we have not a particle of evidence, would not draw Mercury to the sun's surface for at least ten million millions of years. The real danger would be in the effects which the perturbing action of the larger planets might produce on the orbit of Mercury. That orbit is even now very eccentric, and must at times become still more so. It might, but for the actual adjustment of the planetary system, become so eccentric that Mercury could not keep clear of the sun; and a blow from even small Mercury (only weighing, in fact, 390 millions of millions of millions of tons), with a velocity of some 300 miles per second, would warm our sun considerably. But there is no risk of this happening in Mercury's case—though the unseen and much more shifty Vulcan (in which planet I beg to express here my utter disbelief) might, perchance, work mischief if he really existed.

As for star clouds lying in the sun's course, we may feel equally confident. The telescope assures us that there are none immediately on the track, and we know, also, that, swiftly though the sun is carrying us onwards through space,[1] many millions of years must pass before he is among the star families towards which he is rushing.

Of the danger from combustion, or from other causes of ignition than those considered by Meyer and Klein, it still remains to speak. But first, let us consider what new evidence has been thrown upon the subject by the observations made on the star which flamed out last November.

[1] The velocity of three or four miles per second inferred by the elder Struve must now be regarded (as I long since pointed out would prove to be the case) as very far short of the real velocity of our system's motion through stellar space.

The new star was first seen by Professor Schmidt, who has had the good fortune of announcing to astronomers more than one remarkable phenomenon. It was he who discovered in November 1866 that a lunar crater had disappeared, an announcement quite in accordance with the facts of the case. We have seen that he was one of the independent discoverers of the outburst in the Northern Crown. On November 24, at the early hour of 5.41 in the evening (showing that Schmidt takes time by the forelock at his observatory), he noticed a star of the third magnitude in the constellation of the Swan, not far from the tail of that southward-flying celestial bird. He is quite sure that on November 20, the last preceding clear evening, the star was not there. At midnight its light was very yellow, and it was somewhat brighter than the neighbouring star Eta Pegasi, on the Flying Horse's southernmost knee (if anatomists will excuse my following the ordinary usage which calls the wrist of the horse's fore-arm the knee). He sent news of the discovery forthwith to Leverrier, the chief of the Paris observatory; and the observers there set to work to analyse the light of the stranger. Unfortunately the star's suddenly acquired brilliancy rapidly faded. M. Paul Henry estimated the star's brightness on December 2 as equal only to that of a fifth-magnitude star. Moreover, the colour, which had been very yellow on November 24, was by this time 'greenish, almost blue.' On December 2, M. Cornu, observing during a short time when the star was visible through a break between clouds, found that the star's spectrum consisted almost entirely of bright lines. On December 5, he was able to determine the position of these lines, though still much interrupted by clouds. He found three bright lines of hydrogen, the strong (really double) line of sodium, the (really triple) line of magnesium, and two other lines. One of these last seemed to agree exactly in position with a bright line belonging to the corona seen around the sun during total eclipse.[1]

The star has since faded gradually in lustre until, at present, it is quite invisible to the naked eye.

We cannot doubt that the catastrophe which befell this star is of the same general nature as is that which befell the star in the Northern Crown. It is extremely significant that all the elements which manifested signs of intense heat in the case of the star in the Swan, are characteristic of our sun's outer appendages. We know that the coloured flames seen around the sun during total solar eclipse consist of glowing hydrogen, and of glowing matter giving a line so near the sodium line that in the case of a stellar spectrum it would, probably, not be possible to distinguish one from the other. Into the prominences there are thrown from time to time masses of glowing sodium, magnesium, and (in less degree) iron and other metallic vapours. Lastly, in that glorious appendage, the solar corona, which extends for hundreds of thousands of miles from the sun's surface, there are enormous quantities of some element, whose nature is as yet unknown, showing under spectroscopic analysis the bright line which seems to have appeared in the spectrum of the flaming sun in the Swan.

[1] M. Cornu's observations are full of interest, and he deserves considerable credit for his energy in availing himself of the few favourable opportunities he had for making them. But he goes beyond his province in adding to his account of them some remarks, intended apparently as a reflection on Mr. Huggins's speculations respecting the star in the Northern Crown. '*I*,' says M. Cornu, 'will not try to form any hypothesis about the cause of the outburst. To do so would be unscientific, and such speculations, though interesting, cumber science wofully.' This is sheer nonsense, and comes very ill from an observer whose successes in science have been due entirely to the employment of methods of observation which would have had no existence had others been as unready to think out the meaning of observed facts as he appears to be himself.

This evidence seems to me to suggest that the intense heat which suddenly affected this star had its origin from without. At the same time, I cannot agree with Meyer and Klein in considering that the cause of the heat was either the downfall of a planetary mass on the star, or the collision of the star with a star-cloudlet, or nebula, traversing space in one direction while the star swept onwards in another. A planet could not very well come into final conflict with its sun at one fell swoop. It would gradually draw nearer and nearer, not by the narrowing of its path, but by the change of the path's shape. The path would, in fact, become more and more eccentric; until, at length, at its point of nearest approach, the planet would graze its primary, exciting an intense heat where it struck, but escaping actual destruction that time. The planet would make another circuit, and again graze its sun, at or near the same part of the planet's path. For several circuits this would continue, the grazes not becoming more effective each time, but rather less. The interval between them, however, would grow continually less and less. At last the time would come when the planet's path would be reduced to the circular form, its globe touching its sun's all the way round, and then the planet would very quickly be reduced to vapour, and partly burned up, its substance being absorbed by its sun. But all the successive grazes would be indicated to us by accessions in the star's lustre, the period between each seeming outburst being only a few months at first, and becoming gradually less and less (during a long course of years, perhaps even of centuries), until the planet was finally destroyed. Nothing of this sort has happened in the case of any so-called new star.

As for the rush of a star through a nebulous mass, that is a theory which would scarcely be entertained by any one acquainted with the enormous distances separating the gaseous star-clouds properly called nebulæ. There may be small clouds of the same sort scattered much more densely through space; but we have not a particle of evidence that this actually is the case. All we certainly *know* about star-cloudlets suggest that the distances separating them from each other are comparable with those which separate star from star, in which case the idea of a star coming into collision with a star-cloudlet, and still more the idea of this occurring several times in a century, is wild in the extreme.

On the whole, the theory seems more probable than any of these, that enormous flights of large meteoric masses travel around those stars which thus occasionally break forth in conflagration, such flights travelling on exceedingly eccentric paths, and requiring enormously long periods to complete each circuit of their vast orbits. In conceiving this, we are not imagining anything new. Such a meteoric flight would differ only in degree not kind from meteoric flights which are known to circle around our own sun. I am not sure, indeed, that it can be definitely asserted that our sun has no meteoric appendages of the same nature as those which, if this theory be true, excite to intense periodic activity the sun round which they circle. We know that comets and meteors are closely connected, every comet being probably (many certainly) attended by flights of meteoric masses. The meteors which produce the celebrated November showers of falling stars follow in the track of a comet invisible to the naked eye. May we not reasonably suppose, then, that those glorious comets which have not only been visible but conspicuous, shining even in the day-time, and brandishing round tails which, like that of the 'wonder in heaven, the great dragon,' seemed to 'draw the third part of the stars of heaven,' are followed by much denser flights of much more massive meteors? Now some-among these giant comets have paths which carry them very close to our sun. Newton's comet, with its tail a hundred millions of miles in length, all but grazed the sun's globe. The comet of 1843, whose tail, says Sir J. Herschel, 'stretched half-way across the sky,' must actually have grazed the sun, though but lightly, for its nucleus was within 80,000 miles of his surface, and its head was more than 160,000 miles in diameter. And these are only two among the few comets whose paths are known. At any time we might be visited by a comet mightier than either, travelling on an orbit intersecting the sun's surface, followed by flights of meteoric masses enormous in size and many in number, which, falling on the sun's globe with the enormous velocity corresponding to their vast orbital range and their near approach to the sun—a velocity of some 360 miles per second—would, beyond all doubt, excite his whole frame, and especially his surface regions, to a degree of heat far exceeding what he now emits.

We have had evidence of the tremendous heat to which the sun's surface would be excited by the downfall of a shower of large meteoric masses. Carrington and Hodgson, on September 1, 1859, observed (independently) the passage of two intensely bright bodies across a small part of the sun's surface—the bodies first increasing in brightness, then diminishing, then fading away. It is generally believed that these were meteoric masses raised to fierce heat by frictional resistance. Now so much brighter did they appear, or rather did that part of the sun's surface appear through which they had rushed, that Carrington supposed the dark glass screen used to protect the eye had broken, and Hodgson described the brightness of this part of the sun as such that the part shone like a brilliant star on the background of the glowing solar surface. Mark, also, the consequences of the downfall of those two bodies only. A magnetic disturbance affected the whole frame of the earth at the very time when the sun had been thus disturbed. Vivid auroras were seen not only in both hemispheres, but in latitudes where auroras are very seldom witnessed. 'By degrees,' says Sir J. Herschel, 'accounts began to pour in of great auroras seen not only in these latitudes, but at Rome, in the West Indies, in the tropics within eighteen degrees of the equator (where they hardly ever appear); nay, what is still more striking, in South America and in Australia—where, at Melbourne, on the night of September 2, the greatest aurora ever seen there made its appearance. These auroras were accompanied with unusually great electro-magnetic disturbances in every part of the world. In many places the telegraph wires struck work. They had too many private messages of their own to convey. At Washington and Philadelphia, in America, the electric signal-men received severe electric shocks. At a station in Norway the telegraphic apparatus was set fire to; and at Boston, in North America, a flame of fire followed the pen of Bain's electric telegraph, which writes down the message upon chemically prepared paper.' Seeing that where the two meteors fell the sun's surface glowed thus intensely, and that the effect of this accession of energy upon our earth was thus well marked, can it be doubted that a comet, bearing in its train a flight of many millions of meteoric masses, and falling directly upon the sun, would produce an accession of light and heat whose consequences would be disastrous? When the earth has passed through the richer portions (not the actual nuclei, be it remembered) of meteor systems, the meteors visible from even a single station have been counted by tens of thousands, and it has been computed that millions must have fallen upon the whole earth. These were meteors following in the train of very small comets. If a very large comet followed by no denser a flight of meteors, but each meteoric mass much larger, fell directly upon the sun, it would not be the outskirts but the nucleus of the meteoric train which would impinge upon him. They would number thousands of millions. The velocity of downfall of each mass would be more than 360 miles per second. And they would continue to pour in upon him for several days in succession, millions falling every hour. It seems not improbable that, under this tremendous and long-continued meteoric hail, his whole surface would be caused to glow as intensely as that small part whose brilliancy was so surprising in the observation made by Carrington and Hodgson. In that case, our sun, seen from some remote star whence ordinarily he is invisible, would shine out as a new sun, for a few days, while all things living on our earth, and whatever other members of the solar system are the abode of life, would inevitably be destroyed.

The reader must not suppose that this idea has been suggested merely in the attempt to explain outbursts of stars. The following passage from a paper of considerable scientific interest by Professor Kirkwood, of Bloomington, Indiana, a well-known American astronomer, shows that the idea had occurred to him for a very different reason. He speaks here of a probable connection between the comet of 1843 and the great sun-spot which appeared in June 1843. I am not sure, however, but that we may regard the very meteors which seem to have fallen on the sun on September 1, 1859, as bodies travelling in the track of the comet of 1843—just as the November meteors seen in 1867-8, 9, etc., until 1872, were bodies certainly following in the track of the telescopic comet of 1866. 'The opinion has been expressed by more than one astronomer,' he says, speaking of Carrington's observation, 'that this phenomenon was produced by the fall of meteoric matter upon the sun's surface. Now, the fact may be worthy of note that the comet of 1843 actually grazed the sun's atmosphere about three months before the appearance of the great sun-spot of the same year. Had it approached but little nearer, the resistance of the atmosphere would probably have brought its entire mass to the solar surface. Even at its actual distance it must have produced considerable atmospheric disturbance. But the recent discovery that a number of comets are associated with meteoric matter, travelling in nearly the same orbits, suggests the inquiry whether an enormous meteorite following in the comet's train, and having a somewhat less perihelion distance, may not have been precipitated upon the sun, thus producing the great disturbance observed so shortly after the comet's perihelion passage.'

There are those, myself among the number, who consider the periodicity of the solar spots, that tide of spots which flows to its maximum and then ebbs to its minimum in a little more than eleven years, as only explicable on the theory that a small comet having this period, and followed by a meteor train, has a path intersecting the sun's surface. In an article entitled 'The Sun a Bubble,' which appeared in the 'Cornhill Magazine' for October 1874, I remarked that from the observed phenomena of sun-spots we might be led to suspect the existence of some as yet undetected comet with a train of exceptionally large meteoric masses, travelling in a period of about eleven years round the sun, and having its place of nearest approach to that orb so close to the solar surface that, when the main flight is passing, the stragglers fall upon the sun's surface. In this case, we could readily understand that, as this small comet unquestionably causes our sun to be variable to some slight degree in brilliancy, in a period of about eleven years, so some much larger comet circling around Mira, in a period of about 331 days, may occasion those alternations of brightness which have been described above. It may be noticed in passing, that it is by no means certain that the time when the sun is most spotted is the time when he gives out least light. Though at such times his surface is dark where the spots are, yet elsewhere it is probably brighter than usual; at any rate, all the evidence we have tends to show that when the sun is most spotted, his energies are most active. It is then that the coloured flames leap to their greatest height and show their greatest brilliancy, then also that they show the most rapid and remarkable changes of shape.

Supposing there really is, I will not say danger, but a possibility, that our sun may one day, through the arrival of some very large comet travelling directly towards him, share the fate of the suns whose outbursts I have described above, we might be destroyed unawares, or we might be aware for several weeks of the approach of the destroying comet. Suppose, for example, the comet, which might arrive from any part of the heavens, came from out that part of the star-depths which is occupied by the constellation Taurus—then, if the arrival were so timed that the comet, which might reach the sun at any time, fell upon him in May or June, we should know nothing of that comet's approach: for it would approach in that part of the heavens which was occupied by the sun, and his splendour would hide as with a veil the destroying enemy. On the other hand, if the comet, arriving from the same region of the heavens, so approached as to fall upon the sun in November or December, we should see it for several weeks. For it would then approach from the part of the heavens high above the southern horizon at midnight. Astronomers would be able in a few days after it was discovered to determine its path and predict its downfall upon the sun, precisely as Newton calculated the path of *his* comet and predicted its near approach to the sun. It would be known for weeks then that the event which Newton contemplated as likely to cause a tremendous outburst of solar heat, competent to destroy all life upon the surface of our earth, was about to take place; and, doubtless, the minds of many students of science would be exercised during that interval in determining whether Newton was right or wrong. For my own part, I have very little doubt that, though the change in the sun's condition in consequence of the direct downfall upon his surface of a very large comet would be but temporary, and in that sense slight—for what are a few weeks in the history of an orb which has already existed during thousands of millions of years?—yet the effect upon the inhabitants of the earth would be by no means slight. I do not think, however, that any students of science would remain, after the catastrophe, to estimate or to record its effects.

Fortunately, all that we have learned hitherto from the stars favours the belief that, while a catastrophe of this sort may be possible, it is exceedingly unlikely. We may estimate the probabilities precisely in the same way that an insurance company estimates the chance of a railway accident. Such a company considers the number of accidents which occur among a given number of railway journeys, and from the smallness of the number of accidents compared with the largeness of the number of journeys estimates the safety of railway travelling. Our sun is one among many millions of suns, any one of which (though all but a few thousands are actually invisible) would become visible to the naked eye, if exposed to the same conditions as have affected the suns in flames described in the preceding pages. Seeing, then, that during the last two thousand years or thereabouts, only a few instances of the kind, certainly not so many as twenty, have been recorded, while there is reason to believe that some of these relate to the same star which has blazed out more than once, we may fairly consider the chance exceedingly small that during the next two thousand, or even the next twenty thousand years, our sun will be exposed to a catastrophe of the kind.

We might arrive at this conclusion independently of any considerations tending to show that our sun belongs to a safe class of system-rulers, and that all, or nearly all, the great solar catastrophes have occurred among suns of a particular class. There are, however, several considerations of the kind which are worth noting.

In the first place, we may dismiss as altogether unlikely the visit of a comet from the star-depths to our sun, on a course carrying the comet directly upon the sun's surface. But if, among the comets travelling in regular attendance upon the sun, there be one whose orbit intersects the sun's globe, then that comet must several times ere this have struck the sun, raising him temporarily to a destructive degree of heat. Now, such a comet must have a period of enormous length, for the races of animals now existing upon the earth must all have been formed since that comet's last visit—on the assumption, be it remembered, that the fall of a large comet upon the sun, or rather the direct passage of the sun through the meteoric nucleus of a large comet, would excite the sun to destructive heat. If all living creatures on the earth are to be destroyed when some comet belonging to the solar system makes its next return to the sun, that same comet at its last visit must have raised the sun to an equal, or even greater intensity of heat, so that either no such races as at present exist had then come into being, or, if any such existed, they must at that time have been utterly destroyed. We may fairly believe that all comets of the destructive sort have been eliminated. Judging from the evidence we have on the subject, the process of the formation of the solar system was one which involved the utilisation of cometic and meteoric matter; and it fortunately so chanced that the comets likely otherwise to have been most mischievous—those, namely, which crossed the track of planets, and still more those whose paths intersected the globe of the sun—were precisely those which would be earliest and most thoroughly used up in this way.

Secondly, it is noteworthy that all the stars which have blazed out suddenly, except one, have appeared in a particular region of the heavens—the zone of the Milky Way (all, too, on one half of that zone). The single exception is the star in the Northern Crown, and that star appeared in a region which I have found to be connected with the Milky Way by a well-marked stream of stars, not a stream of a few stars scattered here and there, but a stream where thousands of stars are closely aggregated together, though not quite so closely as to form a visible extension of the Milky Way. In my map of 324,000 stars this stream can be quite clearly recognised; but, indeed, the brighter stars scattered along it form a stream recognisable with the naked eye, and have long since been regarded by astronomers as such, forming the stars of the Serpent and the Crown, or a serpentine streak followed by a loop of stars shaped like a coronet. Now the Milky Way, and the outlying streams of stars connected with it, seem to form a region of the stellar universe where fashioning processes are still at work. As Sir W. Herschel long since pointed out, we can recognise in various parts of the heavens various stages of development, and chief among the regions where as yet Nature's work seems incomplete, is the Galactic zone—

especially that half of it where the Milky Way consists of irregular streams and clouds of stellar light. As there is no reason for believing that our sun belongs to this part of the galaxy, but on the contrary good ground for considering that he belongs to the class of insulated stars, few of which have shown signs of irregular variation, while none have ever blazed suddenly out with many hundred times their former lustre, we may fairly infer a very high degree of probability in favour of the belief that, for many ages still to come, the sun will continue steadily to discharge his duties as fire, light, and life of the solar system.

VII.

THE RINGS OF SATURN.

THE rings of Saturn, always among the most interesting objects of astronomical research, have recently been subjected to close scrutiny under high telescopic powers by Mr. Trouvelot, of the Harvard Observatory, Cambridge, U.S. The results which he has obtained afford very significant evidence respecting these strange appendages, and even throw some degree of light on the subject of cosmical evolution. The present time, when Saturn is the ruling planet of the night, seems favourable for giving a brief account of recent speculations respecting the Saturnian ring-system, especially as the observations of Mr. Trouvelot appear to remove all doubt as to the true nature of the rings, if indeed any doubt could reasonably be entertained after the investigations made by European and American astronomers when the dark inner ring had but recently been recognised.

It may be well to give a brief account of the progress of observation from the time when the rings were first discovered.

In passing, I may remark that the failure of Galileo to ascertain the real shape of these appendages has always seemed to me to afford striking evidence of the importance of careful reasoning upon all observations whose actual significance is not at once apparent. If Galileo had been thus careful to analyse his observations of Saturn, he could not have failed to ascertain their real meaning. He had seen the planet apparently attended by two large satellites, one on either side, 'as though supporting the aged Saturn upon his slow course around the sun.' Night after night he had seen these attendants, always similarly placed, one on either side of the planet, and at equal distances from it. Then in 1612 he had again examined the planet, and lo, the attendants had vanished, 'as though Saturn had been at his old tricks, and had devoured his children.' But after a while the attendant orbs had reappeared in their former positions, had seemed slowly to grow larger, until at length they had presented the appearance of two pairs of mighty arms encompassing the planet. If Galileo had reasoned upon these changes of appearance, he could not have failed, as it seems to me, to interpret their true meaning. The three forms under which the rings had been seen by him sufficed to indicate the true shape of the appendage. Because Saturn was seen with two attendants of apparently equal size and always equi-distant from him, it was certain that there must be some appendage surrounding him, and extending to that distance from his globe. Because this appendage disappeared, it was certain that it must be thin and flat. Because it appeared at another time with a dark space between the arms and the planet, it was certain that the appendage is separated by a wide gap from the body of the planet. So that Galileo might have concluded—not doubtfully, but with assured confidence—that the appendage is a thin flat ring nowhere attached to the planet, or, as Huyghens said some forty years later, Saturn '*annulo cingitur tenui, plano, nusquam cohærente.*' Whether such reasoning would have been accepted by the contemporaries of Galileo may be doubtful. The generality of men are not content with reasoning which is logically sound, but require evidence which they can easily understand. Very likely Huyghens' proof from direct observation, though in reality not a whit more complete and far rougher, would have been regarded as the first true proof of the existence of Saturn's ring, just as Sir W. Herschel's observation of one star actually moving round another was regarded as the first true proof of the physical association of certain stars, a fact which Michell had proved as completely and far more neatly half a century earlier, by a method, however, which was 'caviare to the general.'

However, as matters chanced, the scientific world was not called upon to decide between the merits of a discovery made by direct observation and one effected by means of abstract reasoning. It was not until Saturn had been examined with much higher telescopic power than Galileo could employ, that the appendage which had so perplexed the Florentine astronomer was seen to be a thin flat ring, nowhere touching the planet, and considerably inclined to the plane in which Saturn travels. We cannot wonder that the discovery was regarded as a most interesting one. Astronomers had heretofore had to deal with solid masses, either known to be spheroidal, like the earth, the sun, the moon, Jupiter, and Venus, or presumed to be so, like the stars. The comets might be judged to be vaporous masses of various forms; but even these were supposed to surround or to attend upon globe-shaped nuclear masses. Here, however, in the case of Saturn's ring, was a quoit-shaped body travelling around the sun in continual attendance upon Saturn, whose motions, no matter how they varied in velocity or direction, were so closely followed by this strange attendant that the planet remained always centrally poised within the span of its ring-girdle. To appreciate the interest with which this strange phenomenon was regarded, we must remember that as yet the law of gravity had not been recognised. Huyghens discovered the ring (or rather perceived its nature) in 1659, but it was not till 1666 that Newton first entertained the idea that the moon is retained in its orbit about the earth by the attractive energy which causes unsupported bodies to fall earthwards; and he was unable to demonstrate the law of gravity before 1684. Now, in a general sense, we can readily understand in these days how a ring around a planet continues to travel along with the planet despite all changes of velocity or direction of motion. For the law of gravity teaches that the same causes which tend to change the direction and velocity of the planet's motion tend in precisely the same degree to change the direction and velocity of the ring's motion. But when Huyghens made his discovery it must have appeared a most mysterious circumstance that a ring and planet should be thus constantly associated—that during thousands of years no collision should have occurred whereby the relatively delicate structure of the ring had been destroyed.

Only six years later a discovery was made by two English observers, William and Thomas Ball, which enhanced the mystery. Observing the northern face of the ring, which was at that time turned earthwards, they perceived a black stripe of considerable breadth dividing the ring into two concentric portions. The discovery did not attract so much attention as it deserved, insomuch that when Cassini, ten years later, announced the discovery of a corresponding dark division on the southern surface, none recalled the observation made by the brothers Ball. Cassini expressed the opinion that the ring is really divided into two, not merely marked by a dark stripe on its southern face. This conclusion would, of course, have been an assured one, had the previous observation of a dark division on the northern face been remembered.

With the knowledge which we now possess, indeed, the darkness of the seeming stripe would be sufficient evidence that there must be a real division there between the rings; for we know that no mere darkness of the ring's substance could account for the apparent darkness of the stripe. It has been well remarked by Professor Tyndall, that if the moon's whole surface could be covered with black velvet, she would yet appear white when seen on the dark background of the sky. And it may be doubted whether a circular strip of black velvet 2000 miles wide, placed where we see the dark division between the rings, would appear nearly as dark as that division. Since we could only admit the possibility of some substance resembling our darker rocks occupying this position (for we know of nothing to justify the supposition that a substance as dark as lampblack or black velvet could be there), we are manifestly precluded from supposing that the dark space is other than a division between two distinct rings.

Yet Sir W. Herschel, in examining the rings of Saturn with his powerful telescopes, for a long time favoured the theory that there is no real division. He called it the 'broad black mark,' and argued that it can neither indicate the existence of a zone of hills upon the ring, nor of a vast cavernous groove, for in either case it would present changes of appearance (according to the ring's changes of position) such as he was unable to detect. It was not until the year 1790, eleven years after his observations had commenced, that, perceiving a corresponding broad black mark upon the ring's southern face, Herschel expressed a 'suspicion' that the ring is divided into two concentric portions by a circular gap nearly 2000 miles in width. He expressed at the same time, very strongly, his belief that this division was the only one in Saturn's ring-system.

A special interest attached at that time to the question

whether the ring is divided or not, for Laplace had then recently published the results of his mathematical inquiry into the movements of such a ring as Saturn's, and, having *proved* that a single solid ring of such enormous width could not continue to move around the planet, had expressed the *opinion* that Saturn's ring consists in reality of many concentric rings, each turning, with its own proper rotation rate, around the central planet. It is singular that Herschel, who, though not versed in the methods of the higher mathematics, had considerable native power as a mathematician, was unable to perceive the force of Laplace's reasoning. Indeed, this is one of those cases where clearness of perception rather than profundity of mathematical insight was required. Laplace's equations of motion did not express all the relations involved, nor was it possible to judge, from the results he deduced, how far the stability of the Saturnian rings depended on the real structure of these appendages. One who was well acquainted with mechanical matters, and sufficiently versed in mathematics to understand how to estimate generally the forces acting upon the ring-system, could have perceived as readily the general conditions of the problem as the most profound mathematician. One may compare the case to the problem of determining whether the action of the moon in causing the tidal wave modifies in any manner the earth's motion of rotation. We know that as a mathematical question this is a very difficult one. The Astronomer Royal, for example, not long ago dealt with it analytically, and deduced the conclusion that there is no effect on the earth's rotation, presently however, discovering by a lucky chance a term in the result which indicates an effect of that kind. But if we look at the matter in its mechanical aspect, we perceive at once, without any profound mathematical research, that the retardation so hard no detect mathematically must necessarily take place. As Sir E. Beckett says in his masterly work, ***Astronomy without Mathematics***, 'the conclusion is as evident without mathematics as with them, when once it has been suggested.' So when we consider the case of a wide flat ring surrounding a mighty planet like Saturn, we perceive that nothing could possibly save such a ring from destruction if it were really one solid structure.

To recognise this the more clearly, let us first notice the dimensions of the planet and rings.

We have in Saturn a globe about 70,000 miles in mean diameter, an equatorial diameter being about 73,000 miles, the polar diameter 66,000 miles. The attractive force of this mighty mass upon bodies placed on its surface is equal to about one-fifth more than terrestrial gravity if the body is near the pole of Saturn, and is almost exactly the same as terrestrial gravity if the body is at the planet's equator. Its action on the matter of the ring is, of course, very much less, because of the increased distance, but still a force is exerted on every part of the ring which is comparable with the familiar force of terrestrial gravity. The outer edge of the outer ring lies about 83,500 miles from the planet's centre, the inner edge of the inner ring (I speak throughout of the ring-system as known to Sir W. Herschel and Laplace) about 54,500 miles from the centre, the breadth of the system of bright rings being about 29,000 miles. Between the planet's equator and the inner edge of the innermost bright ring there intervenes a space of about 20,000 miles. Roughly speaking, it may be said that the attraction of the planet on the substance of the ring's inner edge is less than gravity at Saturn's equator (or, which is almost exactly the same thing, is less than terrestrial gravity) in about the proportion of 9 to 20; or, still more roughly, the inner edge of Saturn's inner bright ring is drawn inwards by about half the force of gravity at the earth's surface. The outer edge is drawn towards Saturn by a force less than terrestrial gravity in the proportion of about 3 to 16—say roughly that the force thus exerted by Saturn on the matter of the outer edge of the ring-system is equivalent to about one-fifth of the force of gravity at the earth's surface.

It is clear, first, that if the ring-system did not rotate, the forces thus acting on the material of the rings would immediately break them into fragments, and, dragging these down to the planet's equator, would leave them scattered in heaps upon that portion of Saturn's surface. The ring would in fact be in that case like a mighty arch, each portion of which would be drawn towards Saturn's centre by its own weight. This weight would be enormous if Bessel's estimate of the mass of the ring-system is correct. He made the mass of the ring rather greater than the mass of the earth—an estimate which I believe to be greatly in excess of the truth. Probably the rings do not amount in mass to more than a fourth part of the earth's mass. But even that is enormous, and subjected as is the material of the rings to forces varying from one-half to a fifth of terrestrial gravity, the strains and pressures upon the various parts of the system would exceed thousands of times those which even the strongest material built up into their shape could resist. The system would no more be able to resist such strains and pressures than an arch of iron spanning the Atlantic would be able to sustain its own weight against the earth's attraction.

It would be necessary then that the ring-system should rotate around the planet. But it is clear that the proper rate of rotation for the outer portion would be very different from the rate suited for the inner portion. In order that the inner portion should travel around Saturn entirely relieved of its weight, it should complete a revolution in about seven hours twenty-three minutes. The outer portion, however, should revolve in about thirteen hours fifty-eight minutes, or nearly fourteen hours. Thus the inner part should rotate in little more than half the time required by the outer part. The result would necessarily be that the ring-system would be affected by tremendous strains, which it would be quite unable to resist. The existence of the great division would manifestly go far to diminish the strains. It is easily shown that the rate of turning where the division is, would be once in about eleven hours and twenty-five minutes, not differing greatly from the mean between the rotation-periods for the outside and for the inside edges of the system. Even then, however, the strains would be hundreds of times greater than the material of the ring could resist. A mass comparable in weight to our earth, compelled to rotate in (say) nine hours when it ought to rotate in eleven or in seven, would be subjected to strains exceeding many times the resistances which the cohesive power of its substance could afford. That would be the condition of the inner ring. And in like manner the outer ring, if it rotated in about twelve hours and three-quarters, would have its outer portions rotating too fast and its inner portions too slowly, because their proper periods would be fourteen hours and eleven hours and a half respectively. Nothing but the division of the ring into a number of narrow hoops could possibly save it from destruction through the internal strains and pressures to which its material would be subjected.

Even this complicated arrangement, however, would not save the ring-system. If we suppose a fine hoop to turn around a central attracting body as the rings of Saturn rotate around the planet, it may be shown that unless the hoop is so weighted that its centre of gravity is far from the planet, there will be no stability in the resulting motions; the hoop will before long be made to rotate eccentrically, and eventually be brought into destructive collision with the central planet.

It was here that Laplace left the problem. Nothing could have been more unsatisfactory than his result, though it was accepted for nearly half a century unquestioned. He had shown that a weighted fine hoop may possibly turn around a central attracting mass without destructive changes of position, but he had not proved more than the bare possibility of this, while nothing in the appearance of Saturn's rings suggests that any such arrangement exists. Again, manifestly a multitude of narrow hoops, so combined as to form a broad flat system of rings, would be constantly in collision *inter se.* Besides, each one of them would be subjected to destructive strains. For though a fine uniform hoop set rotating at a proper rate around an attracting mass at its centre would be freed from all strains, the case is very different with a hoop so weighted as to have its centre of gravity greatly displaced. Laplace had saved the theoretical stability of the motions of a fine ring at the expense of the ring's power of resisting the strains to which it would be exposed. It seems incredible that such a result (expressed, too, very doubtingly by the distinguished mathematician who had obtained it) should have been accepted so long almost without question. There is nothing in nature in the remotest degree resembling the arrangement imagined by Laplace, which indeed appears on *à priori* grounds impossible. It was not claimed for it that it removed the original difficulties of the problem; and it introduced others fully as serious. So strong, however, is authority in the scientific world that none ventured to express any doubts except Sir W. Herschel, who simply denied that the two rings were divided into many, as

Laplace's theory required. As time went on and the signs of many divisions were at times recognised, it was supposed that Laplace's reasoning had been justified; and despite the utter impossibility of the arrangement he had suggested, that arrangement was ordinarily described as probably existing.

At length, however, a discovery was made which caused the whole question to be reopened.

On November 10, 1850, W. Bond, observing the planet with the telescope of the Harvard Observatory, perceived within the inner bright ring a feeble illumination which he was at a loss to understand. On the next night the faint light was better seen. On the 15th, Tuttle, who was observing with Bond, suggested the idea that the light within the inner bright ring was due to a dusky ring inside the system of bright rings. On November 25, Mr. Dawes in England perceived this dusky ring, and announced the discovery before the news had reached England that Bond had already seen the dark ring. The credit of the discovery is usually shared between Bond and Dawes, though the usual rule in such matters would assign the discovery to Bond alone. It was found that the dark ring had already been seen at Rome so far back as 1828, and again by Galle at Berlin in May 1838. The Roman observations were not satisfactory. Those by Galle, however, were sufficient to have established the fact of the ring's existence; indeed, in 1839 Galle measured the dark ring. But very little attention was attracted to this interesting discovery, insomuch that when Bond and Dawes announced their observation of the dark ring in 1850, the news was received by astronomers with all the interest attaching to the detection of before unnoted phenomena.

It may be well to notice under what conditions the dark ring was detected in 1850. In September 1848 the ring had been turned edgewise towards the sun, and as rather more than seven years are occupied in the apparent gradual opening out of the ring from that edge view to its most open appearance (when the outline of the ring-system is an eclipse whose lesser axis is nearly equal to half the greater), it will be seen that in November 1850 the rings were but slightly opened. Thus the recognition of the dark ring within the bright system was made under unfavourable conditions. For four preceding years—that is, from the year 1846—the rings had been as little or less opened; and again for several years preceding 1846, though the rings had been more open, the planet had been unfavourably placed for observation in northern latitudes, crossing the meridian at low altitudes. Still, in 1838 and 1839, when the rings were most open, although the planet was never seen under favourable conditions, the opening of the rings, then nearly at its greatest, made the recognition of the dark ring possible; and we have seen that Galle then made the discovery. When Bond rediscovered the dark ring, everything promised that before long the appendage would be visible with telescopes far inferior in power to the great Harvard refractor. Year after year the planet was becoming more favourably placed for observation, while all the time the rings were opening out. Accordingly it need not surprise us to learn that in 1853 the dark ring was seen with a telescope less than three inches and a half in aperture. Even so early as 1851, Mr. Hartnup, observing the planet with a telescope eight inches and a half in aperture, found that 'the dark ring could not be overlooked for an instant.'

But while this increase in the distinctness of the dark ring was to be expected, from the mere fact that the ring was discovered under relatively unfavourable conditions, yet the fact that Saturn was thus found to have an appendage of a remarkable character, perfectly obvious even with moderate telescopic power, was manifestly most surprising. The planet had been studied for nearly two centuries with telescopes exceeding in power those with which the dark ring was now perceived. Some among these telescopes were not only of great power, but employed by observers of the utmost skill. The elder Herschel had for a quarter of a century studied Saturn with his great reflectors eighteen inches in aperture, and had at times turned on the planet his monstrous (though not mighty) four-feet mirror. Schröter had examined the dark space within the inner bright ring for the special purpose of determining whether the ring-system is really disconnected from the globe. He had used a mirror nineteen inches in aperture, and he had observed that the dark space seen on either side of Saturn inside the ring-system not only appeared dark, but actually darker than the surrounding sky. This was presumably (though not quite certainly) an effect of contrast only, the dark space being bounded all round by bright surfaces. If real, the phenomenon signified that whereas the space outside the ring, where the satellites of the planet travel, was occupied by some sort of cosmical dust, the space within the ring-system was, as it were, swept and garnished, as though all the scattered matter which might otherwise have occupied that region had been either attracted to the body of the planet or to the rings.[1] But manifestly the observation was entirely inconsistent with the supposition that there existed in Schröter's time a dark or dusky ring within the bright system. Again, the elder Struve made the most careful measurement of the whole of the ring-system in 1826, when the system was as

[1] The same peculiarity has been noticed since the discovery of the dark ring, the space within that ring being observed by Coolidge and G. Bond at Harvard in 1856 to be apparently darker than the surrounding sky.

well placed for observation as in 1856 (or, in other words, as well placed as it can possibly be); but though he used a telescope nine inches and a half in aperture, and though his attention was specially attracted to the inner edge of the inner bright ring (*which seemed to him indistinct*), he did not detect the dark ring. Yet we have seen that in 1851, under much less favourable conditions, a less practised observer, using a telescope of less aperture, found that the dark ring could not be overlooked for an instant. It is manifest that all these considerations point to the conclusion that the dark ring is a new formation, or, at the least, that it has changed notably in condition during the present century.

I have hitherto only considered the appearance of the dusky ring as seen on either side of the planet's globe within the bright rings. The most remarkable feature of the appendage remains still to be mentioned—the fact, namely, that the bright body of the planet can be seen through this dusky ring. Where the dark ring crosses the planet, it appears as a rather dark belt, which might readily be mistaken for a belt upon the planet's surface; for the outline of the planet can be seen through the ring as through a film of smoke or a crape veil.

Now it is worthy of notice that whereas the dark ring was not detected outside the planet's body until 1838, nor generally recognised by astronomers until 1850, the dark belt across the planet, really caused by the dusky ring, was observed more than a century earlier. In 1715 the younger Cassini saw it, and perceived that it was not curved enough for a belt really belonging to the planet. Hadley again observed that the belt attended the ring as this opened out and closed, or, in other words, that the dark belt belonged to the ring, not to the body of the planet. And in many pictures of Saturn's system a dark band is shown along the inner edge of the inner bright ring where it crosses the body of the planet. It seems to me that we have here a most important piece of evidence respecting the rings. It is clear that the inner part of the inner bright ring has for more than a century and a half (how much more we do not know) been partially transparent, and it is probable that within its inner edge there has been all the time a ring of matter; but this ring has only within the last half-century gathered consistency enough to be discernible. It is manifest that the existence of the dark belt shown in the older pictures would have led directly to the detection of the dark ring, had not this appendage been exceedingly faint. Thus, while the observation of the dark belt across the planet's face proves the dusky ring to have existed in some form long before it was perceived, the same fact only helps to render us certain that the dark ring has changed notably in condition during the present century.

The discovery of this singular appendage, an object unique in the solar system, naturally attracted fresh attention to the question of the stability of the rings. The idea was thrown out by the elder Bond that the new ring may be fluid, or even that the whole ring-system may be fluid, and the dark ring simply thinner than the rest. It was thought possible that the ring-system is of the nature of a vast ocean, whose waves are steadily advancing upon the planet's globe. The mathematical investigation of the subject was also resumed by Professor Benjamin Pierce, of Harvard, and it was satisfactorily demonstrated that the stability of a system of actual rings of solid matter required so nice an adjustment of so many narrow rings as to render the system far more complex than even Laplace had supposed. 'A stable formation can,' he said, 'be nothing other than a very great number of separate narrow rigid rings, each revolving with its proper relative velocity.' As was well remarked by the late Professor Nichol, 'If this arrangement or anything like it were real, how many new conditions of instability do we introduce. Observation tells us that the division between such rings must be extremely narrow, so that the slightest disturbance by external or internal causes would cause one ring to impinge upon another; and we should thus have the seed of perpetual catastrophes.' Nor would such a constitution protect the system against dissolution. 'There is no escape from the difficulties, therefore, but through the final rejection of the idea that Saturn's rings are rigid or in any sense a solid formation.'

The idea that the ring-system may be fluid came naturally next under mathematical scrutiny. Strangely enough, the physical objections to the theory of fluidity appear to have been entirely overlooked. Before we could accept such a theory, we must admit the existence of elements differing entirely from those with which we are familiar. No fluid known to us could retain the form of the rings of Saturn under the conditions to which they are exposed. But the mathematical examination of the subject disposed so thoroughly of the theory that the rings can consist of continuous fluid masses, that we need not now discuss the physical objections to the theory.

There remains only the theory that the Saturnian ring-system consists of discrete masses analogous to the streams of meteors known to exist in great numbers within the solar system. The masses may be solid or fluid, may be strewn in relatively vacant space, or may be surrounded by vaporous envelopes; but that they are discrete, each free to travel on its own course, seemed as completely demonstrated by Pierce's calculations as anything not actually admitting of direct observation could possibly be. The matter was placed beyond dispute by the independent analysis to which Clerk Maxwell subjected the mathematical problem. It had been selected in 1855 as the subject for the Adams Prize Essay at Cambridge, and Clerk Maxwell's essay, which obtained the prize, showed conclusively that only a system of many small bodies, each free to travel upon its course under the varying attractions to which it was subjected by Saturn itself, and by the Saturnian satellites, could possibly continue to girdle a planet as the rings of Saturn girdle him.

It is clear that all the peculiarities hitherto observed in the Saturnian ring-system are explicable so soon as we regard that system as made up of multitudes of small bodies. Varieties of brightness simply indicate various degrees of condensation of these small satellites. Thus the outer ring had long been observed to be less bright than the inner. Of course it did not seem impossible that the outer ring might be made of different materials; yet there was something bizarre in the supposition that two rings forming the same system were thus different in substance. It would not have been at all noteworthy if different parts of the same ring differed in luminosity—in fact, it was much more remarkable that each zone of the system seemed uniformly bright all round. But that one zone should be of one tint, another of an entirely different tint, was a strange circumstance so long as the only available interpretation seemed to be that one zone was made (throughout) of one substance, the other of another. If this was strange when the difference between the inner and outer bright rings was alone considered, how much stranger did it seem when the multitudinous divisions in the rings were taken into account! Why should the ring-system, 30,000 miles in width, be thus divided into zones of different material? An arrangement so artificial is quite unlike all that is elsewhere seen among the subjects of the astronomer's researches. But when the rings are regarded as made up of multitudes of small bodies, we can quite readily understand how the nearly circular movements of all of these, at different rates, should result in the formation of rings of aggregation and rings of segregation, appearing at the earth's distance as bright rings and faint rings. The dark ring clearly corresponds in appearance with a ring of thinly scattered satellites. Indeed, it seems impossible otherwise to account for the appearance of a dusky belt across the globe of the planet where the dark ring crosses the disc. If the material of the dark ring were some partly transparent solid or fluid substance, the light of the planet received through the dark ring added to the light reflected by the dark ring itself, would be so nearly equivalent to the light received from the rest of the planet's disc, that either no dark belt would be seen, or the darkening would be barely discernible. In some positions a bright belt would be seen, not a dark one. But a ring of scattered satellites would cast as its shadow a multitude of black spots, which would give to the belt in shadow a dark grey aspect. A considerable proportion of these spots would be hidden by the satellites forming the dark ring, and in every case where a spot was wholly or partially hidden by a satellite, the effect (at our distant station where the separate satellites of the dark ring are not discernible) would simply be to reduce *pro tanto* the darkness of the grey belt of shadow. But certainly more than half the shadows of the satellites would remain in sight; for the darkness of the ring at the time of its discovery showed that the satellites were very sparsely strewn. And these shadows would be sufficient to give to the belt a dusky hue, such as it presented when first discovered.[1]

[1] I cannot understand why Mr. Webb, in his interesting little

The observations which have recently been made by Mr. Trouvelot indicate changes in the ring-system, and especially in the dark ring, which place every other theory save that to which we have thus been led entirely out of the question. It should be noted that Mr. Trouvelot has employed telescopes of unquestionable excellence and varying in aperture from six inches to twenty-six inches, the latter aperture being that of the great telescope of the Washington Observatory (the largest refractor in the world).

He has noted in the first place that the interior edge of the outer bright ring, which marks the outer limit of the great division, is irregular, but whether the irregularity is permanent or not he does not know. The great division itself is found not to be actually black, but, as was long since noted by Captain Jacob, of the Madras Observatory, a very dark brown, as though a few scattered satellites travelled along this relatively vacant zone of the system. Mr. Trouvelot has further noticed that the shadow of the planet upon the rings, and especially upon the outer ring, changes continually in shape, a circumstance which he attributes to irregularities in the surface of the rings. For my own part, I should be disposed to attribute these changes in the shape of the planet's shadow (noted by other observers also) to rapid changes in the deep cloud-laden atmosphere of the planet. Passing on, however, to less doubtful observations, we find that the whole system of rings has presented a clouded and spotted aspect during the last four years. Mr. Trouvelot specially describes this appearance as observed on the parts of the ring outside the

work, *Celestial Objects for Common Telescopes*, says that the satellite theory of the rings certainly seems insufficient to account for the phenomena of the dark ring. It seems, on the contrary, manifest that the dark ring can scarcely be explained in any other way. The observations recently made are altogether inexplicable on any other theory.

disc, called by astronomers the *ansæ* (because of their resemblance to handles), and it would seem, therefore, that the spotted and cloudy portions are seen only where the background on which the rings are projected is black. This circumstance clearly suggests that the darkness of these parts is due to the background, or, in other words, that the sky is in reality seen through those parts of the ring-system, just as the darkness of the slate-coloured interior ring is attributed, on the satellite theory, to the background of sky visible through the scattered flight of satellites forming the dark ring. The matter composing the dark ring has been observed by Mr. Trouvelot to be gathered in places into compact masses, which prevent the light of the planet from being seen through those portions of the dark ring where the matter is thus massed together. It is clear that such peculiarities could not possibly present themselves in the case of a continuous solid or fluid ring-system, whereas they would naturally occur in a ring formed of multitudes of minute bodies travelling freely around the planet.

The point next to be mentioned is still more decisive. When the dark ring was carefully examined with powerful telescopes during the ten years following its discovery by Bond, at which time it was most favourably placed for observation, it was observed that the outline of the planet could be seen across the entire breadth of the dark ring. All the observations agreed in this respect. It was, indeed, noticed by Dawes that outside the planet's disc the dark ring showed varieties of tint, its inner half being darker than its outer portion. Lassell, observing the planet under most favourable conditions with his two-feet mirror at Malta, could not perceive these varieties of tint, which therefore we may judge to have been either not permanent or very slightly marked. But, as I have said, all observers agreed that the outline of the planet could be seen athwart the entire width of the dark ring. Mr. Trouvelot, however, has found that during the last four years the planet has not been visible through the whole width of the dark ring, but only through the inner half of the ring's breadth. It appears, then, that either the inner portion is getting continually thinner and thinner—that is, the satellites composing it are becoming continually more sparsely strewn—or that the outer portion is becoming more compact, doubtless by receiving stray satellites from the interior of the inner bright ring.

It is clear that in Saturn's ring-system, if not in the planet itself, mighty changes are still taking place. It may be that the rings are being so fashioned under the forces to which they are subjected as to be on their way to becoming changed into separate satellites, inner members of that system which at present consists of eight secondary planets. But, whatever may be the end towards which these changes are tending, we see processes of evolution taking place which may be regarded as typifying the more extensive and probably more energetic processes whereby the solar system itself reached its present condition. I ventured more than ten years ago, in the preface to my treatise upon the planet Saturn, to suggest the possibility 'that in the variations perceptibly proceeding in the Saturnian ring-system a key may one day be found to the law of development under which the solar system has reached its present condition.' This suggestion seems to me strikingly confirmed by the recent discoveries. The planet Saturn and its appendages, always interesting to astronomers, are found more than ever worthy of close investigation and scrutiny. We may here, as it were, seize nature in the act, and trace out the actual progress of developments which at present are matters rather of theory than of observation.

VIII.

COMETS AS PORTENTS

The blazing star,
Threat'ning the world with famine, plague, and war;
To princes death; to kingdoms many curses;
To all estates inevitable losses;
To herdsmen rot; to ploughmen hapless seasons;
To sailors storms; to cities civil treasons.

ALTHOUGH comets are no longer regarded with supersti tious awe as in old times, mystery still clings to them. Astronomers can tell what path a comet is travelling upon, and say whence it has come and whither it will go, can even in many cases predict the periodic returns of a comet, can analyse the substance of these strange wanderers, and have recently discovered a singular bond of relationship between comets and those other strange visitants from the celestial depths, the shooting stars. But astronomy has hitherto proved unable to determine the origin of comets, the part they perform in the economy of the universe, their real structure, the causes of the marvellous changes of shape which they undergo as they approach the sun, rush round him, and then retreat. As Sir John Herschel has remarked: 'No one, hitherto, has been able to assign any single point in which we should be a bit better or worse off, materially speaking, if there were no such thing as a comet. Persons, even thinking persons, have busied them selves with conjectures; such as that they may serve for fuel for the sun (into which, however, they never fall), or that they may cause warm summers, which is a mere fancy, or that they may give rise to epidemics, or potato-blights, and so forth.' And though, as he justly says, 'this is all wild talking,' yet it will probably continue until astronomers have been able to master the problems respecting comets which hitherto have foiled their best efforts. The unexplained has ever been and will ever be marvellous to the general mind. Just as unexplored regions of the earth have been tenanted in imagination by

> anthropophagi and men whose heads
> Do grow beneath their shoulders,

so do wondrous possibilities exist in the unknown and the ill-understood phenomena of nature.

In old times, when the appearance and movements of comets were supposed to be altogether uncontrolled by physical laws, it was natural that comets should be regarded as signs from heaven, tokens of Divine wrath towards some, and of the interposition of Divine providence in favour of others. As Seneca well remarked: 'There is no man so dull, so obtuse, so turned to earthly things, who does not direct all the powers of his mind towards things Divine when some novel phenomenon appears in the heavens. While all follows its usual course up yonder, familiarity robs the spectacle of its grandeur. For so is man made. However wonderful may be what he sees day after day, he looks on it with indifference; while matters of very little importance attract and interest him if they depart from the accustomed order. The host of heavenly constellations beneath the vault of heaven, whose beauty they adorn, attract no attention; but if any unusual appearance be noticed among them, at once all eyes are turned heavenwards. The sun is only looked on with interest when he is undergoing eclipse. Men observe the moon only under like conditions. . . . So thoroughly is it a part of our nature to admire the new rather than the great. The same is true of comets. When one of these fiery bodies of unusual form appears, every one is eager to know what it means; men forget other objects to inquire about the new arrival; they know not whether to wonder or to tremble; for many spread fear on all sides, drawing from the phenomenon most grave prognostics.'

There is no direct reference to comets in the Bible, either in the Old Testament or the New. It is possible that some of the signs from heaven recorded in the Bible pages were either comets or meteors, and that even where in some places an angel or messenger from God is said to have appeared and delivered a message, what really happened was that some remarkable phenomenon in the heavens was interpreted in a particular manner by the priests, and the interpretation afterwards described as the message of an angel. The image of the 'flaming sword which turned every way' may have been derived from a comet; but we can form no safe conclusion about this, any more than we can upon the question whether the 'horror of great darkness' which fell upon Abraham (Genesis xv. 12) when the sun was going down, was caused by an eclipse;[1] or whether the going back of the shadow upon the dial of Ahaz was

[1] A gentleman, whose acquaintance I made in returning from America last spring, assured me that he had found demonstrative evidence showing that a total eclipse of the moon then occurred; for he could prove that Abraham's vision occurred at the time of full moon, so that it could not otherwise have been dark when the sun went down (v. 17). But the horror of great darkness occurred when the sun was going down, and total eclipses of the moon do not behave that way—at least, in our time.

caused by a mock sun. The star seen by the wise men from the east may have been a comet, since the word translated 'star' signifies any bright object seen in the heavens and is in fact the same word which Homer, in a passage frequently referred to, uses to signify either a comet or a meteor. The way in which it appeared to go before them, when (directed by Herod, be it noticed) they went to Bethlehem, almost due south of Jerusalem, would correspond to a meridian culmination low down—for the star had manifestly not been visible in the earlier evening, since we are told that they rejoiced when they saw the star again. It was probably a comet travelling southwards; and, as the wise men had travelled from the east, it had very likely been first seen in the west as an evening star, wherefore its course was retrograde—that is, supposing it *was* a comet.[1] It may possibly have been an apparition of Halley's comet, following a course somewhat similar to that which it followed in the year 1835, when the perihelion passage was made on November 15, and the comet running southwards disappeared from northern astronomers, though in January it was '*received*' by Sir J. Herschel, to use his own expression, 'in the southern hemisphere.' There was an apparition of Halley's comet in the year 66, or seventy years after the Nativity; and the period of the comet varies, according to the perturbing influences affecting the comet's motion, from sixty-nine to eighty years.

Homer does not, to the best of my recollection, refer

[1] It is not easy to understand what else it could have been. The notion that a conjunction of three planets, which took place shortly before the time of Christ's birth, gave rise to the tradition of the star in the east, though propounded by a former president of the Astronomical Society, could hardly be entertained by an astronomer, unless he entirely rejected Matthew's account, which the author of this theory, being a clergyman, can scarcely have done.

anywhere directly to comets. Pope, indeed, who made very free with Homer's references to the heavenly bodies,[1] introduces a comet—and a red one, too!—into the simile of the heavenly portent in Book IV.:—

> As the red comet from Saturnius sent
> To fright the nations with a dire portent
> (A fatal sign to armies in the plain,
> Or trembling sailors on the wintry main),
> With sweeping glories glides along in air,
> And shakes the sparkles from its blazing hair:
> Between two armies thus, in open sight,
> Shot the bright goddess in a trail of light.

But Homer says nothing of this comet. If Homer had introduced a comet, we may be sure it would not have shaken sparkles from its blazing tail. Homer said simply that 'Pallas rushed from the peaks of heaven, like the bright star sent by the son of crafty-counselled Kronus (as a sign either to sailors, or the broad array of the nations), from which many sparks proceed.' Strangely enough, Pingré and Lalande, the former noted for his researches into ancient comets, the latter a skilful astronomer, agree in considering that Homer really referred to a comet, and they even regard this comet as an apparition of the comet

[1] As, for instance, when he makes Homer say of the moon that

> Around her throne the vivid planets roll,
> And stars unnumbered gild the glowing pole.

It is difficult, indeed, to understand how so thorough an astronomer as the late Admiral Smyth could have called the passage in which these lines occur one of the finest bursts of poetry in our language, except on the principle cleverly cited by Waller when Charles II. upbraided him for the warmth of his panegyric on Cromwell, that 'poets succeed better with fiction than with truth.' Macaulay, though not an astronomer, speaks more justly of the passage in saying that this single passage contains more inaccuracies than can be found in all Wordsworth's 'Excursion.'

of 1680. They cite in support of this opinion the portent which followed the prayer of Anchises, 'Æneid,' Book II. 692, etc.: 'Scarce had the old man ceased from praying, when a peal of thunder was heard on the left, and a star, gliding from the heavens amid the darkness, rushed through space followed by a long train of light; we saw the star,' says Æneas, 'suspended for a moment above the roof, brighten our home with its fires, then, tracing out a brilliant course, disappear in the forests of Ida; then a long train of flame illuminated us, and the place around reeked with the smell of sulphur. Overcome by these startling portents, my father arose, invoked the gods, and worshipped the holy star.' It is impossible to recognise here the description of a comet. The noise, the trail of light, the visible motion, the smell of sulphur, all correspond with the fall of a meteorite close by; and doubtless Virgil simply introduced into the narrative the circumstances of some such phenomenon which had been witnessed in his own time. To base on such a point the theory that the comet of 1680 was visible at the time of the fall of Troy, the date of which is unknown, is venturesome in the extreme. True, the period calculated for the comet of 1680, when Pingré and Lalande agreed in this unhappy guess, was 575 years; and if we multiply this period by five we obtain 2875 years, taking 1680 from which leaves 1195 years B.C., near enough to the supposed date of the capture of Troy. Unfortunately, Encke (the eminent astronomer to whom we owe that determination of the sun's distance which for nearly half a century held its place in our books, but has within the last twenty years been replaced by a distance three millions of miles less) went over afresh the calculations of the motions of that famous comet, and found that, instead of 575 years, the most probable period is about 8814 years. The difference amounts only to 8239 years; but even this small difference rather impairs the theory of Lalande and Pingré.[1]

Three hundred and seventy-one years before the Christian era, a comet appeared which Aristotle (who was a boy at the time) has described. Diodorus Siculus writes thus respecting it: 'In the first year of the 102d Olympiad, Alcisthenes being Archon of Athens, several prodigies announced the approaching humiliation of the Lacedæmonians; a blazing torch of extraordinary size, which was compared to a flaming beam, was seen during several nights.' Guillemin, from whose interesting work on Comets I have translated the above passage, remarks that this same comet was regarded by the ancients as having not merely presaged but produced the earthquakes which caused the towns of Helice and Bura to be submerged. This was clearly in the thoughts of Seneca when he said of this comet that as soon as it appeared it brought about the submergence of Bura and Helice.

[1] It may be necessary to throw in here a few words of explanation, lest the non-astronomical reader should run away with the idea that the so-called exact science is a very inexact science indeed, so far as comets are concerned. The comet of 1680 was one of those which travel on a very eccentric orbit. Coming, indeed, from out depths many times more remote than the path even of the remotest planet, Neptune, this comet approached nearer to the sun than any which astronomers have ever seen, except only the comet of 1843. When at its nearest its nucleus was only a sixth part of the sun's diameter from his surface. Thus the part of the comet's orbit along which astronomers traced its motion was only a small part at one end of an enormously long oval, and very slight errors of observation were sufficient to produce very large errors in the determination of the nature of the comet's orbit. Encke admitted that the period might, so far as the comparatively imperfect observations made in 1680 were concerned, be any whatever, from 805 years to many millions of years, or even to infinity—that is, the comet might have a path not re-entering into itself, but carrying the comet for ever away from the sun after its one visit to our system.

In those times, however, comets were not regarded solely as signs of disaster. As the misfortunes of one nation were commonly held to be of advantage to other nations, so the same comet might be regarded very differently by different nations or different rulers. Thus the comet of the year 344 B.C. was regarded by Timoleon of Corinth as presaging the success of his expedition against Corinth. 'The gods announced,' said Diodorus Siculus, 'by a remarkable portent, his success and future greatness; a blazing torch appeared in the heavens at night, and went before the fleet of Timoleon until he arrived in Sicily.' The comets of the years 134 B.C. and 118 B.C. were not regarded as portents of death, but as signalising, the former the birth, the latter the accession, of Mithridates. The comet of 43 B.C. was held by some to be the soul of Julius Cæsar on its way to the abode of the gods. Bodin, a French lawyer of the sixteenth century, regarded this as the usual significance of comets. He was, indeed, sufficiently modest to attribute the opinion to Democritus, but the whole credit of the discovery belonged to himself. He maintained that comets only indicate approaching misfortunes because they are the spirits or souls of illustrious men, who for many years have acted the part of guardian angels, and, being at last ready to die, celebrate their last triumph by voyaging to the firmament as flaming stars. 'Naturally,' he says, 'the appearance of a comet is followed by plague, pestilence, and civil war; for the nations are deprived of the guidance of their worthy rulers, who, while they were alive, gave all their efforts to prevent intestine disorders.' Pingré comments justly on this, saying that 'it must be classed among base and shameful flatteries, not among philosophic opinions.'

Usually, however, it must be admitted that the ancients, like the men of the Middle Ages, regarded comets as harbingers of evil. 'A fearful star is the comet,' says Pliny, 'and not easily appeased, as appeared in the late civil troubles when Octavius was consul; a second time by the intestine war of Pompey and Cæsar; and, in our own time, when, Claudius Cæsar having been poisoned, the empire was left to Domitian, in whose reign there appeared a blazing comet.' Lucan tells us of the second event here referred to, that during the war 'the darkest nights were lit up by unknown stars' (a rather singular way of saying that there were no dark nights); 'the heavens appeared on fire, flaming torches traversed in all directions the depths of space; a comet, that fearful star which overthrows the powers of the earth, showed its horrid hair.' Seneca also expressed the opinion that some comets portend mischief: 'Some comets,' he said, 'are very cruel and portend the worst misfortunes; they bring with them and leave behind them the seeds of blood and slaughter.'

It was held, indeed, by many in those times a subject for reproach that some were too hard of heart to believe when these signs were sent. It was a point of religious faith that 'God worketh' these 'signs and wonders in heaven.' When troubles were about to befall men, 'nation rising against nation, and kingdom against kingdom, with great earthquakes in divers places, and famines, and pestilences, and fearful sights,' then 'great signs shall there be from heaven.' Says Josephus, commenting on the obstinacy of the Jews in such matters, 'when they were at any time premonished from the lips of truth itself, by prodigies and other premonitory signs of their approaching ruin, they had neither eyes nor ears nor understanding to make a right use of them, but passed them over without heeding or so much as thinking of them; as, for example, what shall we say of the comet in the form of a sword that hung over Jerusalem for a whole year together?' This was probably the comet described by Dion Cassius (*Hist. Roman.* lxv. 8) as having been visible between the months of April and December in the year 69 A.D. This or the comet of 66 A.D. might have been Halley's comet. The account of Josephus as to the time during which it was visible would not apply to Halley's, or, indeed, to any known comet whatever; doubtless he exaggerated. He says: 'The comet was of the kind called *Xiphias*, because their tail resembles the blade of a sword,' and this would apply fairly well to Halley's comet as seen in 1682, 1759, and 1835; though it is to be remembered that comets vary very much even at successive apparitions, and it would be quite unsafe to judge from the appearance of a comet seen eighteen centuries ago that it either was or was not the same as some comet now known to be periodic.

The comet of 79 A.D. is interesting as having given rise to a happy retort from Vespasian, whose death the comet was held to portend. Seeing some of his courtiers whispering about the comet, 'That hairy star,' he said, 'does not portend evil to me. It menaces rather the king of the Parthians. He is a hairy man, but I am bald.'

Anna Comnena goes even beyond Josephus. He only rebuked other men for not believing so strongly as he did himself in the significance of comets—a rebuke little needed, indeed, if we can judge from what history tells us of the terrors excited by comets. But the judicious daughter of Alexius was good enough to approve of the wisdom which provided these portents. Speaking of a remarkable comet which appeared before the irruption of the Gauls into the Roman empire, she says: 'This happened by the usual administration of Providence in such cases; for it is not fit that so great and strange an alteration of things as was brought to pass by that irruption of theirs should be without some previous denunciation and admonishment from heaven.'

Socrates, the historian (b. 6, c. 6), says that when Gainas besieged Constantinople, 'so great was the danger which hung over the city, that it was presignified and portended by a huge blazing comet which reached from heaven to the earth, the like whereof no man had ever seen before.' And Cedrenus, in his 'Compendium of History,' states that a comet appeared before the death of Johannes Tzimicas, the emperor of the East, which foreshadowed not alone his death, but the great calamities which were to befall the Roman empire by reason of their civil wars. In like manner, the comet of 451 announced the death of Attila, that of 455 the death of Valentinian. The death of Merovingius was announced by the comet of 577, of Chilperic by that of 584, of the Emperor Maurice by that of 602, of Mahomet by that of 632, of Louis the Debonair by that of 837, and of the Emperor Louis II. by that of 875. Nay, so confidently did men believe that comets indicated the approaching death of great men, that they did not believe a very great man *could* die without a comet. So they inferred that the death of a very great man indicated the arrival of a comet; and if the comet chanced not to be visible, so much the worse—not for the theory, but—for the comet. 'A comet of this kind,' says Pingré, 'was that of the year 814, presaging the death of Charlemagne.' So Guillemin quotes Pingré; but he should rather have said, such was the comet whose arrival was announced by Charlemagne's death—and in no other way, for it was not seen by mortal man.

The reader who chances to be strong as to his dates may have observed that some of the dates above mentioned for comets do not accord exactly with the dates of the events associated with those comets. Thus Louis the Debonair did not die in 837, but in 840. This, however, is a matter of very little importance. If some men, after their comet has called for them, are 'an unconscionable time in dying,' as Charles II. said of himself, it surely must not be considered the fault of the comet. Louis himself regarded the comet of 837 as his death-warrant; the astrologers admitted as much: what more could be desired? The account of the matter given in a chronicle of the time, by a writer who called himself 'The Astronomer,' is curious enough: 'During the holy season of Easter, a phenomenon, ever fatal and of gloomy foreboding, appeared in the heavens. As soon as the emperor, who paid attention to such phenomena, received the first announcement of it, he gave himself no rest until he had called a certain learned man and myself before him. As soon as I arrived, he anxiously asked me what I thought of such a sign. I asked time of him, in order to consider the aspect of the stars, and to discover the truth by their means, promising to acquaint him on the morrow; but the emperor, persuaded that I wished to gain time, which was true, in order not to be obliged to announce anything fatal to him, said to me: "Go on the terrace of the palace, and return at once to tell me what you have seen, for I did not see this star last evening, and you did not point it out to me; but I know that it is a comet; tell me what you think it announces to me." Then, scarcely allowing me time to say a word, he added: "There is still another thing you keep back: it is that a change of reign and the death of a prince are announced by this sign." And as I advanced the testimony of the prophet, who said: "Fear not the signs of the heavens as the nations fear them," the prince, with his grand nature and the wisdom which never forsook him, said: "We must only fear Him who has created both us and this star. But, as this phenomenon may refer to us, let us acknowledge it as a warning from heaven."' Accordingly, Louis himself and all his court fasted and prayed, and he built churches and monasteries. But all was of no avail.

In little more than three years he died; showing, as the historian Raoul Glaber remarked, that 'these phenomena of the universe are never presented to man without surely announcing some wonderful and terrible event.' With a range of three years in advance, and so many kings and princes as there were about in those days, and are still, it would be rather difficult for a comet to appear without announcing some such wonderful and terrible event as a royal death.

The year 1000 A.D. was by all but common consent regarded as the date assigned for the end of the world. For a thousand years Satan had been chained, and now he was to be loosened for a while. So that when a comet made its appearance, and, terrible to relate, continued visible for nine days, the phenomenon was regarded as something more than a nine days' wonder. Besides the comet, a very wonderful meteor was seen. 'The heavens opened, and a kind of flaming torch fell upon the earth, leaving behind a long track of light like the path of a flash of lightning. Its brightness was so great that it frightened not only those who were in the fields, but even those who were in their houses. As this opening in the sky slowly closed men saw with horror the figure of a dragon, whose feet were blue, and whose head' [like that of Dickens's dwarf] 'seemed to grow larger and larger.' A picture of this dreadful meteor accompanies the account given by the old chronicler. For fear the exact likeness of the dragon might not be recognised (and, indeed, to see it one must 'make believe a good deal'), there is placed beside it a picture of a dragon to correspond, which picture is in turn labelled 'Serpens cum ceruleis pedibus.' It was considered very wicked in the year 1000 to doubt that the end of all things was at hand. But somehow the world escaped that time.

In the year 1066 Halley's comet appeared to announce to the Saxons the approaching conquest of England by William the Norman. A contemporary poet made a singular remark, which may have some profound poetical meaning, but certainly seems a little indistinct on the surface. He said that 'the comet had been more favourable to William than nature had been to Cæsar; the latter had no hair, but William had received some from the comet.' This is the only instance, so far as I know, in which a comet has been regarded as a peruquier. A monk of Malmesbury spoke more to the purpose, according to then received ideas, in thus apostrophising the comet: 'Here art thou again, cause of tears to many mothers! It is long since I saw thee last, but I see thee now more terrible than ever; thou threatenest my country with complete ruin.'

Halley's comet, with its inconveniently short period of about seventy-seven years, has repeatedly troubled the nations and been regarded as a sign sent from Heaven:

> Ten million cubic miles of head,
> Ten billion leagues of tail,

all provided for the sole purpose of warning one petty race of earth-folks against the evils likely to be brought against them by another. This comet has appeared twenty-four times since the date of its first recorded appearance, which some consider to have been 12 B.C., and others refer to a few years later. It may be interesting to quote here Babinet's description of the effects ascribed in 1455 to this comet, often the terror of nations, but the triumph of mathematicians, as the first whose motions were brought into recognisable obedience to the laws of gravity.[1]

[1] For a portion of the passages which I have quoted in this essay I am indebted to Guillemin's 'Treatise on Comets,' a useful contribution to the literature of the subject, though somewhat inadequate so far as exposition is concerned.

'The Mussulmans, with Mahomet II. at their head, were besieging Belgrade, which was defended by Huniade, surnamed the Exterminator of the Turks. Halley's comet appeared and the two armies were seized with equal fear. Pope Calixtus III., himself seized by the general terror, ordered public prayers and timidly anathematised the comet and the enemies of Christianity. He established the prayer called the noon *Angelus*, the use of which is continued in all Catholic churches. The Franciscans (*Frères Mineurs*) brought 40,000 defenders to Belgrade, besieged by the conqueror of Constantinople, the destroyer of the Eastern Empire. At last the battle began; it continued two days without ceasing. A contest of two days caused 40,000 combatants to bite the dust. The Franciscans, unarmed, crucifix in hand, were in the front rank, invoking the papal exorcism against the comet, and turning upon the enemy that heavenly wrath of which none in those times dared doubt.'

The great comet of 1556 has been regarded as the occasion of the Emperor Charles V.'s abdication of the imperial throne; a circumstance which seems rendered a little doubtful by the fact that he had already abdicated when the comet appeared—a mere detail, perhaps, but suggesting the possibility that cause and effect may have been interchanged by mistake, and that it was Charles's abdication which occasioned the appearance of the comet. According to Gemma's account the comet was conspicuous rather from its great light than from the length of its tail or the strangeness of its appearance. 'Its head equalled Jupiter in brightness, and was equal in diameter to nearly half the apparent diameter of the moon.' It appeared about the end of February, and in March presented a terrible appearance, according to Ripamonte. 'Terrific indeed,' says Sir J. Herschel, 'it might well have been to the mind of a prince prepared by the most abject superstition to receive its appearance as a warning of approaching death, and as specially sent, whether in anger or in mercy, to detach his thoughts from earthly things, and fix them on his eternal interests. Such was its effect on the Emperor Charles V., whose abdication is distinctly ascribed by many historians to this cause, and whose words on the occasion of his first beholding it have even been recorded—

"His ergo indiciis me mea fata vocant"—

the language and the metrical form of which exclamation afford no ground for disputing its authenticity, when the habits and education of those times are fairly considered.' It is quite likely that, having already abdicated the throne, Charles regarded the comet as signalling his retirement from power—an event which he doubtless considered a great deal too important to be left without some celestial record. But the words attributed to him are in all probability apocryphal.

The comet of 1577 was remarkable for the strangeness of its aspect, which in some respects resembled that of the comet of 1858, called Donati's. It required only the terror with which such portentous objects were witnessed in the Middle Ages to transform the various streamers, curved and straight, extending from such an object, into swords and spears, and other signs of war and trouble. Doubtless, we owe to the fears of the Middle Ages the strange pictures claiming to present the actual aspect of some of the larger comets. Halley's comet did not escape. It was compared to a straight sword at one visit, to a curved scimitar in 1456, and even at its last return in 1835 there were some who recognised in the comet a resemblance to a misty head. Other comets have been compared to swords of fire, bloody crosses, flaming daggers, spears, serpents, fiery dragons, fish, and so forth. But in this respect no comet would seem to have been comparable with that of 1528, of which Andrew Paré writes as follows: 'This comet was so horrible and dreadful, and engendered such terror in the minds of men, that they died, some from fear alone, others from illness engendered by fear. It was of immense length and blood-red colour; at its head was seen the figure of a curved arm, holding a large sword in the hand as if preparing to strike. At the point of this sword were three stars; and on either side a number of axes, knives, and swords covered with blood, amongst which were many hideous human faces with bristling beards and hair.'

Such peculiarities of shape, and also those affecting the position and movements of comets, were held to be full of meaning. As Bayle pointed out in his 'Thoughts about the Comet of 1680,' these fancies are of great antiquity. Pliny tells us that in his time astrologers claimed to interpret the meaning of a comet's position and appearance, and that also of the direction towards which its rays pointed. They could, moreover, explain the effects produced by the fixed stars whose rays were conjoined with the comet's. If a comet resembles a flute, then musicians are aimed at; when comets are in the less dignified parts of the constellations, they presage evil to immodest persons; if the head of a comet forms an equilateral triangle or a square with fixed stars, then it is time for mathematicians and men of science to tremble. When they are in the sign of the Ram, they portend great wars and widespread mortality, the abasement of the great and the elevation of the small, besides fearful droughts in regions over which that sign predominates; in the Virgin, they imply many grievous ills to the female portion of the population; in the Scorpion, they portend a plague of reptiles, especially locusts; in the Fishes, they indicate great troubles from religious differences, besides war and pestilence. When, like the one described by Milton, they 'fire the length of Ophiuchus huge,' they show that there will be much mortality caused by poisoning.

The comet of 1680, which led Bayle to write the treatise to which reference has just been made, was one well calculated to inspire terror. Indeed, if the truth were known, that comet probably brought greater danger to the inhabitants of the earth than any other except the comet of 1843—the danger not, however, being that derived from possible collision between the earth and a comet, but that arising from the possible downfall of a large comet upon the sun, and the consequent enormous increase of the sun's heat. That, according to Newton, is the great danger men have to fear from comets; and the comet of 1680 was one which in that sense was a very dangerous one. There is no reason why a comet from outer space should not fall straight towards the sun, as at one time the comet of 1680 was supposed to be doing. All the comfort that science can give the world on that point is that such a course for a comet is only one out of many millions of possible courses, all fully as likely; and that, therefore, the chance of a comet falling upon the sun is only as one in many millions. Still, the comet of 1680 made a very fair shot at the sun, and a very slight modification of its course by Jupiter or Saturn might have brought about the catastrophe which Newton feared. Whether, if a comet actually fell upon the sun, anything very dreadful would happen, is not so clear. Newton's ideas respecting comets were formed in ignorance of many physical facts and laws which in our day render reasoning upon the subject comparatively easy Yet, even in our time, it is not possible to assert confidently that such fears are idle. During the solar outburst witnessed by Carrington and Hodgson in September 1859, it is supposed that the sun swallowed a large meteoric mass; and, as great comets are probably followed by many such masses, it seems reasonable to infer that if such a comet fell upon the sun, his surface being pelted with such exceptionally large masses, stoned with these mighty meteoric balls, would glow all over (or nearly so) as brightly as a small spot of that surface glowed upon that occasion. Now that portion was so bright that Carrington thought 'that by some chance a ray of light had penetrated a hole in the screen attached to the object-glass by which the general image is thrown in shade, for the brilliancy was fully equal to that of direct sunlight.' Manifestly, if the whole surface of the sun, or any large portion of the surface, were caused to glow with that exceeding brilliancy, surpassing ordinary sunlight in the same degree that ordinary sunlight surpassed the shaded solar image in Carrington's observations, the result would be disastrous in the extreme for the inhabitants of that half of the earth which chanced to be in sunlight at the time; and if (as could scarcely fail to happen) the duration of that abnormal splendour were more than half a day, then the whole earth would probably be depopulated by the intense heat. The danger, as I have said, is slight —partly because there is small chance of a collision between the sun and a comet, partly because we have no certain reasons for assuming that a collision would be followed by the heating of the sun for a while to a very high temperature. Looking around at the suns which people space, and considering their history, so far as it has been made known to us, for the last two thousand years, we find small occasion for fear. Those suns seem to have been for the most part safe from any sudden or rapid accessions of heat; and if they travel thus safely in their mighty journeys through space, we may well believe that our sun also is safe. Nevertheless, there *have* been catastrophes here and there. Now one sun and now another has blazed out with a hundred times its usual lustre, gradually losing its new fires and returning to its customary brightness; but after what destruction among those peopling its system of worlds who shall say? Spectroscopic analysis, that powerful help to the modern astronomical inquirer, has shown in one of these cases that just such changes had taken place as we might fairly expect would follow if a mighty comet fell into the sun. If this interpretation be correct, then we are not wholly safe. Any day might bring us news of a comet sailing full upon our sun from out the depths of space. Then astronomers would perhaps have the opportunity of ascertaining the harmlessness of a collision between the ruler of our system and one of the long-tailed visitors from the celestial spaces. Or possibly, astronomers and the earth's inhabitants generally might find out the reverse, though the knowledge would not avail them much, seeing that the messenger who would bring it would be the King of Terrors himself.

It was well, perhaps, that Newton's discovery of the law of gravitation, and the application of this law to the comets of 1680 and 1682 (the latter our old friend Halley's comet, then properly so called as studied by him), came in time to aid in removing to some slight degree the old superstitions respecting comets. For in England many remembered the comets of the Great Plague and of the Great Fire of London. These comets came so closely upon the time of the Plague and the Fire respectively, that it was not wonderful if even the wiser sort were struck by the coincidence and could scarcely regard it as accidental. It is not easy for the student of science in our own times, when the movements of comets are as well understood as those of the most orderly planets, to place himself in the position of men in the times when no one knew on what paths comets came, or whither they retreated after they had visited our sun.

Taught as men were, on the one hand, that it was wicked to question what seemed to be the teaching of the Scriptures, that changes or new appearances in the heavens were sent to warn mankind of approaching troubles, and perplexed as they were, on the other, by the absence of any real knowledge respecting comets and meteors, it was not so easy as we might imagine from our own way of viewing these matters, to shake off a superstition which had ruled over men's minds for thousands of years.

No sect had been free from this superstition. Popes and priests had taught their followers to pray against the evil influences of comets and other celestial portents; Luther and Melanchthon had condemned in no measured terms the rashness and impiety of those who had striven to show that the heavenly bodies and the earth move in concordance with law—those 'fools who wish to reverse the entire science of astronomy.' A long interval had elapsed between the time when the Copernican theory was struggling for existence—when, but that more serious heresies engaged men's attention and kept religious folk by the ears, that astronomical heresy would probably have been quenched in blood—and the forging by Newton of the final link of the chain of reasoning on which modern astronomy is based; but in those times the minds of men moved more slowly than in ours. The masses still held to the old beliefs about the heavenly bodies. Defoe, indeed, speaking of the terror of men at the time of the Great Plague, says that they 'were more addicted to prophecies and astrological conjurations, dreams, and old wives' tales, than ever they were before or since.' But in reality, it was only because of the great misery then prevailing that men seemed more superstitious than usual; for misery brings out the superstitions—the fetishisms, if we may so speak—which are inherent in many minds, but concealed from others in prosperous times, out of shame, or perhaps a worthier feeling. Even in our own times great national calamities would show that many superstitions exist which had been thought extinct, and we should see excited among the ill-educated that particular form of persecution which arises, not from zeal for religion and not from intolerance, but from the belief that the troubles have been sent because of unbelief and the fear that unless some expiation be made the evil will not pass away from the midst of the people. It is at such times of general affliction that minds of the meaner sort have proved 'zealous even to slaying.'

The influence of strange appearances in the heavens on even thoughtful and reasoning minds, at such times of universal calamity, is well shown by Defoe's remarks on the comets of the years 1664 and 1666. 'The old women,' he says, 'and the phlegmatic, hypochondriacal part of the other sex, whom I could almost call old women too, remarked that those two comets passed directly over the city' [though that appearance must have depended on the position whence these old women, male and female, observed the comet], 'and that so very near the houses, that it was plain they imported something peculiar to the city alone; and that the comet before the Pestilence was of a faint, dull, languid colour, and its motion very heavy, solemn, and slow; but that the comet before the Fire was bright and sparkling, or, as others said, flaming, and its motion swift and furious: and that accordingly one foretold a heavy judgment, slow but severe, terrible and frightful, as was the Plague; but the other foretold a stroke, sudden, swift, and fiery, as was the Conflagration. Nay, so particular some people were, that, as they looked upon that comet preceding the Fire, they fancied that they not only saw it pass swiftly and fiercely, and could perceive the motion with their eye, but even that they heard it; that it made a mighty rushing noise, fierce and terrible, though at a distance and but just perceivable. I saw both these stars, and must confess had I had so much the common notion of such things in my head, that I was apt to look upon them as the forerunners and warnings of God's judgments, and especially when, the Plague having followed the first, I yet saw another of the same kind, I could not but say, God had not yet sufficiently scourged the city' [London].

The comets of 1680 and 1682, though they did not bring plagues or conflagrations immediately, yet were not supposed to have been altogether without influence. The convenient fiction, indeed, that some comets operate quickly and others slowly, made it very difficult for a comet to appear to which some evil effects could not be ascribed. If any one can find a single date, since the records of history have been carefully kept, which was so fortunately placed that, during no time following it within five years, no prince, king, emperor, or pope died, no war was begun, or ended disastrously for one side or the other engaged in it, no revolution was effected, neither plague nor pestilence occurred, neither droughts nor floods afflicted any nation, no great hurricanes, earthquakes, volcanic outbursts, or other trouble was recorded, he will then have shown the bare possibility that a comet might have appeared which seemed to presage neither abrupt nor slow-moving calamities. But it is not possible to name such a date, nor even a date which was not followed within two years at the utmost by a calamity such as superstition might assign to a comet. And so closely have such calamities usually followed, that scarce a comet could appear which might not be regarded as the precursor of very quickly approaching calamity. Even if a comet had come which seemed to bring no trouble, nay, if many such comets had come, men would still have overlooked the absence of any apparent fulfilment of the predicted troubles. Henry IV. well remarked, when he was told that astrologers predicted his death because a certain comet had been observed: 'One of these days they will predict it truly, and people will remember better the single occasion when the prediction will be fulfilled than the many other occasions when it has been falsified by the event.'

The troubles connected with the comets of 1680 and 1682 were removed farther from the dates of the events themselves than usual, at least so far as the English interpretation of the comets was concerned. 'The great comet in 1680,' says one, 'followed by a lesser comet in 1682, was evidently the forerunner of all those remarkable and disastrous events that ended in the revolution of 1688. It also evidently presaged the revocation of the edict of Nantes, and the cruel persecution of the Protestants, by the French king Louis XIV., afterwards followed by those terrible wars which, with little intermission, continued to ravage the finest parts of Europe for nearly twenty-four years.'

If in some respects the fears inspired by comets have been reduced by modern scientific discoveries respecting these bodies, yet in other respects the very confidence engendered by the exactness of modern astronomical computations has proved a source of terror. There is nothing more remarkable, for instance, in the whole history of cometary superstition, than the panic which spread over France in the year 1773, in consequence of a rumour that the mathematician Lalande had predicted the occurrence of a collision between a comet and the earth, and that disastrous effects would inevitably follow. The foundation of the rumour was slight enough in all conscience. It had simply been announced that Lalande would read before the Academy of Sciences a paper entitled 'Reflections on those Comets which can approach the Earth.' That was absolutely all; yet, from that one fact, not only were vague rumours of approaching cometic troubles spread abroad, but the statement was definitely made that on May 20 or 21, 1773, a comet would encounter the earth.'[1] So great was the fear thus excited, that, in order to calm it, Lalande inserted in the 'Gazette de France' of May 7, 1773, the following advertisement :—'M. Lalande had not time to read his memoir upon comets which may approach the earth and cause changes in her motions; but he would observe that it is impossible to assign the epochs of such events. The next comet whose return is expected is the one which should return in eighteen years; but it is not one of those which can hurt the earth.'

This note had not the slightest effect in restoring peace to the minds of unscientific Frenchmen. M. Lalande's study was crowded with anxious persons who came to inquire about his memoir. Certain devout folk, 'as ignorant as they were imbecile,' says a contemporary journal, begged the Archbishop of Paris to appoint forty hours' prayer to

[1] Something very similar happened only a few years ago, so that we cannot afford to laugh too freely at the terrors of France in 1773. It was reported during the winter of 1871-1872, that Plantamour, the Swiss astronomer, had predicted the earth's destruction by a comet on August 12, 1872. Yet there was no other foundation for this rumour than the fact that Plantamour, in a lecture upon comets and meteors, had stated that the meteors seen on August 10, 11, and 12 are bodies following in the track of a comet whose orbit passes very near to the earth's. It was very certainly known to astronomers that there could be no present danger of a collision with this comet, for the comet has a period of at least 150 years, and had last passed close to the earth's orbit (not to the earth herself, be it understood) in 1862. But it was useless to point this out. Many people insisted on believing that on August 12, 1872, the earth would come into collision, possibly disastrous, with a mighty comet, which Plantamour was said to have detected and to have shown by a profound calculation to be rushing directly upon our unfortunate earth.

avert the danger and prevent the terrible deluge. For this was the particular form most men agreed that the danger would take. That prelate was on the point, indeed, of complying with their request, and would have done so, but that some members of the Academy explained to him that by so doing he would excite ridicule.

Far more effective, and, to say truth, far better judged, was the irony of Voltaire, in his deservedly celebrated 'Letter on the Pretended Comet.' It ran as follows :—

'Grenoble, May 17, 1773.

'Certain Parisians who are not philosophers, and who, if we are to believe them, will not have time to become such, have informed me that the end of the world approaches, and will occur without fail on the 20th of this present month of May. They expect, that day, a comet, which is to take our little globe from behind and reduce it to impalpable powder, according to a certain prediction of the Academy of Sciences which has not yet been made.

'Nothing is more likely than this event; for James Bernouilli, in his "Treatise upon the Comet" of 1680, predicted expressly that the famous comet of 1680 would return with terrible uproar (*fracas*) on May 19, 1719; he assured us that in truth its peruque would signify nothing mischievous, but that its tail would be an infallible sign of the wrath of heaven. If James Bernouilli mistook, it is, after all, but a matter of fifty-four years and three days.

'Now, so small an error as this being regarded by all geometricians as of little moment in the immensity of ages, it is manifest that nothing can be more reasonable than to hope (*sic, espérer*) for the end of the world on the 20th of this present month of May 1773, or in some other year. If the thing should not come to pass, "omittance is no quittance" (*ce qui est différé, n'est pas perdu*).

'There is certainly no reason for laughing at M. Trissotin, triple idiot though he is (*tout Trissotin qu'il est*), when he says to Madame Philaminte (Molière's "Femmes Savantes," acte iv. scène 3),

> 'Nous l'avons en dormant, madame, échappé belle ;
> Un monde près de nous a passé tout du long,
> Est chu tout au travers de notre tourbillon ;
> Et, s'il eût en chemin rencontré notre terre,
> Elle eût été brisée en morceaux comme verre.

'A comet coursing along its parabolic orbit may come full tilt against our earth. But then, what will happen? Either that comet will have a force equal to that of our earth, or greater, or less. If equal, we shall do the comet as much harm as it will do us, action and reaction being equal; if greater, the comet will bear us away with it; if less, we shall bear away the comet.

'This great event may occur in a thousand ways, and no one can affirm that our earth and the other planets have not experienced more than one revolution, through the mischance of encountering a comet on their path.

'The Parisians will not desert their city on the 20th inst.; they will sing songs, and the play of "The Comet and the World's End" will be performed at the Opéra Comique.'

The last touch is as fine in its way as Sydney Smith's remark that, if London were destroyed by an earthquake, the surviving citizens would celebrate the event by a public dinner among the ruins. Voltaire's prediction was not fulfilled exactly to the letter, but what actually happened was even funnier than what his lively imagination had suggested. It was stated by a Parisian Professor in 1832 (as a reason why the Academy of Sciences should refute an assertion then rife to the effect that Biela's comet would encounter the earth that year) that during the cometic panic of 1773 'there were not wanting people who knew too well the art of turning to their advantage the alarm inspired by the approaching comet, and *places in Paradise were sold at a very high rate*.[1] The announcement of the comet of 1832 may produce similar effects,' he said, 'unless the authority of the Academy apply a prompt remedy; and this salutary intervention is at this moment implored by many benevolent persons.'

In recent years the effects produced on the minds of men by comets have been less marked than of yore, and appear to have depended a good deal on circumstances. The comet of the year 1858 (called Donati's), for example, occasioned no special fears, at least until Napoleon III. made his famous New-Year's day speech, after which many began to think the comet had meant mischief. But the comet of 1861, though less conspicuous, occasioned more serious fears. It was held by many in Italy to presage a very great misfortune indeed, viz. the restoration of Francis II. to the throne of the Two Sicilies. Others thought that the downfall of the temporal power of the Papacy and the death of Pope Pius IX. were signified. I have not heard that any very serious consequences were expected to follow

1 A rather amusing mistake was made by the stenographers of a New York paper in reporting the above sentence, which I happened to quote in a lecture upon Comets and Meteors. Instead of Paradise they wrote Paris. Those acquainted with Pitman's system of short-hand, the one most commonly employed by reporters, will easily understand how the mistake was made, the marks made to represent the consonants p, r, d, and s differing little from those made to represent the consonants p, r, and s (the 'd' or 't' sound is represented, or may be represented, by simply shortening the length of the sign for the preceding consonant). The mistake led naturally to my remarking in my next lecture that I had not before known how thoroughly synonymous the words are in America, though I had heard it said that 'Good Americans, when they die, go to Paris.'

the appearance of Coggia's comet in 1874. The great heat which prevailed during parts of the summer of 1876 was held by many to be connected in some way with a comet which some very unskilful telescopist constructed in his imagination out of the glare of Jupiter in the object-glass of his telescope. Another benighted person, seeing the Pleiades low down through a fog, turned them into a comet, about the same time. Possibly the idea was, that since comets are supposed to cause great heats, great heats may be supposed to indicate a comet somewhere; and with minds thus prepared, it was not wonderful, perhaps, that telescopic glare, or an imperfect view of our old friends the Pleiades, should have been mistaken for a vision of the heat-producing comet.

It should be a noteworthy circumstance to those who still continue to look on comets as signs of great catastrophes, that a war more remarkable in many respects than any which has ever yet been waged between two great nations—a war swift in its operations and decisive in its effects—a war in which three armies, each larger than all the forces commanded by Napoleon I. during the campaign of 1813, were captured bodily—should have been begun and carried on to its termination without the appearance of any great comet. The civil war in America, a still more terrible calamity to that great nation than the success of Moltke's operations to the French, may be regarded by believers as presignified by the great comet of 1861. But it so chances that the war between France and Germany occurred near the middle of one of the longest intervals recorded in astronomical annals as unmarked by a single conspicuous comet—the interval between the years 1862 and 1874.

If the progress of just ideas respecting comets has been slow, it must nevertheless be regarded as on the whole satisfactory. When we remember that it was not a mere idle fancy which had to be opposed, not mere terrors which had to be calmed, but that the idea of the significance of changes in the heavens had come to be regarded by mankind as a part of their religion, it cannot but be thought a hopeful sign that all reasoning men in our time have abandoned the idea that comets are sent to warn the inhabitants of this small earth. Obeying in their movements the same law of gravitation which guides the planets in their courses, the comets are tracked by the skilful mathematician along those remote parts of their course where even the telescope fails to keep them in view. Not only are they no longer regarded as presaging the fortunes of men on this earth, but men on this earth are able to predict the fortunes of comets. Not only is it seen that they cannot influence the fates of the earth or other planets, but we perceive that the earth and planets by their attractive energies influence, and in no unimportant degree, the fates of these visitants from outer space. Encouraging, truly, is the lesson taught us by the success of earnest study and careful inquiry in determining some at least among the laws which govern bodies once thought the wildest and most erratic creatures in the whole of God's universe.

IX.

THE LUNAR HOAX.

Then he gave them an account of the famous moon hoax, which came out in 1835. It was full of the most barefaced absurdities, yet people swallowed it all; and even Arago is said to have treated it seriously as a thing that could not well be true, for Mr. Herschel would have certainly notified him of these marvellous discoveries. The writer of it had not troubled himself to invent probabilities, but had borrowed his scenery from the 'Arabian Nights' and his lunar inhabitants from 'Peter Wilkins.'—OLIVER WENDELL HOLMES (in *The Poet at the Breakfast-Table*).

IN one of the earliest numbers of 'Macmillan's Magazine, the late Professor De Morgan, in an article on Scientific Hoaxing, gave a brief account of the so-called 'lunar hoax'—an instance of scientific trickery frequently mentioned, though probably few are familiar with the real facts. De Morgan himself possessed a copy of the second English edition of the pamphlet, published in London in 1836. But the original pamphlet edition, published in America in September 1835, is not easily to be obtained. The proprietors of the New York 'Sun,' in which the fictitious narrative first appeared, published an edition of 60,000 copies, and every copy was sold in less than a month. Lately a single copy of that edition was sold for three dollars seventy-five cents.[1]

[1] On the occasion of my first visit to America, in 1873, I for the first time succeeded in obtaining a copy of this curious pamphlet. It

The pamphlet is interesting in many respects, and I propose to give here a brief account of it. But first it may be well to describe briefly the origin of the hoax.

It is said that after the French revolution of 1830 Nicollet, a French astronomer of some repute, especially for certain lunar observations of a very delicate and difficult kind, left France in debt and also in bad odour with the republican party. According to this story, Arago the astronomer was especially obnoxious to Nicollet, and it was as much with the view of revenging himself on his foe as from a wish to raise a little money that Nicollet wrote the moon-fable. It is said further that Arago was entrapped, as Nicollet desired, and circulated all over Paris the wonders related in the pamphlet, until Nicollet wrote to his friend Bouvard explaining the trick. So runs the story, but the story cannot be altogether true. Nicollet may have prepared the narrative and partly written it, but there are passages in the pamphlet as published in America which no astronomer could have written. Possibly there is some truth in De Morgan's supposition that the original work was French. This may have been Nicollet's: and the American edition was probably enlarged by the translator, who, according to this account, was Richard Alton Locke,[1] to whom in America the whole credit, or discredit, of the hoax is commonly attributed. There can be no doubt that either the French version was much more carefully designed than the American, or there was no truth in the

had been mentioned to me (by Emerson, I think) as an amusing piece of trickery played off by a scientific man on his brethren; and Dr. Wendell Holmes, who was present, remarked that he had a copy in his possession. This he was good enough to lend me. Soon after, a valued friend in New York presented me with a copy.

[1] This Locke must not be confounded with Richard Lock, the circle-squarer and general paradoxist, who flourished a century earlier.

story that Arago was deceived by the narrative; for in its present form the story, though clever, could not for an instant have deceived any one acquainted with the most elementary laws of optics. The whole story turns on optical rather than on astronomical considerations; but every astronomer of the least skill is acquainted with the principles on which the construction of optical instruments depends. Though the success of the deception recently practised on M. Chasles by the forger of the Pascal papers has been regarded as showing how easily mathematicians may be entrapped, yet even M. Chasles would not have been deceived by bad mathematics; and Arago, a master of the science of optics, could not but have detected optical blunders which would be glaring to the average Cambridge undergraduate.

But let us turn to the story itself.

The account opens with a passage unmistakably from an American hand, though purporting, be it remembered, to be quoted from the 'Supplement to the Edinburgh Journal of Science.' 'In this unusual addition to our journal, we have the happiness of making known to the British public, and thence to the whole civilised world, recent discoveries in astronomy which will build an imperishable monument to the age in which we live, and confer upon the present generation of the human race a proud distinction through all future time. It has been poetically said' [where and by whom?] 'that the stars of heaven are the hereditary regalia of man, as the intellectual sovereign of the animal creation. He may now fold the zodiac around him with a loftier consciousness of his mental supremacy.' To the American mind enwrapment in the star-jewelled zodiac may appear as natural as their ordinary oratorical references to the star-spangled banner; but the idea is essentially transatlantic, and not even the most poetical European astronomer could have risen to such a height of imagery.

Passing over several pages of introductory matter, we come to the description of the method by which a telescope of sufficient magnifying power to show living creatures in the moon was constructed by Sir John Herschel. It had occurred, it would seem, to the elder Herschel to construct an improved series of parabolic and spherical reflectors 'uniting all the meritorious points in the Gregorian and Newtonian instruments, with the highly interesting achromatic discovery of Dolland'(*sic*). [This is much as though one should say that a clever engineer had conceived the idea of constructing an improved series of railway engines, combining all the meritorious points in stationary and locomotive engines, with *Isaac* Watts' highly ingenious discovery of screw propulsion. For the Gregorian and Newtonian instruments simply differ in sending the rays received from the great mirror in different directions, and Dolland's discovery relates to the ordinary forms of telescopes with large lens, not with large mirror.] However, accumulating infirmities and eventually death prevented Sir William Herschel from applying his plan, which 'evinced the most profound research in optical science, and the most dexterous ingenuity in mechanical contrivance. But his son, Sir John Herschel, nursed and cradled in the observatory, and a practical astronomer from his boyhood, determined upon testing it at whatever cost. Within two years of his father's death he completed his new apparatus, and adapted it to the old telescope with nearly perfect success.' A short account of the observations made with this instrument, now magnifying six thousand times, follows, in which most of the astronomical statements are very correctly and justly worded, being, in fact, borrowed from a paper by Sir W. Herschel on observation of the moon with precisely that power.

But this great improvement upon all former telescopes still left the observer at a distance of forty miles from the moon; and at that distance no object less than about twenty yards in diameter could be distinguished, and even objects of that size 'would appear only as feeble, shapeless points.' Sir John 'had the satisfaction to know that if he could leap astride a cannon-ball, and travel upon its wings of fury for the respectable period of several millions of years, he would not obtain a more enlarged view of the more distant stars than he could now possess in a few minutes of time; and that it would require an ultra-railroad speed of fifty miles an hour for nearly the livelong year, to secure him a more favourable inspection of the gentle luminary of the night;' but 'the exciting question whether this "observed" of all the sons of men, from the days of Eden to those of Edinburgh, be inhabited by beings, like ourselves, of consciousness and curiosity, was left to the benevolent index of natural analogy, or to the severe tradition that the moon is tenanted only by the hoary *solitaire*, whom the criminal code of the nursery had banished thither for collecting fuel on the Sabbath-day.'[1] But the time had arrived when the great discovery was to be made, by which at length the moon could be brought near enough, by telescopic power, for living creatures on her surface to be seen if any exist.

The account of the sudden discovery of the new method,

[1] The nurses' tale is, that the man was sent to the moon by Moses for gathering sticks on the Sabbath, and they refer to the cheerful story in Numbers xv. 32-36. According to German nurses the day was not the Sabbath, but Sunday. Their tale runs as follows: 'Ages ago there went one Sunday an old man into the woods to hew sticks. He cut a faggot and slung it on a stout staff, cast it over his shoulder, and began to trudge home with his burthen. On his way he met a handsome man in Sunday suit, walking towards the church. The man stopped, and asked the faggot-bearer; "Do you know that this is Sunday on earth, when all must rest from their labours?" "Sunday

during a conversation between Sir John Herschel and Sir David Brewster, is one of the most cleverly conceived (though also one of the absurdest) passages in the pamphlet. 'About three years ago, in the course of a conversational discussion with Sir David Brewster upon the merits of some ingenious suggestions by the latter, in his article on Optics in the "Edinburgh Encyclopædia," p. 644, for improvements in Newtonian reflectors, Sir John Herschel adverted to the convenient simplicity of the old astronomical telescopes that were without tubes, and the object-glass of which, placed upon a high pole, threw the focal image to a distance of 150 and even 200 feet. Dr. Brewster readily admitted that a tube was not necessary, provided the focal image were conveyed into a dark apartment and there properly received by reflectors. . . . The conversation then became directed to that all-invincible enemy, the paucity of light in powerful magnifiers. After a few moments' silent thought, Sir John diffidently enquired whether it would not be possible to effect *a transfusion of artificial light through the focal object of vision!* Sir David, somewhat startled at the originality of the idea, paused awhile, and then hesitatingly referred to the refrangibility of rays, and the angle of incidence. Sir John, grown more confident, adduced the example of the Newtonian reflector, in which the refrangibility was corrected by the second speculum, and the angle of incidence restored by the third.'

on earth or Monday in heaven, it's all one to me?" laughed the woodcutter. "Then bear your bundle for ever!" answered the stranger. "And as you value not Sunday on earth, yours shall be a perpetual Moon-day in heaven; you shall stand for eternity in the moon, a warning to all Sabbath-breakers." Thereupon the stranger vanished; and the man was caught up with his staff and faggot into the moon, where he stands yet.' According to some narrators the stranger was Christ; but whether from German laxity in such matters or for some other reason, no text is quoted in evidence, as by the more orthodox British nurses. Luke vi. 1-5 might serve.

All this part of the narrative is simply splendid in absurdity. Hesitating references to refrangibility and the angle of incidence would have been sheerly idiotic under the supposed circumstances; and in the Newtonian reflector (which has only two specula or mirrors) there is no refrangibility to be corrected; apart from which, 'correcting refrangibility' has no more meaning than 'restoring the angle of incidence.'

'"And," continued Sir John, "why cannot the illuminating microscope, say the hydro-oxygen, be applied to render distinct, and, if necessary, even to magnify, the focal object?" Sir David sprung from his chair' [and well he might, though not] 'in an ecstasy of conviction, and, leaping half-way to the ceiling, exclaimed, "Thou art the man!" Each philosopher anticipated the other in presenting the prompt illustration that if the rays of the hydro-oxygen microscope, passed through a drop of water containing the larvæ of a gnat and other objects invisible to the naked eye, rendered them not only keenly but firmly magnified to dimensions of many feet; so could the same artificial light, passed through the faintest focal object of a telescope, both distinctify (to coin a new word for an extraordinary occasion) and magnify its feeblest component members. The only apparent desideratum was a recipient for the focal image which should transfer it, without refranging it, to the surface on which it was to be viewed under the revivifying light of the microscopic reflectors.'

Singularly enough, the idea here mentioned does not appear to many so absurd as it is in reality. It is known that the image formed by the large lens of an ordinary telescope or the large mirror of a reflecting telescope is a real image; not a merely virtual image like that which is seen in a looking-glass. It can be received on a sheet of paper or other white surface just as the image of surrounding objects can be thrown upon the white table of the camera obscura. It is this real image, in fact, which we look at in using a telescope of any sort, the portion of such a telescope nearest to the eye being in reality a microscope for viewing the image formed by the great lens or mirror, as the case may be. And it does not seem to some altogether absurd to speak of illuminating this image by transfused light, or of casting by means of an illuminating microscope a vastly enlarged picture of this image upon a screen. But of course the image being simply formed by the passage of rays (which originally came from the object whose image they form) through a certain small space, to send *other* rays (coming from some other luminous object) through the same small space, is not to improve, but, so far as any effect is produced at all, to impair, the distinctness of the image. In fact, if these illuminating rays reached the eye, they would seriously impair the distinctness of the image. Their effect may be compared exactly with the effect of rays of light cast upon the image in a camera obscura; and, to see what the effect of such rays would be, we need only consider why it is that the camera *is* made 'obscura,' or dark. The effect of the transfusion of light through a telescopic image may be easily tried by any one who cares to make the experiment. He has only to do away with the tube of his telescope (substituting two or three straight rods to hold the glass in its place), and then in the blaze of a strong sun to direct the telescope on some object lying nearly towards the sun. Or if he prefer artificial light for the experiment, then at night let him direct the telescope so prepared upon the moon, while a strong electric light is directed upon the place where the focal image is formed (close in front of the eye). The experiment will not suggest very sanguine hopes of good result from the transfusion of artificial light. Yet, to my own knowledge, not a few who were perfectly well aware that the lunar hoax was not based on facts, have gravely reasoned that the principle suggested might be sound, and, in fact, that they could see no reason why astronomers should not try it, even though it had been first suggested as a joke.

To return, however, to the narrative. 'The co-operative philosophers, having hit upon their method, determined to test it practically. They decided that a medium of the purest plate-glass (which it is said they obtained, by consent, be it observed, from the shop-window of M. Desanges, the jeweller to his ex-majesty Charles X., in High Street) was the most eligible they could discover. It answered perfectly with a telescope which magnified a hundred times, and a microscope of about thrice that power.' Thus fortified by experiment, and 'fully sanctioned by the high optical authority of Sir David Brewster, Sir John laid his plan before the Royal Society, and particularly directed to it the attention of his Royal Highness the Duke of Sussex, the ever munificent patron of science and the arts. It was immediately and enthusiastically approved by the committee chosen to investigate it, and the chairman, who was the Royal President' (this continual reference to royalty is manifestly intended to give a British tone to the narrative), 'subscribed his name for a contribution of £10,000, with a promise that he would zealously submit the proposed instrument as a fit object for the patronage of the privy purse. He did so without delay; and his Majesty, on being informed that the estimated expense was £70,000, naïvely enquired if the costly instrument would conduce to any improvement in *navigation*. On being informed that it undoubtly would, the sailor king promised a *carte blanche* for any amount which might be required.'

All this is very clever. The 'sailor king' comes in as effectively to give *vraisemblance* to the narrative as 'Crabtree's little bronze Shakspeare that stood over the fireplace,' and the 'postman just come to the door with a double letter from Northamptonshire.'

Then comes a description of the construction of the object-glass, twenty-four feet in diameter, 'just six times the size of the elder Herschel's;' who, by the way, never made a telescope with an object-glass. The account of Sir John Herschel's journey from England, and even some details of the construction of the observatory, were based on facts, indeed, so many persons in America as well as in England were acquainted with some of these circumstances, that it was essential to follow the facts as closely as possible. Of course, also, some explanation had to be given of the circumstance that nothing had before been heard respecting the gigantic instrument taken out by Sir John Herschel. 'Whether,' says the story, 'the British Government were sceptical concerning the promised splendour of the discoveries, or wished them to be scrupulously veiled until they had accumulated a full-orbed glory for the nation and reign in which they originated, is a question which we can only conjecturally solve. But certain it is that the astronomer's royal patrons enjoined a masonic taciturnity upon him and his friends until he should have officially communicated the results of his great experiment.'

It was not till the night of January 10, 1835, that the mighty telescope was at length directed towards our satellite. The part of the moon selected was on the eastern part of her disc. 'The whole immense power of the telescope was applied, and to its focal image about one half of the power of the microscope. On removing the screen of the latter, the field of view was covered throughout its entire area with a beautifully distinct and even vivid representation of *basaltic rock*. Its colour was a greenish brown; and the width of the columns, as defined by their interstices on the canvas, was invariably twenty-eight inches. No fracture whatever appeared in the mass first presented; but in a few seconds a shelving pile appeared, of five or six columns' width, which showed their figure to be hexagonal, and their articulations similar to those of the basaltic formation at Staffa. This precipitous cliff was profusely covered with a dark red flower, precisely similar, says Dr. Grant, to the Papaver Rhœus, or Rose Poppy, of our sublunary corn-fields; and this was the first organic production of nature in a foreign world ever revealed to the eyes of men.'

It would be wearisome to go through the whole series of observations thus fabled, and only a few of the more striking features need be indicated. The discoveries are carefully graduated in interest. Thus we have seen how, after recognising basaltic formations, the observers discovered flowers: they next see a lunar forest, whose 'trees were of one unvaried kind, and unlike any on earth except the largest kind of yews in the English churchyards.' (There is an American ring in this sentence, by the way, as there is in one, a few lines farther on, where the narrator having stated that by mistake the observers had the Sea of Clouds instead of a more easterly spot in the field of view, proceeds to say: 'However, the moon was a free country, and we not as yet attached to any particular province.') Next a lunar ocean is described, 'the water nearly as blue as that of the deep sea, and breaking in large white billows upon the strand, while the action of very high tides was quite manifest upon the face of the cliffs for more than a hundred miles.' After a description of several valleys, hills, mountains and forests, we come to the discovery of animal life. An oval valley surrounded by hills, red as the purest vermilion, is selected as the scene. 'Small collections of trees, of every imaginable kind, were scattered about the whole of this luxuriant area; and here our magnifiers blessed our panting hopes with specimens of conscious existence. In the shade of the woods we beheld brown quadrupeds having all the external characteristics of the bison, but more diminutive than any species of the bos genus in our natural history.' Then herds of agile creatures like antelopes are described, 'abounding on the acclivitous glades of the woods.' In the contemplation of these sprightly animals the narrator becomes quite lively. 'This beautiful creature,' says he, 'afforded us the most exquisite amusement. The mimicry of its movements upon our white painted canvas was as faithful and luminous as that of animals within a few yards of the camera obscura. Frequently, when attempting to put our fingers upon its beard, it would suddenly bound away as if conscious of our earthly impertinence; but then others would appear, whom we could not prevent nibbling the herbage, say or do to them what we would.'

A strange amphibious creature, of a spherical form, rolling with great velocity along a pebbly beach, is the next object of interest, but is presently lost sight of in a strong current setting off from the angle of an island. After this there are three or four pages descriptive of various lunar scenes and animals, the latter showing a tendency, singular considering the circumstances, though very convenient for the narrator, to become higher and higher in type as the discoveries proceed, until an animal somewhat of the nature of the missing link is discovered. It is found in the Endymion (a circular walled plain) in company with a small kind of reindeer, the elk, the moose, and the horned bear, and is described as the biped beaver. It 'resembles the beaver of the earth in every other respect than in its destitution of a tail, and its invariable habit of walking upon only two feet. It carries its young in its arms like a human being, and moves with an easy gliding motion. Its huts are constructed better and higher than those of many tribes of human savages, and, from the appearance of smoke in nearly all of them, there is no doubt of its being acquainted with the use of fire. Still, its head and body differ only in the points stated from that of the beaver; and it was never seen except on the borders of lakes and rivers, in which it has been observed to immerse for a period of several seconds.'

The next step towards the climax brings us to domestic animals, 'good large sheep, which would not have disgraced the farms of Leicestershire or the shambles of Leadenhall Market; we fairly laughed at the recognition of so familiar an acquaintance in so distant a land. Presently they appeared in great numbers, and, on reducing the lenses, we found them in flocks over a great part of the valley. I need not say how desirous we were of finding shepherds to these flocks, and even a man with blue apron and rolled-up sleeves would have been a welcome sight to us, it not to the sheep; but they fed in peace, lords of their own pastures, without either protector or destroyer in human shape.'

In the meantime, discussion had arisen as to the lunar locality where men, or creatures resembling them, would most likely be found. Herschel had a theory on the subject —viz., that just where the balancing or libratory swing of the moon brings into view the greatest extent beyond the eastern or western parts of that hemisphere which is turned earthwards in the moon's mean or average position, lunar inhabitants would probably be found, and nowhere else. This, by the way (speaking seriously), is a rather curious anticipation of a view long subsequently advanced by Hansen, and for a time adopted by Sir J. Herschel, that possibly the remote hemisphere of the moon may be a fit abode for living creatures, the oceans and atmosphere which are wanting on the nearer hemisphere having been (on this hypothesis) drawn over to the remoter because of a displacement of the moon's centre of gravity. I ventured in one of my first books on astronomy to indicate objections to this theory, the force of which Sir J. Herschel admitted in a letter addressed to me on the subject.

Taking, then, an opportunity when the moon had just swung to the extreme limit of her balancing, or, to use technical terms, when she had attained her maximum libration in longitude, the observers approached the level opening to Lake Langrenus, as the narrator calls this fine walled plain, which, by the way, is fully thirty degrees of lunar longitude within the average western limit of the moon's visible hemisphere. 'Here the valley narrows to a mile in width, and displays scenery on both sides picturesque and romantic beyond the powers of a prose description. Imagination, borne on the wings of poetry, could alone gather similes to portray the wild sublimity of this landscape, where dark behemoth crags stood over the brows of lofty precipices, as if a rampart in the sky; and forests seemed suspended in mid-air. On the eastern side there was one soaring crag, crested with trees, which hung over in a curve like three-fourths of a Gothic arch, and being of a rich crimson colour, its effect was most strange upon minds unaccustomed to the association of such grandeur with such beauty. But, whilst gazing upon them in a perspective of about half a mile, we were thrilled with astonishment to perceive four successive flocks of large winged creatures, wholly unlike any kind of birds, descend with a slow even motion from the cliffs on the western side and alight upon the plain. They were first noticed by Dr. Herschel, who exclaimed: "Now, gentlemen, my theories against your proofs, which you have often found a pretty even bet, we have here something worth looking at. I was confident that if ever we found beings in human shape it would be in this longitude, and that they would be provided by their Creator with some extraordinary powers of locomotion." . . . We counted three parties of these creatures, of twelve, nine, and fifteen in each, walking erect towards a small wood near the base of the eastern precipices. Certainly they *were* like human beings, for their wings had now disappeared, and their attitude in walking was both erect and dignified. . . . They averaged four feet in height, were covered, except on the face, with short and glossy copper-coloured hair, lying snugly upon their backs, from the top of the shoulders to the calves of the legs. The face, which was of a yellowish flesh colour, was a slight improvement upon that of the large orang outang, being more open and intelligent in its expression, and having a much greater expansion of forehead. The mouth, however, was very prominent, though somewhat relieved by a thick beard upon the lower jaw, and by lips far more human than those of any species of the simia genus. In general symmetry of body and limbs they were infinitely superior to the orang outang; so much so, that, but for their long wings, Lieutenant Drummond said they would look as well on a parade ground as some of the old Cockney militia. . . . These creatures were evidently engaged in conversation; their gesticulation, more particularly the varied action of their hands and arms, appeared impassioned and emphatic. We hence inferred that they were rational beings, and, although not perhaps of so high an order as others which we discovered the next month on the shores of the Bay of Rainbows, that they were capable of producing works of art and contrivance. . . . They possessed wings of great expansion, similar in construction to those of the bat, being a semi-transparent membrane united in curvilinear divisions by means of straight radii, united at the back by the dorsal integuments. But what astonished us very much was the circumstance of this membrane being continued from the shoulders to the legs, united all the way down, though gradually decreasing in width' (very much as Fuseli depicted the wings of his Satanic Majesty, though H.S.M. would seem to have the advantage of the lunar Bat-men in not being influenced by gravity[1]). 'The wings seemed completely under the command of volition, for those of the

[1] Milton's opinion may be quoted against me here; and as received ideas respecting angels, good and bad, the fall of man, and many other such matters, are due quite as much to Milton as to any other authority, his opinion must not be lightly disregarded. But though, when Milton's Satan 'meets a vast vacuity' where his wings are of no further service to him,

> 'All unawares
> Flutt'ring his pennons vain, plumb down he drops
> Ten thousand fathoms deep, and to this hour
> Down had been falling, had not by ill chance
> The strong rebuff of some tumultuous cloud,
> Instinct with fire and nitre, hurried him
> As many miles aloft,'

yet this was written nearly a quarter of a century before Newton had established the law of gravity. Moreover, there is no evidence to show in what direction Satan fell; 'above is below and below above,' says Richter, 'to one stripped of gravitating body;' and whether Satan was under the influence of gravity or not, he would be practically exempt from its action when in the midst of that 'dark, illimitable ocean' of space,

> 'Without bound,
> Without dimensions, where length, breadth, and height,
> And time and place are lost.'

His lighting 'on Niphates' top,' and overleaping the gate of Paradise, may be used as arguments either way. On the whole, I must (according to my present lights) claim for Satan a freedom from all scientific restraints. This freedom is exemplified by his showing all the kingdoms of the world from an exceeding high mountain, thus affording the first practical demonstration of the flat-earth theory, the maintenance of which led to poor Mr. Hampden's incarceration.

creatures whom we saw bathing in the water spread them instantly to their full width, waved them as ducks do theirs to shake off the water, and then as instantly closed them again in a compact form. Our further observation of the habits of these creatures, who were of both sexes, led to results so very remarkable, that I prefer they should be first laid before the public in Dr. Herschel's own work, where I have reason to know they are fully and faithfully stated, however incredulously they may be received. . . . We scientifically denominated them the Vespertilio-homo or Bat-man; and they are doubtless innocent and happy creatures, notwithstanding that some of their amusements would but ill comport with our terrestrial notions of decorum.' The omitted passages were suppressed in obedience to Dr. Grant's private injunction. 'These, however, and other prohibited passages,' were to be presently 'published by Dr. Herschel, with the certificates of the civil and military authorities of the colony, and of several Episcopal, Wesleyan, and other ministers, who in the month of March last were permitted, under stipulation of temporary secrecy, to visit the observatory, and become eye-witnesses of the wonders which they were requested to attest. We are confident that his forthcoming volumes will be at once the most sublime in science, and the most intense in general interest, that ever issued from the press.'

The actual climax of the narrative, however, is not yet reached. The inhabitants of Langrenus, though rational, do not belong to the highest orders of intelligent Lunarians. Herschel, ever ready with theories, had pointed out that probably the most cultivated races would be found residing on the slopes of some active volcano, and, in particular, that the proximity of the flaming mountain Bullialdus (about twenty degrees south and ten east of the vast crater Tycho, the centre whence extend those great radiations which give to the moon something of the appearance of a peeled orange) 'must be so great a local convenience to dwellers in this valley during the long periodical absence of solar light, as to render it a place of popular resort for the inhabitants of all the adjacent regions, more especially as its bulwark of hills afforded an infallible security against any volcanic eruption that could occur.' Our observers therefore applied their full power to explore it. 'Rich, indeed, was our reward. The very first object in this valley that appeared upon our canvas was a magnificent work of art. It was a temple—a fane of devotion or of science, which, when consecrated to the Creator, is devotion of the loftiest order, for it exhibits His attributes purely, free from the masquerade attire and blasphemous caricature of controversial creeds, and has the seal and signature of His own hand to sanction its aspirations. It was an equi-angular temple, built of polished sapphire, or of some resplendent blue stone, which, like it, displayed a myriad point of golden light twinkling and scintillating in the sunbeams. . . The roof was composed of yellow metal, and divided into three compartments, which were not triangular planes inclining to the centre, but subdivided, curved, and separated so as to present a mass of violently agitated flames rising from a common source of conflagration, and terminating in wildly waving points. This design was too manifest and too skilfully executed to be mistaken for a single moment. Through a few openings in these metallic flames we perceived a large sphere of a darker kind of metal nearly of a clouded copper colour, which they enclosed and seemingly raged around, as if hieroglyphically consuming it. . . . What did the ingenious builders mean by the globe surrounded by flames? Did they, by this, record any past calamity of *their* world, or predict any future one of *ours?*' (Why, by the way, should the past theory be assigned to the moon and the future one to our earth?) 'I by no means despair of ultimately solving not only these but a thousand other questions which present themselves respecting the objects in this planet; for not the millionth part of her surface has yet been explored, and we have been more desirous of collecting the greatest possible number of new facts than of indulging in speculative theories, however seductive to the imagination.'

After this we have an account of the behaviour of the Vespertilio-homo at meals. 'They seemed eminently happy, and even polite; for individuals would select large and bright specimens of fruit, and throw them archwise across to some friend who had extracted the nutriment from those scattered around him.' However, the lunar men are not on the whole particularly interesting beings according to this account. 'So far as we could judge, they spent their happy hours in collecting various fruits in the woods, in eating, flying, bathing, and loitering about the summits of precipices.' One may say of them what Huxley is reported to have said of the spirits as described by spiritualists, that no student of science would care to waste his time inquiring about such a stupid set of people.

Such are the more interesting and characteristic portions of a narrative, running in the original to forty or fifty large octavo pages. In its day the story attracted a good deal of notice, and, even when every one had learned the trick, many were still interested in a *brochure* which was so cleverly conceived and had deceived so many. To this day the lunar hoax is talked of in America, where originally it had its chief—or, one may rather say, its only real—success as a hoax. It reached England too late to deceive any but those who were unacquainted with Herschel's real doings, and no editors of public journals, I believe, gave countenance to it at all. In America, on the contrary, many editors gave the narrative a distinguished place in their columns. Some indeed expressed doubts, and others followed the safe course of the 'Philadelphia Inquirer,' which informed its readers that 'after an attentive perusal of the whole story they could decide for themselves;' adding that, 'whether true or false, the narrative is written with consummate ability and possesses intense interest.' But others were more credulous. According to the 'Mercantile Advertiser' the story carried 'intrinsic evidence of being an authentic document.' The 'Albany Daily Advertiser' had read the article 'with unspeakable emotions of pleasure and astonishment.' The 'New York Times' announced that 'the writer (Dr. Andrew Grant) displays the most extensive and accurate knowledge of astronomy; and the description of Sir John's recently improved instruments, the principle on which the inestimable improvements were founded, the account of the wonderful discoveries in the moon, etc., all are probable and plausible, and have an air of intense verisimilitude.' The 'New Yorker' considered the discoveries 'of astounding interest, creating a new era in astronomy and science generally.'[1]

[1] The *Sun* itself claimed to have established the veracity of the account in a manner strongly recalling a well-known argument used by orthodox believers in the Bible account of the cosmogony. Either, say these, Moses discovered how the world was made, or the facts were revealed to him by some one who had made the discovery: but Moses could not have made the discovery, knowing nothing of the higher departments of science; therefore, the account came from the only Being who could rationally be supposed to know anything about the beginning of the world. 'Either,' said the *New York Sun*, speaking of a mathematical problem discussed in the article, 'that problem was predicated by us or some other person, who has thereby made the greatest of all modern discoveries in mathematical astronomy. We did not make it, for we know nothing of mathematics whatever; therefore, it was made by the only person to whom it can rationally be ascribed, namely Herschel the astronomer, its only avowed and undeniable

In our time a trick of the kind could hardly be expected to succeed so well, even if as cleverly devised and as well executed. The facts of popular astronomy and of general popular science have been more widely disseminated. America, too, more than any other great nation, has advanced in the interval. It was about two years after this pamphlet had appeared, that J. Quincy Adams used the following significant language in advocating the erection of an astronomical observatory at Washington: 'It is with no feeling of pride as an American that the remark may be made, that on the comparatively small territorial surface of Europe there are existing more than 130 of these lighthouses of the skies; while throughout the whole American hemisphere there is but one.' At present, some of the finest observatories in the world belong to American cities, or are attached to American colleges; and much of the most interesting astronomical work of this country has been achieved by American observers.

Yet we still hear from time to time of the attempted publication of hoaxes of greater or less ingenuity. It is singular (and I think significant) how often these relate to the moon. There would seem to be some charm about our satellite for the minds of paradoxists and hoaxers generally. Nor are these tricks invariably detected at once by the general public, or even by persons of some culture. I remember being gravely asked (in January 1874) whether an account given in the 'New York World,' purporting to describe how the moon's frame was gradually cracking, threatening eventually to fall into several separate fragments, was in reality based on fact. In the far West,

author.' In reality, notwithstanding this convincing argument, the problem was stolen by Locke from a paper by Olbers, shortly before published, and gave the method followed by Beer and Mädler throughout their selenographical researches in 1833-37.

at Lincoln, Nebraska, a lawyer asked me, not long since, why I had not described the great discoveries recently made by means of a powerful reflector erected near Paris. According to the 'Chicago Times,' this powerful instrument had shown buildings in the moon, and bands of workers could be seen with it who manifestly were undergoing some kind of penal servitude, for they were chained together. It was clear, from the presence of these and the absence of other inhabitants, that the side of the moon turned earthwards is a dreary and unpleasant place of abode, the real 'happy hunting grounds' of the moon lying on her remote and unseen hemisphere.

As gauges of general knowledge, scientific hoaxes have their uses, just as paradoxical works have. No one, certainly no student of science, can thoroughly understand how little some persons know about science, until he has observed how much will be believed, if only published with the apparent authority of a few known names, and announced with a sufficient parade of technical verbiage; nor is it so easy as might be thought, even for those who are acquainted with the facts, to disprove either a hoax or a paradox. Nothing, indeed, can much more thoroughly perplex and confound a student of science than to be asked to prove, for example, that the earth is not flat, or the moon not inhabited by creatures like ourselves; for the circumstance that such a question is asked implies ignorance so thorough of the very facts on which the proof must be based, as to render argument all but hopeless from the outset. I have had a somewhat wide experience of paradoxists, and have noted the experience of De Morgan and others who, like him, have tried to convince them of their folly. The conclusion at which I have arrived is, that to make a rope of sand were an easy task compared with the attempt to instil the simpler facts of science into paradoxical heads.

I would make some remarks, in conclusion, upon scientific or quasi-scientific papers not intended to deceive, but yet presenting imaginary scenes, events, and so forth, described more or less in accordance with scientific facts. Imaginary journeys to the sun, moon, planets, and stars; travels over regions on the earth as yet unexplored; voyages under the sea, through the bowels of the earth, and other such narratives, may, perhaps, be sometimes usefully written and read, so long as certain conditions are fulfilled by the narrator. In the first place, while adopting, to preserve the unities, the tone of one relating facts which actually occurred, he should not suffer even the simplest among his readers to lie under the least misapprehension as to the true nature of the narrative. Again, since of necessity established facts must in such a narrative appear in company with the results of more or less probable surmise, the reader should have some means of distinguishing where fact ends and surmise begins. For example, in a paper I once wrote, entitled 'A Journey to Saturn,' I was not sufficiently careful to note that while the appearances described in the approach towards the planet were in reality based on the observed appearances as higher and higher telescopic powers are applied to the planet, others supposed to have been seen by the visitors to Saturn when actually within his system, were only such as might possibly or probably be seen, but for which we have no real evidence. In consequence of this omission, I received several inquiries about these matters. 'Is it true,' some wrote, 'that the small satellite Hyperion' (scarce discernible in powerful telescopes, while Titan and Japetus on either side are large) 'is only one of a ring of small satellites travelling between the orbits of the larger moons?'—as the same planets travel between the paths of Mars and Jupiter. Others asked on what grounds it was said that the voyagers found small moons circling about Titan, the giant moon of the Saturnian system, as the moons of Jupiter and Saturn circle around those giant members of the solar system. In each case, I was reduced to the abject nececsity of explaining that there was no evidence for the alleged state of things, which, however, might nevertheless exist. Scientific fiction which has to be interpreted in that way is as bad as a joke that has to be explained. In my 'Journey to the Sun' I was more successful (it was the earlier essay, however); insomuch that Professor Young, of Dartmouth College (Hanover, N.H.), one of the most skilful solar observers living, assured me that, with scarcely a single exception, the various phenomena described corresponded exactly with the ideas he had formed respecting the probable condition of our luminary.[1]

But I must confess that my own experience has not been, on the whole, favourable to that kind of popular science writing. It appears to me that the more thoroughly the writer of such an essay has studied any particular scientific subject, the less able must he be to write a fictitious narrative respecting it. Just as those ignorant of any subject are often the readiest to theorise about it, because least hampered by exact knowledge, so I think that the careful avoidance of any exact study of the

[1] I had at the same time the good fortune to satisfy in equal degree, though quite unexpectedly, an English student of the sun, who at that time bore me no great good-will. Something in the article chanced to suggest that it came from another, presumably a rival, hand; while an essay which appeared about the same time (the spring of 1872) was commonly but erroneously attributed to me. Accordingly, a leading article in *Nature* was devoted to the annihilation of the writer supposed to be myself, and to the lavish and quite undeserved laudation of the article I had written, which was selected as typifying all the good qualities which an article of the kind should possess. Those acquainted with the facts were not a little amused by the mistake.

details of a scientific subject must greatly facilitate the writing of a fictitious narrative respecting it. But unfortunately a narrative written under such conditions, however interesting to the general reader, can scarcely forward the propagation of scientific knowledge, one of the qualities claimed for fables of the kind. As an instance in point, I may cite Jules Verne's 'Voyage to the Moon,' where (apart, of course, from the inherent and intentional absurdity of the scheme itself), the circumstances which are described are calculated to give entirely erroneous ideas about the laws of motion. Nothing could be more amusing, but at the same time nothing more scientifically absurd, than the story of the dead dog Satellite, which, flung out of the travelling projectile, becomes a veritable satellite, moving always beside the voyagers; for, with whatever velocity the dog had been expelled by them, with that same velocity would he have retreated continually from their projectile abode, whose own attraction on the dog would have had no appreciable effect in checking his departure. Again, the scene when the projectile reaches the neutral point between the earth and moon, so that there is no longer any gravity to keep the travellers on the floor of their travelling car, is well conceived (though, in part, somewhat profane); but in reality the state of things described as occurring there would have prevailed throughout the journey. The travellers would no more be drawn earthwards (as compared with the projectile itself) than we travellers on the earth are drawn sunwards with reference to the earth. The earth's attracting force on the projectile and on the travellers would be equal all through the journey, not solely when the projectile reached the neutral point; and being equal on both, would not draw them together. It may be argued that the attractions were equal before the projectile set out on its journey, and therefore, if the reasoning just given were correct, the travellers ought not to have had any weight keeping them on the floor of the projectile before it started, 'which is absurd.' But the pressure upon the floor of the projectile at rest is caused by the floor being kept from moving; let it be free to obey gravity, and there will no longer be any pressure: and throughout the journey to the moon, the projectile, like the travellers it contains, is obeying the action of gravity. Unfortunately, those who are able to follow the correct reasoning in such matters are not those to whom Jules Verne's account would suggest wrong ideas about matters dynamical; the young learner who *is* misled by such narratives is neither able to reason out the matter for himself, nor to understand the true reasoning respecting it. He is, therefore, apt to be set quite at sea by stories of the kind, and especially by the specious reasoning introduced to explain the events described. In fine, it would seem that such narratives must be valued for their intrinsic interest, just like other novels or romances, not for the quality sometimes claimed for them of combining instruction with amusement.

X.

ON SOME ASTRONOMICAL PARADOXES.

For many years the late Professor De Morgan contributed to the columns of the 'Athenæum' a series of papers in which he dealt with the strange treatises in which the earth is flattened, the circle squared, the angle divided into three, the cube doubled (the famous problem which the Delphic oracle set astronomers), and the whole of modern astronomy shown to be a delusion and a snare. He treated these works in a quaint fashion: not unkindly, for his was a kindly nature; not even earnestly, though he was thoroughly in earnest; yet in such sort as to rouse the indignation of the unfortunate paradoxists. He was abused roundly for what he said, but much more roundly when he declined further controversy. Paradoxists of the ignorant sort (for it must be remembered that not all are ignorant) are, indeed, well practised in abuse, and have long learned to call mathematicians and astronomers cheats and charlatans. They freely used their vocabulary for the benefit of De Morgan, whom they denounced as a scurrilous scribbler, a defamatory, dishonest, abusive, ungentlemanly, and libellous trickster.

He bore this shower of abuse with exceeding patience and good nature. He had not been wholly unprepared for it, in fact; and, as he had a purpose in dealing with the paradoxists, he was satisfied to continue that quiet analysis of their work which so roused their indignation. He found in them a curious subject of study; and he found an equally curious subject of study in their disciples. The simpler—not to say more foolish—paradoxists, whose wonderful discoveries are merely amazing misapprehensions, were even more interesting to De Morgan than the craftier sort who make a living, or try to make a living, out of their pretended theories. Indeed, these last he treated, as they deserved, with a scathing satire quite different from his humorous and not ungenial comments on the wonderful theories of the honest paradoxists.

There is one special use to which the study of paradox-literature may be applied, which—so far as I know—has not hitherto been much attended to. It may be questioned whether half the strange notions into which paradoxists fall must not be ascribed to the vagueness of too many of our scientific treatises. A half-understood explanation, or a carelessly worded account of some natural phenomenon, leads the paradoxist, whose nature is compounded of conceit and simplicity, to originate a theory of his own on the subject. Once such a theory has been devised, it takes complete possession of the paradoxist's mind. All the facts of which he thenceforward hears, which bear in the least on his favourite craze, appear to give evidence in its favour, even though in reality they are most obviously opposed to it He learns to look upon himself as an unappreciated Newton, and to see the bitterest malevolence in those who venture to question his preposterous notions. He is fortunate if he do not suffer his theories to withdraw him from his means of earning a livelihood, or if he do not waste his substance in propounding and defending them.

One of the favourite subjects for paradox-forming is the accepted theory of the solar system. Our books on astronomy too often present this theory in such sort that it seems only a *successor* of Ptolemy's: and the impression is conveyed that, like Ptolemy's, it may be one day superseded by some other theory. This is quite enough for the paradoxist. If a new theory is to replace the one now accepted, why should not *he* be the new Copernicus? He starts upon the road without a tithe of the knowledge that old Ptolemy possessed, unaware of the difficulties which Ptolemy met and dealt with—free, therefore, because of his perfect ignorance, to form theories at which Ptolemy would have smiled. He has probably heard of the

> centrics and eccentrics scribbled o'er
> Cycle and epicycle, orb in orb,

which disfigured the theories of the ancients; but he is quite unconscious that every one of those scribblings had a real meaning, each being intended to account for some observed peculiarity of planetary motion, which *must* be accounted for by any theory which is to claim acceptance. In this happy unconsciousness that there are any peculiarities requiring explanation, knowing nothing of the strange paths which the planets are seen to follow on the heavenly vault,

> Their wand'ring course now high, now low, then hid,
> Progressive, retrograde, or standing still,

he placidly puts forward—and presently very vehemently urges—a theory which accounts for none of these things.

It has often seemed to me that a large part of the mischief—for let it be remembered that the published errors of the paradoxist are indicative of much unpublished misapprehension—arises from the undeserved contempt with which our books of astronomy too often treat the labours of Ptolemy, Tycho Brahe, and others who advocated erroneous theories. If the simple truth were told, that the theory of Ptolemy was a masterpiece of ingenuity and that it was worked out by his followers in a way which merits the highest possible praise, while the theory of Tycho Brahe was placed in reality on a sounder basis than that of Copernicus, and accounted as well and as simply for observed appearances, the student would begin to realise the noble nature of the problem which those great astronomers dealt with. And again, if stress were laid upon the fact that Tycho Brahe devoted years upon years of his life to secure such observations of the planets as might settle the questions at issue, the student would learn something of the spirit in which the true lover of science proceeds.

It seems to me, also, that far too little is said about the kind of work by which Kepler and Newton finally established the accepted theories. There is a strange charm in the history of those twenty years of Kepler's life during which he was analysing the observations made by Tycho Brahe. Surrounded with domestic trials and anxieties, which might well have claimed his whole attention, tried grievously by ill-health and bodily anguish, he laboured all those years upon erroneous theories. The very worst of these had infinitely more evidence in its favour than the best which the paradoxists have brought forth. There was not one of those theories which nine out of ten of his scientific contemporaries would not have accepted ungrudgingly. Yet he wrought these theories one after another to their own disproof. *Nineteen* of them he tried and rejected—the twentieth was the true theory of the solar system. Perhaps nothing in the whole history of astronomy affords a nobler lesson to the student of science —unless, indeed, it be the calm philosophy with which Newton for eighteen years suffered the theory of the universe to remain in abeyance, because faulty measurements of the earth prevented his calculations from agreeing with observed facts. But, as Professor Tyndall has well remarked—and the paradoxist should lay the lesson well to heart—'Newton's action in this matter was the normal action of the scientific mind. If it were otherwise—if scientific men were not accustomed to demand verification, if they were satisfied with the imperfect while the perfect is attainable—their science, instead of being, as it is, a fortress of adamant, would be a house of clay, ill fitted to bear the buffetings of the theologic storms to which it has been from time to time, and is at present, exposed.'

The fame of Newton has proved to many paradoxists an irresistible attraction ; it has been to these unfortunates as the candle to the fluttering moth. Circle-squaring, as we shall presently see, has had its attractions, nor have earth-fixing and earth-flattening been neglected ; but attacking the law of gravitation has been the favourite work of paradoxists. Newton has been praised as surpassing the whole human race in genius ; mathematicians and astronomers have agreed to laud him as unequalled ; why should not Paradoxus displace him and be praised in like manner? . It would be unfair, perhaps, to say that the paradoxist consciously argues thus. He doubtless in most instances convinces himself that he has really detected some flaw in the theory of gravitation. Yet it is impossible not to recognise, as the real motive of every paradox-monger, the desire to have that said of him which has been said of Newton : '*Genus humanum ingenio superavit.*'

I remember a curious instance of this which occurred soon after the appearance of the comet of 1858. It chanced that, while that object was under discussion, reference was made to the action of a repulsive force exerted by the sun upon the matter of the comet's tail. On this, some one addressed a long letter to a Glasgow newspaper, announcing that he had long ago proved that the sun's attraction alone is insufficient to account for the planetary motions. His reasoning was amazingly simple. If the sun's attraction is powerful enough to keep the outer planets in their course, it must be too powerful for Venus and Mercury close by the sun; if it only just suffices to keep these in their course, it cannot possibly be powerful enough to restrain the outer planets. The writer of this letter said that he had been very badly treated by scientific bodies. He had announced his discovery to the Royal Astronomical Society, the Royal Society, the Imperial Academy at Paris, and other scientific bodies; but they had one and all refused to listen to him. He had forsaken or neglected his trade for several years in order to give attention to the new and (as he thought) the true theory of the universe. He complained in a specially bitter manner of the unfavourable comments which men of science had made upon his views in private letters addressed to him in reply to his communications.

There is something melancholy even in what is most ridiculous in cases of this sort. The simplicity which supposes that considerations so obvious as those adduced could escape the scrutiny, not of Newton only, but of all who have followed in the same track during two centuries, is certainly stupendous; nor can one fail to smile at seeing a difficulty, such as might naturally suggest itself to a beginner, and such as half-a-dozen words from an expert would clear up, regarded gravely as a discovery calculated to make its author famous for all time. Yet, when one considers the probable consequences of the blunder to the unhappy enthusiast, and perchance to his family, it is difficult not to feel a sense of pity, quite apart from that pity allied to contempt which is excited by his mistake. A few words added to the account of Newton's theory, which the paradoxist had probably read in some astronomical treatise, would have prevented all this mischief. Indeed, this difficulty, which, as we have said, is a natural one, should be dealt with and removed in any account of the planetary system intended for beginners. The simple statement that the outer planets move more slowly than the inner, and so *require* a smaller force to keep them in their course, would have sufficed, not, perhaps, altogether to remove the difficulty, but to show the beginner where the explanation was to be looked for.

It was in connection with this subject of gravitation that one of the most well-meaning of the paradoxists—the late Mr. James Reddie—came under Professor De Morgan's criticism. Mr. Reddie was something more than well-meaning. He was earnestly desirous of advancing the interests of science, as well as of defending religion from what he mistakenly supposed to be the dangerous teachings of the Newtonians. He founded for these purposes the Victoria Institute, of which society he was the secretary from the time of its institution until his decease, some years since; and, probably, many who declined to join that society because of the Anti-Newtonian proclivities of its secretary, were unaware that to that secretary the institute owed its existence.

It so chanced that I had myself a good deal of correspondence with Mr. Reddie (who was, however, personally unknown to me). This correspondence served to throw quite a new light on the mental habitudes and ways of thinking of the honest paradoxist. I believe that Professor De Morgan hardly gave Mr. Reddie credit for the perfect honesty which he really possessed. It may have been that a clear reasoner like De Morgan could hardly (despite his wide experience) appreciate the confusion of mind which is the normal characteristic of the paradoxist. But certainly the very candid way in which Mr. Reddie admitted, in the correspondence above named, that he had not known some facts and had misunderstood others, afforded to my mind the most satisfactory proofs of his straightforwardness.

It may be instructive to consider a few of those paradoxes of Mr. Reddie's which Professor De Morgan found chief occasion to pulverise.

In a letter to the Astronomer-Royal Mr. Reddie announced that he was about to write 'a paper intended to be hereafter published, elaborating more minutely and discussing more rigidly than before the glaring fallacies, dating from the time of Newton, relating to the motion of the moon.' He proceeded to 'indicate the nature of the issues he intended to raise.' He had discovered that the moon does not, as a matter of fact, go round the earth at the rate of 2288 miles an hour, as astronomers say, but follows an undulatory path round the sun at a rate varying between 65,000 and 70,000 miles an hour; because, while the moon seems to go round the earth, the latter is travelling onwards at the rate of 67,500 miles an hour round the sun. Of course he was quite right in his facts, and quite wrong in his inferences; as the Astronomer-Royal pointed out in a brief letter, closing with the remark that, 'as a very closely occupied man,' Mr. Airy could 'not enter further into the matter.' But further Mr. Reddie persisted in going, though he received no more letters from Greenwich. His reply to Sir G. Airy contained, in fact, matter enough for a small pamphlet.

Now here was certainly an amazing fact. A well-known astronomical relation, which astronomers have over and over again described and explained, is treated as though it were something which had throughout all ages escaped attention. It is not here the failure to comprehend the *rationale* of a simple explanation which is startling, but the notion that an obvious fact had been wholly overlooked.

Of like nature was the mistake which brought Mr

Reddie more especially under Professor De Morgan's notice. It is known that the sun, carrying with him his family of planets, is speeding swiftly through space—his velocity being estimated as probably not falling short of 20,000 miles per hour. It follows, of course, that the real paths of the planets in space are not closed curves, but spirals of different orders. How, then, can the theory of Copernicus be right, according to which the planets circle in closed orbits round the sun? Here was Mr. Reddie's difficulty; and like the other, it appeared to his mind as a great discovery. He was no whit concerned by the thought that astronomers ought surely to have noticed the difficulty before. It did not seem in the least wonderful that he, lightly reading a book or two of popular astronomy, should discover that which Laplace, the Herschels, Leverrier, Airy, Adams, and a host of others, who have given their whole lives to astronomy, had failed to notice. Accordingly, Mr. Reddie forwarded to the British Association (in session at Newcastle) a paper controverting the theory of the sun's motion. The paper was declined with thanks by that bigoted body 'as opposed to Newtonian astronomy.' 'That paper I published,' says Mr. Reddie, 'in September 1863, with an appendix, in both thoroughly exhibiting the illogical reasoning and absurdities involved in the theory; and with what result? The members of Section A of the British Association, and Fellows of the Royal Society and of the Royal Astronomical Society, to whom I sent copies of my paper, were, without exception, *dumb.*' Professor De Morgan, however, having occasion to examine Mr. Reddie's publications some time after, was in no sort dumb, but in very plain and definite terms exhibited their absurdity. After all, however, the real absurdity consisted, not in the statements which Mr. Reddie made, nor even in the conclusions which he drew from them, but in the astounding simplicity which could suppose that astronomers were unaware of the facts which their own labours had revealed.

In my correspondence with Mr. Reddie I recognised the real source of the amazing self-complacency displayed by the true paradoxist. The very insufficiency of the knowledge which a paradoxist possesses of his subject, affords the measure of his estimate of the care with which other men have studied that subject. Because the paradoxist is ready to pronounce an opinion about matters he has not studied, it does not seem strange to him that Newton and his followers should be equally ready to discuss subjects they had not inquired into.

Another very remarkable instance was afforded by Mr. Reddie's treatment of the subject of comets. And here, by the way, I shall quote a remark made by Sir John Herschel soon after the appearance of the comet of 1861. 'I have received letters,' he said, 'about the comets of the last few years, enough to make one's hair stand on end at the absurdity of the theories they propose, and at the ignorance of the commonest laws of optics, of motion, of heat, and of general physics, they betray in their writers.' In the present instance, the correspondence showed that the paradoxist supposed the parabolic paths of some comets to be regarded by astronomers as analogous to the parabolic paths traversed by projectiles. He expressed considerable astonishment when I informed him that, in the first place, projectiles do not travel on truly parabolic paths; and secondly, that in all respects their motion differs essentially from that which astronomers ascribe to comets. These last move more and more quickly until they reach what is called the vertex of the parabola (the point of such a path which lies nearest to the sun): projectiles, on the contrary, move more and more slowly as they approach the corresponding point of their path; and further, the comet first approaches and then recedes from the centre of attraction—the projectile first recedes from and then approaches the attracting centre.

The earth-flatteners form a considerable section of the paradoxical family. They experienced a practical rebuff, a few years since, which should to some degree have shaken their faith in the present chief of their order. To do this chief justice, he is probably far less confident about the flatness of the earth than any of his disciples. Under the assumed name of Parallax he visited most of the chief towns of England, propounding what he calls his system of zetetic astronomy. Why he should call himself Parallax it would be hard to say; unless it be that the verb from which the word is derived signifies primarily to shift about or dodge, and secondarily to alter a little, especially for the worse. His employment of the word zetetic is less doubtful, as he claims for his system that it alone is founded on the true seeking out of Nature's secrets.

The experimental basis of the theory of Parallax is mainly this: Having betaken himself to a part of the Bedford Canal, where there is an uninterrupted water-line of about six miles, he tested the water surface for signs of curvature, and (as he said) found none.

It chanced, unfortunately, that a disciple—Mr. John Hampden, of Swindon—accepted the narrative of this observation in an unquestioning spirit; and was so confident that the Bedford Canal has a truly plane surface, that he wagered five hundred pounds on his opinion, challenging the believers in the earth's rotundity to repeat the experiment. The challenge was accepted by Mr. Wallace, the eminent naturalist; and the result may be anticipated. Three boats were to be moored in a line, three miles or so between each. Each carried a mast of given length. If, when the summits of the first and last masts were seen in a line through a telescope, the summit of the middle mast was not found to be above the line, then Mr. Hampden was to receive five hundred pounds from Mr. Wallace. If, on the contrary, the top of the middle mast was found, as the accepted theory said it should be, to be several feet above the line joining the tops of the two outer masts, then Mr. Hampden was to lose the five hundred pounds he had so rashly ventured. Everything was conducted in accordance with the arrangements agreed upon. The editor of a well-known sporting paper acted as stakeholder, and unprejudiced umpires were to decide as to what actually was seen through the telescope. It need scarcely be said that the accepted theory held its own, and that Mr. Hampden lost his money. He scarcely bore the loss with so good a grace as was to have been expected from a philosopher merely desirous of ascertaining the truth. His wrath was not expended on Parallax, whom he might have suspected of having led him astray; nor does he seem to have been angry with himself, as would have seemed natural. All his anger was reserved for those who still continued to believe in the earth's rotundity. Whether he believed that the Bedford water had risen under the middle boat to oblige Mr. Wallace, or how it came to pass that his own chosen experiment had failed him, does not appear.

The subsequent history of this matter has been unpleasant. It illustrates, unfortunately but too well, the mischief which may ensue from the tricks of those who make a trade of paradox—tricks which would be scarce possible, however, if text-books of science were more carefully written, and by those only who are really acquainted with the subject of which they treat.

The book which originally led to Mr. Hampden's misfortunes, and has misled not a few, ought to have deceived none. I have already mentioned the statement on which

Parallax (whose true name is Rowbotham) rested his theory. Of course, if that statement had been true—if he had, with his eye a few inches from the surface of the water of the Bedford Canal, seen an object close to the surface six miles from him—there manifestly would have been something wrong in the accepted theory about the earth's rotundity. So, also, if a writer were to announce a new theory of gravity, stating as the basis of his theory that a heavy missile which he had thrown into the air had gone upwards on a serpentine course to the moon, any one who accepted the statement would be logically bound to admit at least that the fact described was inconsistent with the accepted theory. But no one would accept such a statement; and no one should have accepted Mr. Rowbotham's statement.

His statement was believed, however, and perhaps is still believed by many. Twenty years ago De Morgan wrote that 'the founder of the zetetic astronomy gained great praise from provincial newspapers for his ingenuity in proving that the earth is a flat, surrounded by ice,' with the north polar ice in the middle. 'Some of the journals rather incline to this view; but the "Leicester Advertiser" thinks that the statement "would seem to invalidate some of the most important conclusions of modern astronomy;" while the "Northfolk Herald" is clear that "there must be great error on one side or the other." . . . . The fact is worth noting that from 1849-1857 arguments on the roundness or flatness of the earth did itinerate. I have no doubt they did much good, for very few persons have any distinct idea of the evidence for the rotundity of the earth. The "Blackburn Standard" and "Preston Guardian" (December 12 and 16, 1849) unite in stating that the lecturer ran away from his second lecture at Burnley, having been rather too hard pressed, at the end of his first lecture, to explain why the large hull of a ship disappeared before the masts. The persons present and waiting for the second lecture assuaged their disappointment by concluding that the lecturer had slipped off the ice edge of his flat disc, and that he would not be seen again till he peeped up on the opposite side.' . . . 'The zetetic system,' proceeds De Morgan, 'still lives in lectures and books; as it ought to do, for there is no way of teaching a truth comparable to opposition. The last I heard of it was in lectures at Plymouth, in October 1864. Since this time a prospectus has been issued of a work entitled "The Earth not a Globe;" but whether it has been published I do not know.'

The book was published soon after the above was written, and De Morgan gives the following quaint account of it: 'August 28, 1865. The zetetic astronomy has come into my hands. When in 1851 I went to see the Great Exhibition I heard an organ played by a performer who seemed very desirous of exhibiting one particular stop. "What do you think of that stop?" I was asked. "That depends on the name of it," said I. "Oh! what can the name of it have to do with the sound? 'that which we call a rose,' etc." "The name has everything to do with it: if it be a flute stop I think it very harsh; but if it be a railway-whistle stop, I think it very sweet." So as to this book: if it be childish, it is clever; if it be mannish, it is unusually foolish. The flat earth floating tremulously on the sea; the sun moving always over the flat, giving day when near enough, and night when too far off; the self-luminous moon, with a semi-transparent invisible moon created to give her an eclipse now and then; the new law of perspective, by which the vanishing of the hull before the masts, usually thought to prove the earth globular, really proves it flat;—all these and other things are well fitted to form exercises for a person who is learning the elements of astronomy. The manner in which the sun dips into the sea, especially in tropical climates, upsets the whole. Mungo Park, I think, gives an African hypothesis which explains phenomena better than this. The sun dips into the Western ocean, and the people there cut him in pieces, fry him in a pan, and then join him together again; take him round the under way, and set him up in the East. I hope this book will be read, and that many will be puzzled by it; for there are many whose notions of astronomy deserve no better fate. There is no subject on which there is so little accurate conception as on that of the motions of the heavenly bodies.[1] The author, though confident in the extreme, neither impeaches the honesty of those whose opinion he assails, nor allots them any future inconvenience: in these points he is worthy to live on a globe and to rotate in twenty-four hours.'

I chanced to reside near Plymouth when Mr. Rowbotham lectured there in October 1864. It will readily be understood that, in a town where there are so many naval men, his lectures were not altogether so successful as they have sometimes been in small inland towns. Numbers of naval officers, however, who were thoroughly well assured of the fact that the earth is a globe, were not able to demolish the crafty arguments of Parallax publicly, during the discussions which he challenged at the close of each

[1] The Astronomer-Royal once told me that he had found that few persons have a clear conception of the fact that the stars rise and set. Still fewer know how the stars move, which stars rise and set, which are always above the horizon, which move on large circles, which on small ones; though a few hours' observation on half-a-dozen nights in the year (such observations being continuous, but made only at hourly intervals) would show clearly how the stars move. It is odd to find even some who write about astronomy making mistakes on matters so elementary. For instance, in a primer of astronomy recently published, it is stated that the stars which pass overhead in London rise and set on a slant—the real fact being that *those* stars never rise or set at all, never coming within some two dozen moon-breadths of the horizon.

lecture. He was too skilled in that sort of evasion which his assumed name (as interpreted by Liddell and Scott) suggests, to be readily cornered. When an argument was used which he could not easily meet, or seem to meet, he would say simply: 'Well, sir, you have now had your fair share of the discussion; let some one else have his turn.' It was stated in the newspapers that one of his audience was so wrathful with the lecturer on account of these evasions, that he endeavoured to strike Parallax with a knobbed stick at the close of the second lecture; but probably there was no real foundation for the story.

Mr. Rowbotham did a very bold thing, however, at Plymouth. He undertook to prove, by observations made with a telescope upon the Eddystone Lighthouse from the Hoe and from the beach, that the surface of the water is flat. From the beach usually only the lantern can be seen. From the Hoe the whole of the lighthouse is visible under favourable conditions. Duly on the morning appointed, Mr. Rowbotham appeared. From the Hoe a telescope was directed towards the lighthouse, which was well seen, the morning being calm and still, and tolerably clear. On descending to the beach it was found that, instead of the whole lantern being visible as usual, only half could be seen —a circumstance doubtless due to the fact that the air's refractive power, which usually diminishes the dip due to the earth's curvature by about one-sixth part, was less efficient that morning than usual. The effect of the peculiarity was manifestly unfavourable to Mr. Rowbotham's theory. The curvature of the earth produced a greater difference than usual between the appearance of a distant object as seen from a certain high station and from a certain low station (though still the difference fell short of that which would be shown if there were no air). But Parallax claimed the peculiarity observable that morning as an argument in favour of his flat earth. It is manifest, he said, that there is something wrong about the accepted theory; for it tells us that so much less of the lighthouse should be seen from the beach than from the Hoe, whereas less still was seen. And many of the Plymouth folk went away from the Hoe that morning, and from the second lecture, in which Parallax triumphantly quoted the results of the observation, with the feeling which had been expressed seven years before in the 'Leicester Advertiser,' that 'some of the most important conclusions of modern astronomy had been seriously invalidated.' If our books of astronomy, in referring to the effects of the earth's curvature, had only been careful to point out how surveyors and sailors and those who build lighthouses take into account the modifying effects of atmospheric refraction, and how these effects have long been known to vary with the temperature and pressure of the air, this mischief would have been avoided. It would not be fair to say of the persons misled on that occasion by Parallax that they deserved no better; since the fault is not theirs as readers, but that of careless or ill-informed writers.

Another experiment conducted by Parallax the same morning was creditable to his ingenuity. Nothing better, perhaps, was ever devised to deceive people, apparently by ocular evidence, into the belief that the earth is flat—nor is there any clearer evidence of the largeness of the earth's globe compared with our ordinary measures. On the Hoe, some ninety or a hundred feet above the sea-level, he had a mirror suspended in a vertical position facing the sea, and invited the bystanders to look in that mirror at the sea-horizon. To all appearance the line of the horizon corresponded exactly with the level of the eye-pupils of the observer. Now, of course, when we look into a mirror whose surface is exactly vertical, the line of sight to the eye-pupils of our image in the mirror is exactly horizontal;

whereas the line of sight from the eyes to the image of the sea-horizon is depressed exactly as much as the line from the eyes to the real sea-horizon. Here, then, seemed to be proof positive that there is no depression of the sea-horizon; for the horizontal line to the image of the eye-pupil seemed to coincide exactly with the line to the image of the sea-horizon. It is not necessary to suppose here that the mirror was wrongly adjusted, though the slightest error of adjustment would affect the result either favourably or unfavourably for Parallax's flat-earth theory. It is a matter of fact that, if the mirror were perfectly vertical, only very acute vision could detect the depression of the image of the sea-horizon below the image of the eye-pupil. The depression can easily be calculated for any given circumstances. Parallax encouraged observers to note very closely the position of the eye-pupil in the image, so that most of them approached the image within about ten inches, or the glass within about five. Now, in such a case, for a height of one hundred feet above the sea-level the image of the sea-horizon would be depressed below the image of the eye-pupil by less than three hundredths of an inch—an amount which could not be detected by one eye in a hundred. The average diameter of the pupil itself is one-fifth of an inch, or about seven times as great as the depression of the sea-horizon in the case supposed. It would require very close observation and a good eye to determine whether a horizontal line seen on either side of the head were on the level of the centres of the eye-pupils, or lower by about one-seventh of the breadth of either pupil.

The experiment is a pretty one, however, and well worth trying by any one who lives near to the sea-shore and sea-cliffs. But there is a much more effective experiment which can be much more easily tried—only it is open to the disadvantage that it at once demolishes the argument of our friend Parallax. It occurred to me while I was writing the above paragraph. Let a very small mirror (it need not be larger than a sixpence) be so suspended to a small support and so weighted that when left to itself it hangs with its face perfectly vertical—an arrangement which any competent optician will easily secure—and let a fine horizontal line or several horizontal lines be marked on the mirror; which, by the way, should be a metallic one, as its indications will then be altogether more trustworthy. This mirror can be put into the waistcoat pocket and conveniently carried to much greater height than the mirror used by Parallax. Now, at some considerable height—say five or six hundred feet above the sea-level, but a hundred or even fifty will suffice—look into this small mirror while *facing* the sea. The true horizon will then be seen to be visibly below the centre of the eye-pupil—visibly in this case because the horizontal line traced on the mirror can be made to coincide with the sea-horizon exactly, and will then be found *not* to coincide with the centre of the eye-pupil. Such an instrument could be readily made to show the distance of the sea-horizon, which at once determines the height of the observer above the sea-level. For this purpose all that would be necessary would be a means of placing the eye at some definite distance from the small mirror, and a fine vertical scale on the mirror to show the exact depression of the sea-horizon. For balloonists such an instrument would sometimes be useful, as showing the elevation independently of the barometer, whenever any portion of the sea-horizon was in view.

The mention of balloon experiences leads me to another delusive argument of the earth-flatteners.[1] It has been the

[1] In passing let me note that, of course, I am not discussing the arguments of paradoxists with the remotest idea of disproving them. They are not, in reality, worth the trouble. But they show where the

experience of all aeronauts that, as the balloon rises, the appearance of the earth is by no means what would be expected from the familiar teachings in our books of astronomy. There is a picture in most of these books representing the effect of ascent above the sea-level in depressing the line of sight to the horizon, and bringing more and more into view the convexity of the earth's globe. One would suppose, from the picture, that when an observer is at a great height the earth would appear to rise under him, like some great round and well-curved shield whose convexity was towards him. Instead of this, the aeronaut finds the earth presenting the appearance of a great hollow basin, or of the concave side of a well-curved shield. The horizon seems to rise as he rises, while the earth beneath him sinks lower and lower. A somewhat similar phenomenon may be noted when, after ascending the landward side of a high cliff, we come suddenly upon a view of the sea—invariably the sea-horizon is higher than we expected to find it. *Only*, in this case, the surface of the sea seems to rise from the beach below towards the distant horizon convexly not concavely; the reason of which I take to be this, that the waves, and especially long rollers or uniform large ripples, teach the eye to form true conceptions of the shape of the sea-surface even when the eye is deceived as to the position of the sea-horizon. Indeed, I should much like to know what would be the appearance of the sea from a balloon when no land was in sight (though I do not particularly wish to make the observation myself): the convexity discernible, for the reason just named, would contend strangely with the concavity imagined, for the reason now to be indicated.

general reader of astronomical text-books, and other such works, is likely to go astray, and thus conveniently indicate matters whose explanation may be useful or interesting.

The deception arises from the circumstance that the scene displayed below and around the balloon is judged by the eye from the experience of more familiar scenes. The horizon is depressed, but so little that the eye cannot detect the depression, especially where the boundary of the horizon is irregular. It is here that the text-book pictures mislead; for they show the depression as far too great to be overlooked, setting the observer sometimes about two thousand miles above the sea-level. The eye, then, judges the horizon to be where it usually is—on the same level as the observer; but looking downwards, the eye perceives, and at once appreciates if it does not even exaggerate, the great depth at which the earth lies below the balloon. The appearance, then, as judged by the eye, is that of a mighty basin whose edge rises up all round to the level of the balloon, while its bottom lies two or three miles or more below the balloon.

The zetetic faithful reason about this matter as though the impressions of the senses were trustworthy under all conditions, familiar or otherwise; whereas, in point of fact, we know that the senses often deceive, even under familiar conditions, and almost always deceive under conditions, which are not familiar. A person, for example, accustomed to the mist and haze of our British air, is told by the sense of sight, when he is travelling where a clearer atmosphere prevails, that a mountain forty miles from him is a hill a few miles away. On the other hand, an Italian travelling through the Highlands is impressed with the belief that all the features of the scenery are much larger (because he supposes them much more remote) than they really are. A hundred such instances of deception might easily be cited. The conditions under which the aeronaut observes the earth are certainly less familiar than those under which the Briton views the Alps and Apennines, or the Italian views Ben Lomond or Ben Lawers. It would be rash, therefore, even if no other evidence were available, to reject the faith that the earth is a globe because, as seen from a balloon, it looks like a basin. Indeed, to be strictly logical, the followers of Parallax ought on this account to adopt the faith that the earth is not flat, but basin-shaped, which hitherto they have not been ready to do.

We have seen that Parallax describes a certain experiment on the Bedford Level, which, if made as he states, would have shown certainly that something was wrong in the accepted system—for a six-mile straight-edge along water would be as severe a blow to the belief in a round earth, as a straight line on the sea-surface from Queenstown to New York. Another curious experiment adorns his little book, which, if it could be repeated successfully before a dozen trustworthy witnesses, would rather astonish men of science. Having, he says, by certain reasoning—altogether erroneous, but that is a detail—convinced himself that, on the accepted theory, a bullet fired vertically upwards ought to fall far to the west of the place whence it was fired, he carefully fixed an air-gun in a vertical position, and fired forty bullets vertically upwards. All these fell close to the gun—which is not surprising, though it must have made such an experiment rather dangerous; but two fell back into the barrel itself—which certainly was very surprising indeed. One might fairly challenge the most experienced gunner in the world to achieve one such vertical shot in a thousand trials; two in forty bordered on the miraculous.

The earth-flatteners I have been speaking of claim, as one of their objects, the defence of Scripture. But some of the earth-flatteners of the last generation (or a little farther back) took quite another view of the matter. For instance, Sir Richard Phillips, a more vehement earth-flattener than Parallax, was so little interested in defending the Scriptures, that in 1793 he was sentenced to a year's imprisonment for selling a book regarded as atheistic. In 1836 he attempted the conversion of Professor De Morgan, opening the correspondence with the remark that he had 'an inveterate abhorrence of all the pretended wisdom of philosophy derived from the monks and doctors of the Middle Ages, and not less those of higher name who merely sought to make the monkish philosophy more plausible, or so to disguise it as to mystify the mob of small thinkers.' He seems himself to have succeeded in mystifying many of those whom he intended to convert. Admiral Smyth gives the following account of an interview he had with Phillips: 'This pseudo-mathematical knight once called upon me at Bedford, without any previous acquaintance, to discuss "those errors of Newton, which he almost blushed to name," and which were inserted in the "Principia" to "puzzle the vulgar." He sneered with sovereign contempt at the "Trinity of Gravitating Force, Projectile Force, and Void Space," and proved that all change of place is accounted for by motion.' [Startling hypothesis!] 'He then exemplified the conditions by placing some pieces of paper on a table, and slapping his hand down close to them, thus making them fly off, which he termed applying the momentum. All motion, he said, is in the direction of the forces; and atoms seek the centre by "terrestrial centripetation"—a property which causes universal pressure; but in what these attributes of pushing and pulling differ from gravitation and attraction was not expounded. Many of his "truths" were as mystified as the conundrums of Rabelais; so nothing was made of the motion.'

A favourite subject of paradoxical ideas has been the moon's motion of rotation. Strangely enough, De Morgan, who knew more about past paradoxists than any man of his time, seems not to have heard of the dispute between Keill and Bentley over this matter in 1690. He says, 'there was a dispute on the subject, in 1748, between James Ferguson and an anonymous opponent; and I think there have been others;' but the older and more interesting dispute he does not mention. Bentley, who was no mathematician, pointed out in a lecture certain reasons for believing that the moon does not turn on her axis, or has no axis on which she turns. Keill, then only nineteen years old, pointed out that the arguments used by Bentley proved that the moon does rotate instead of showing that she does not. (Twenty years later Keill was appointed Savilian Professor of Astronomy at Oxford. He was the first holder of that office to teach the Newtonian astronomy.)

In recent times, as most of my readers know, the paradox that the moon does not rotate has been revived more than once. In 1855 it was sustained by Mr. Jellinger Symons, one of whose staunchest supporters, Mr. H. Perigal, had commenced the attack a few years earlier. Of course, the gist of the argument against the moon's rotation lies in the fact that the moon always keeps the same face turned towards the earth, or very nearly so. If she did so exactly, and if her distance from the earth were constantly the same, then her motion would be exactly the same as though she were rigidly connected with the earth, and turned round an axis at the earth. The case may be thus illustrated: Through the middle of a large orange thrust one short rod vertically, and another long rod horizontally; thrust the further end of the latter through a small apple, and now turn the whole affair round the short vertical rod as an axis. Then the apple will move with respect to the orange as the moon would move with respect to the earth on the suppositions just made. No one in this case would say that the apple was turning round on its axis, since its motion would be one of rotation round the upright axis through the orange. Therefore, say the opponents of the moon's rotation, no one should say that the moon turns round on her axis.

Of course, the answer would be obvious even if the moon's motions were as supposed. The moon is not connected with the earth as the apple is with the orange in the illustrative case. If the apple, without rigid connection with the orange, were carried round the orange so as to move precisely as if it were so connected, it would unquestionably have to rotate on its axis, as any one will find who may try the experiment. Thus for the straight rod thrust through the apple substitute a straight horizontal bar carrying a small basin of water in which the apple floats. Sway the bar steadily and slowly round, and it will be found (if a mark is placed on the apple) that the apple no longer keeps the same face towards the centre of motion; but that, to cause it to do so, a slow motion of rotation must be communicated to the apple in the same direction and at the same rate (neglecting the effects of the friction of the water against the sides of the basin) as the bar is rotating. In my 'Treatise on the Moon' I have described and pictured a simple apparatus by which this experiment may easily be made.

But, of course, such experiments are not essential to the argument by which the paradox is overthrown. This argument simply is, that the moon as she travels on her orbit round the sun—the real centre of her motion—turns every part of her equator in succession towards him once in a lunar month. At the time of new moon the sun illuminates the face of the moon turned from us; at the time of full moon he illuminates the face which has been gradually brought round to him as the moon has passed through her first two quarters. As she passes onwards to new moon again, the face we see is gradually turned from him until he shines full upon the other face. And so on during successive lunations. This could not happen unless the moon rotated. Again, if we lived on the moon we should find the heaven of the fixed stars turning round from east to west once in rather more than twenty-seven days; and unless we supposed, as we should probably do for a long time, that our small world was the centre of the universe, and that the stars turned round it, we should be compelled to admit that it was turning on its own axis from west to east once in the time just named. There would be no escape. The mere fact that all the time the stars thus seemed to be turning round the moon, the earth would not so seem to move, but would lie always in the same direction, would in no sort help to remove the difficulty. Lunarian paradoxists would probably argue that she was in some way rigidly connected with the moon; but even they would never think of arguing that their world did not turn on its axis, *unless* they maintained that it was the centre of the universe. This, I think, they would very probably do; but as yet terrestrial paradoxists have not, I believe, maintained this hypothesis. I once asked Mr. Perigal whether that was the true theory of the universe—the moon central, the earth, sun, and heavens carried round her. He admitted that his objections to accepted views were by no means limited to the moon's rotation; and, if I remember rightly, he said that the idea I had thrown out in jest was nearer the truth than I thought, or used words to that effect. But as yet the theory has not been definitely enunciated that the moon is the boss of the universe.

Comets, as already mentioned, have been the subjects of paradoxes innumerable; but as yet comets have been so little understood, even by astronomers, that paradoxes respecting them cannot be so readily dealt with as those relating to well-established facts. Among thoroughly paradoxical ideas respecting comets, however, may be mentioned one whose author is a mathematician of well-deserved repute—Professor Tait's 'Sea-Bird Theory' of Comets' Tails. According to this theory, the rapid formation of long tails and the rapid changes of their position may be explained on the same principle that we explain the rapid change of appearance of a flight of sea-birds, when, from having been in a position where the eye looks athwart it, the flight assumes a position where the eye looks at it edgewise. In the former position it is scarcely visible (when at a distance), in the latter it is seen as a well-defined streak; and as a very slight change of position of each bird may often suffice to render an extensive flight thus visible throughout its entire length, which but a few moments before had been invisible, so the entire length of a comet's tail may be brought into view, and apparently be formed in a few hours, through some comparatively slight displacement of the individual meteorites composing it.

This paradox—for paradox it unquestionably is—affords a curious illustration of the influence which mathematical power has on the minds of men. Every one knows that Professor Tait has potential mathematical energy competent to dispose, in a very short time, of all the difficulties involved in his theory; therefore few seem to inquire whether this potential energy has ever been called into action. It is singular, too, that other mathematicians of great eminence have been content to take the theory on trust. Thus Sir W. Thomson, at the meeting of the British Association at Edinburgh, described the theory as disposing easily of the difficulties presented by Newton's comet in 1680. Glashier, in his translation of Guillemin's 'Les Comètes,' speaks of the theory as one not improbably correct, though only to be established by rigid investigation of the mathematical problems involved.

In reality, not five minutes' inquiry is needed to show any one acquainted with the history of long-tailed comets that Tait's theory is quite untenable. Take Newton's comet. It had a tail ninety millions of miles long, extending directly from the sun as the comet approached him, and seen, four days later, extending to the same distance, and still directly from the sun, as the comet receded from him in an entirely different direction. According to Tait's sea-bird theory, the earth was at both these epochs in the plane of a sheet of meteorites forming the tail; but on each occasion the sun also was in the same plane, for the edge of the sheet of meteorites was seen to be directly in a line with the sun. The comet's head, of course, was in the same plane; but three points, not in a straight line, determine a plane. Hence we have, as the definite result of the sea-bird theory, that the layer or stratum of meteorites, forming the tail of Newton's comet, lay in the same plane which contained the sun, the earth, and the comet. But the comet crossed the ecliptic (the plane in which the earth travels round the sun) between the epochs named, crossing it at a great angle. When crossing it, then, the great layer of meteorites was in the plane of the ecliptic; before crossing it the layer was greatly inclined to that plane one way, and after crossing it the layer was greatly inclined to that plane another way. So that we have in no way escaped the difficulty which the sea-bird theory was intended to remove. If it was a startling and, indeed, incredible thing that the particles along a comet's tail should have got round in four days from the first to the second position of the tail considered above, it is as startling and incredible that a mighty layer of meteorites should have shifted bodily in the way required by the sea-bird theory. Nay, there is an element in our result which is still more startling than any of the difficulties yet mentioned; and that is, the singular care which the great layer of meteorites would seem to have shown to keep its plane always passing through the earth, with which it was in no way connected. Why should this preference have been shown by the meteor flock for our earth above all the other members of the solar system?—seeing that the sea-bird theory *requires* that this comet, and not Newton's comet alone but all others having tails, should not only be thus complaisant with respect to our little earth, but should behave in a totally different way with respect to every other member of the sun's family.

We can understand that, while several have been found who have applauded the sea-bird paradox for what it *might* do in explaining comets' tails, its advocates have as yet not done much to reconcile it with cometic observation.

The latest astronomical paradox published is perhaps still more startling. It relates to the planet Venus, and is intended to explain the appearance presented by this planet when crossing the sun's face, or, technically, when in transit. At this time she is surrounded by a ring of light, which appears somewhat brighter than the disc of the sun itself. Before fully entering on the sun's face, also, the part of Venus's globe as yet outside the sun's disc is seen to be girt round by a ring of exceedingly bright light—so bright, indeed, that it has left its record in photographs where the exposure was only for the small fraction of a second allowable in the case of so intensely brilliant a body as the sun. Astronomers have not found it difficult to explain either peculiarity. It has been proved clearly in other ways that Venus has an atmosphere like our own, but probably denser. As the sun is raised into view above the horizon (after he has really passed below the horizon plane) by the bending power of our air upon his rays, so the bending power of Venus's air brings the sun into our view round the dark body of the planet. But the new paradox advances a much bolder theory. Instead of an atmosphere such as ours, Venus has a glass envelope; and instead of a surface of earth and water, in some cases covered with clouds, Venus has a surface shining with metallic lustre.[1]

The author of this theory, Mr. Jos. Brett, startled astronomers by announcing, a few years ago, that with an ordinary telescope he could see the light of the sun's corona without the aid of an eclipse, though astronomers had observed that the delicate light of the corona fades out of view with the first returning rays of the sun after total eclipse.

The latest paradoxist, misled by the incorrect term 'centrifugal force,' proposes to 'modify, if not banish,' the old-fashioned astronomy. What is called centrifugal force is in truth only inertia. In the familiar instance of a body whirled round by a string, the breaking of the string no more implies that an active force has pulled away the body, than the breaking of a rope by which a weight is pulled implies that the weight has exerted an active resistance. Of course, here again the text-books are chiefly in fault.

[1] Sterne anticipated this paradoxist in (jestingly) attributing glassiness to an inferior planet. He made the inhabitants, however, not the air, glassy. 'The intense heat of the country,' he says, speaking of the planet Mercury, 'must, I think, long ago have vitrified the bodies of the inhabitants to suit them for the climate; so that all the tenements of their souls may be nothing else, for aught the soundest philosophy can show to the contrary, but one fine transparent body of clear glass; so that till the inhabitant grows old and tolerably wrinkled, whereby the rays of light become monstrously refracted, or return reflected from the surface, etc., his soul might as well play the fool out o' doors as in her own house.'

Such are a few among the paradoxes of various orders by which astronomers, like the students of other sciences, have been from time to time amused. It is not altogether, as it may seem at first sight, 'a sin against the twenty-four hours' to consider such matters; for much may be learned not only from the study of the right road in science, but from observing where and how men may go astray. I know, indeed, few more useful exercises for the learner than to examine a few paradoxes, when leisure serves, and to consider how, if left to his own guidance, he would confute them.

XI.

ON SOME ASTRONOMICAL MYTHS.

THE expression 'astronomical myth' has recently been used, on the title-page of a translation from the French, as synonymous with false systems of astronomy. It is not, however, in that sense that I here use it. The history of astronomy presents the records of some rather perplexing observations, not confirmed by later researches, but yet not easily to be explained away or accounted for. Such observations Humboldt described as belonging to the myths of an uncritical period; and it is in that sense that I employ the term 'astronomical myth' in this essay. I propose briefly to describe and comment on some of the more interesting of these observations, which, in whatever sense they are to be interpreted, will be found to afford a useful lesson.

It is hardly necessary, perhaps, to point out that the cases which I include here I regard as really cases in which astronomers have been deceived by illusory observations. Other students of astronomy may differ from me as respects some of these instances. I do not wish to dogmatise, but simply to describe the facts as I see them, and the impressions which I draw from them. Those who view the facts differently will not, I think, have to complain that I have incorrectly described them.

At the outset, let me point out that some observations

which were for a long time regarded as mythical have proved to be exact. For instance, when as yet very few telescopes existed, and those very feeble, Galileo's discovery of moons travelling round Jupiter was rejected as an illusion for which Satan received the chief share of credit. There is an amusing and yet in one aspect almost pathetic reference to this in his account of his earlier observations of Saturn. He had seen the planet apparently attended on either side by two smaller planets, as if helping old Saturn along. But on December 4, 1612,[1] turning his telescope on the planet, he found to his infinite amazement not a trace of the companion planets could be seen; there in the field of view of his telescope was the golden-tinted disc of the planet as smoothly rounded as the disc of Mars or Jupiter. 'What,' he wrote, 'is to be said concerning so strange a metamorphosis? Are the two lesser stars consumed after the manner of the solar spots? Have they vanished or suddenly fled? Has Saturn, perhaps, devoured his children? Or were the appearances, indeed, illusion or fraud with which the glasses have so long deceived me as well as many others to whom I have shown them? Now, perhaps, is the time come to revive the well-nigh withered hopes of those who, guided by more profound contemplations, have discovered the fallacy of the new observations, and demonstrated the utter impossibility of the existence of those things which the telescope appears to show. I do not know what to say in a case so surprising, so unlooked for, and so novel. The shortness of the time, the unexpected nature of the event,

[1] It will be seen from Table X. of my treatise on Saturn that the ring disappeared on December 12, remaining invisible (because turning its dark side earthwards) till the spring of 1613. But on December 4, the ring must have been quite invisible in a telescope so feeble as Galileo's. The ring then would have been little more than a fine line of light as seen with one of our powerful modern telescopes.

the weakness of my understanding, and the fear of being mistaken, have greatly confounded me.' We now know that these observations, as well as those made soon after by Hevelius, though wrongly interpreted, were correct enough. Nay, we know that if either Galileo or Hevelius had been at the pains to reason out the meaning of the alternate visibility and disappearance of objects looking like attendant planets, they must have anticipated the discovery made in 1656 by Huyghens, that Saturn's globe is girdled about by a thin flat ring so vast that, if a score of globes like our earth were set side by side, the range of that row of worlds would be less than the span of the Saturnian ring system.

There is a reference in Galileo's letter to the solar spots; 'Are the two lesser stars,' he says, 'consumed after the manner of the solar spots?' When he thus wrote the spots were among the myths or fables of astronomy, and an explanation was offered, by those who did not reject them utterly, which has taken its place among forsaken doctrines, those broken toys of astronomers. It is said that when Scheiner, himself a Jesuit, communicated to the Provincial of the Jesuits his discovery of the spots on the sun, the latter, a staunch Aristotelian, cautioned him not to see these things. 'I have read Aristotle's writings from beginning to end many times,' he said, 'and I can assure you I have nowhere found in them anything similar to what you mention' [amazing circumstances!] 'Go, therefore, my son, tranquillise yourself; be assured that what you take for spots on the sun are the faults of your glasses or your eyes.' As the idea was obviously inadmissible that a celestial body could be marked by spots, the theory was started that the dark objects apparently seen on the sun's body were in reality small planets revolving round the sun, and a contest arose for the possession of these mythical planets. Tardé maintained that they should be called *Astra Borbonia*, in honour of the royal family of France; but C. Malapert in sisted that they should be called *Sidera Austriaca.* Meantime the outside world laughed at the spots, and their names, and the astronomers who were thought to have invented both. 'Fabritius puts only three spots,' wrote Burton in his 'Anatomy of Melancholy,' 'and those in the sun; Apelles 15, and those without the sun, floating like the Cyanean Isles in the Euxine Sea. Tardé the Frenchman hath observed 33, and those neither spots nor clouds as Galileus supposed, but planets concentric with the sun, and not far from him, with regular motions. Christopher Schemer' [a significant way of spelling Scheiner's name], 'a German Suisser Jesuit, divides them *in maculas et faculas*, and will have them to be fixed *in solis superficie* and to absolve their periodical and regular motions in 27 or 28 dayes; holding withall the rotation of the sun upon his centre, and are all so confident that they have made schemes and tables of their motions. The Hollander censures all; and thus they disagree among themselves, old and new, irreconcilable in their opinions; thus Aristarchus, thus Hipparchus, thus Ptolomæus, thus Albategnius, etc., with their followers, vary and determine of these celestial orbs and bodies; and so whilst these men contend about the sun and moon, like the philosophers in Lucian, it is to be feared the sun and moon will hide themselves, and be as much offended as she was with those, and send another message to Jupiter, by some new-fangled Icaromenippus, to make an end of all these curious controversies, and scatter them abroad.'

It is well to notice how in this, as in many other instances, the very circumstance which makes scientific research trustworthy caused the unscientific to entertain doubt. If men of science were to arrange beforehand with each other what observations they should publish, how their accounts should be ended, what theories they would endeavour to establish, their results would seem far more trustworthy, their theories far more probable, than according to the method actually adopted. Science, which should be exact, seems altogether inexact, because one observer seems to obtain one result, another a different result. Scientific theories seem unworthy of reliance because scientific men entertain for a long time rival doctrines. But in another and a worthier sense than as the words are used in the 'Critic,' when men of science do agree their agreement is wonderful. It *is* wonderful, worthy of all admiration, because before it has been attained errors long entertained have had to be honestly admitted; because the taunt of inconsistency is not more pleasant to the student of science than to others, and the man who having a long time held one doctrine adopts and enforces another (one perhaps which he had long resisted), is sure to be accused by the many of inconsistency, the truly scientific nature of his procedure being only recognised by the few. The agreement of men of science ought to be regarded also as most significant in another sense. So long as there is room for refusing to admit an important theory advanced by a student of science, it is natural that other students of science should refuse to do so; for in admitting the new theory they are awarding the palm to a rival. In strict principle, of course, this consideration ought to have no influence whatever; as a matter of fact, however, men of science, being always men and not necessarily strengthened by scientific labours against the faults of humanity, the consideration has and must always have influence. Therefore, when the fellow-writers and rivals of Newton or of his followers gave in their adhesion to the Newtonian theory; when in our own time —but let us leave our own time alone, in this respect— when, speaking generally, a novel doctrine, or some new generalisation, or some great and startling discovery, is admitted by rival students of the branch of astronomy to which it belongs, the probability is great that the weight of evidence has been found altogether overwhelming.

Let us now, however, turn to cases in which, while many observations seem to point to some result, it has appeared that, after all, those observations must have been illusory.

A striking instance in point is found in the perplexing history of the supposed satellite of Venus.

On January 25, 1672, the celebrated astronomer, J. D. Cassini saw a crescent shaped and posited like Venus, but smaller, on the western side of the planet. More than fourteen years later, he saw a crescent east of the planet. The object continued visible in the latter case for half an hour, when the approach of daylight obliterated the planet and this phantom moon from view. The apparent distance of the moon from Venus was in both cases small, viz., only one diameter of the planet in the former case, and only three-fifths of that diameter in the latter.

Next, on October 23, 1740, old style, the optician Short, who had had considerable experience in observation, saw a small star perfectly defined but less luminous than Venus, at a distance from the planet equal to about one-third of the apparent diameter of our moon. This is a long distance, and would correspond to a distance from Venus certainly not less than the moon's distance from the earth. Short was aware of the risk of optical illusion in such matters, and therefore observed Venus with a second telescope; he also used four eye-pieces of different magnifying power. He says that Venus was very distinct, the air very pure, insomuch that he was able to use a power of 240. The seeming moon had a diameter less than a third of Venus's, and showed the same phase as the planet. Its disc was exceedingly well defined. He observed it several times during a period of about one hour.

Still more convincing, to all appearance, is the account of the observations made by M. Montaigne, as presented to the Academy of Sciences at Paris by M. Baudouin in 1761. The transit of Venus which was to take place on June 6 in that year led to some inquiry as to the satellite supposed to have been seen by Cassini and Short, for of course a transit would be a favourable occasion for observing the satellite. M. Montaigne, who had no faith in the existence of such an attendant, was persuaded to look for it early in 1761. On May 3 he saw a little crescent moon about twenty minutes of arc (nearly two-thirds the apparent diameter of our moon) from the planet. He repeated his observation several times that night, always seeing the small body, but not quite certain, despite its crescent shape, whether it might not be a small star. On the next evening, and again on May 7 and 10, he saw the small companion apparently somewhat farther from Venus and in a different position. He found that it could be seen when Venus was not in the field of view. The following remarks were made respecting these observations in a French work, 'Dictionnaire de Physique,' published in 1789:—'The year 1761 will be celebrated in astronomy in consequence of the discovery that was made on May 3 of a satellite circulating round Venus. We owe it to M. Montaigne, member of the Society of Limoges. M. Baudouin read before the Academy of Sciences at Paris a very interesting memoir, in which he gave a determination of the revolution and distance of the satellite. From the calculations of this expert astronomer we learn that the new star has a diameter about one-fourth that of Venus, is distant from Venus almost as far as the moon from our earth, has a period of nine days seven hours' [much too short, by the way, to be true, expert though M. Baudouin is said to have been], 'and its ascending node'—but we need not trouble ourselves about its ascending node.

Three years later Rödkier, at Copenhagen, March 3 and 4, 1764, saw the satellite of Venus with a refracting telescope 38 feet long, which should have been effective if longitude has any virtue. He could not see the satellite with another telescope which he tried. But several of his friends saw it with the long telescope. Amongst others, Horrebow, Professor of Astronomy, saw the satellite on March 10 and 11, after taking several precautions to prevent optical illusion. A few days later Montbaron, at Auxerre, who had heard nothing of these observations, saw a satellite, and again on March 28 and 29 it appeared, always in a different position.

It should be added that Scheuten asserted that during the transit of 1761 Venus was accompanied by a small satellite in her motion across the sun's face.

So confidently did many believe in this satellite of Venus that Frederick the Great, who for some reason imagined that he was entitled to dispose as he pleased of the newly discovered body, proposed to assign it away to the mathematician D'Alembert, who excused himself from accepting the questionable honour in the following terms:—

'Your Majesty does me too much honour in wishing to baptize this new planet with my name. I am neither great enough to become the satellite of Venus in the heavens, nor well enough (*assez bien portant*) to be so on the earth, and I am too well content with the small place I occupy in this lower world to be ambitious of a place in the firmament.'

It is not at all easy to explain how this phantom satellite came to be seen. Father Hell, of Vienna—the same astronomer whom Sir G. Airy suspects of falling asleep during the progress of the transit of Venus in 1769—made some experiments showing how a false image of the planet might be seen beside the true one, the false image being smaller and fainter, like the moons seen by Schort (as Hell called Short), Cassini, and the rest. And more recently Sir David Brewster stated that Wargentin 'had in his possession a good achromatic telescope, which always showed Venus with such a satellite.' But Hell admitted that the falsehood of the unreal Venus was easily detected, and Brewster adds to his account of Wargentin's phantom moon, that 'the deception was discovered by turning the telescope about its axis.' As Admiral Smyth well remarks, to endeavour to explain away in this manner the observations made by Cassini and Short 'must be a mere pleasantry, for it is impossible such accurate observers could have been deceived by so gross a neglect.'. Smyth, by the way, was a believer in the moon of Venus. 'The contested satellite is perhaps extremely minute,' he says, 'while some parts of its body may be less capable of reflecting light than others; and when the splendour of its primary and our inconvenient station for watching it are considered, it must be conceded that, however slight the hope may be, search ought not to be relinquished.'

Setting aside Scheuten's asserted recognition of a dark body near Venus during the transit of 1761, Venus has always appeared without any attendant when in transit. As no one else claimed to have seen what Scheuten saw in 1761, though the transit was observed by hundreds, of whom many used far finer telescopes than he, we must consider that he allowed his imagination to deceive him. During the transit of 1769, and again on December 8-9, 1874, Venus certainly had no companion during her transit.

What, then, was it that Cassini, Short, Montaigne, and the rest supposed they saw? The idea has been thrown out by Mr. Webb that mirage caused the illusion. But he appears to have overlooked the fact that though an image of Venus formed by mirage would be fainter than the planet, it would not be smaller. It might, according to the circumstances, be above Venus or below, or even somewhat towards either side, and it might be either a direct or an inverted image, but it could not possibly be a diminished image.

Single observations like Cassini's or Short's might be explained as subjective phenomena, but this explanation will not avail in the case of the Copenhagen observations.

I reject, as every student of astronomy will reject, the idea of wilful deception. Occasionally an observer may pretend to see what he has not seen, though I believe this very seldom happens. But even if Cassini and the rest had been notoriously untrustworthy persons instead of being some of them distinguished for the care and accuracy with which their observations were made and recorded, these occasional views of a phantom satellite are by no means such observations as they would have invented. No distinction was to be gained by observations which could not be confirmed by astronomers possessing more powerful telescopes. Cassini, for example, knew well that nothing but his well-earned reputation could have saved him from suspicion or ridicule when he announced that he had seen Venus attended by a satellite.

It seems to me probable that the false satellite was an optical illusion brought about in a different way from those referred to by Hell and Brewster, though among the various circumstances which in an imperfect instrument might cause such a result I do not undertake to make a selection. It is certain that Venus's satellite has vanished with the improvement of telescopes, while it is equally certain that even with the best modern instruments illusions occasionally appear which deceive even the scientific elect. Three years have passed since I heard the eminent observer Otto Struve, of Pulkowa, give an elaborate account of a companion to the star Procyon, describing the apparent brightness, distance, and motions of this companion body, for the edification of the Astronomer-Royal and many other observers. I had visited but a few months before the Observatory at Washington, where, with a much more powerful telescope, that companion to Procyon had been systematically but fruitlessly sought for, and I entertained a very strong opinion, notwithstanding the circumstantial nature of Struve's account and his confidence (shared in unquestioningly by the observers present), that he had been in some way deceived. But I could not then see, nor has any one yet explained, how this could be. The fact, however, that he had been deceived is now undoubted. Subsequent research has shown that the Pulkowa telescope, though a very fine instrument, possesses the undesirable quality of making a companion orb for all first-class stars in the position where O. Struve and his assistant Lindenau saw the supposed companion of Procyon.

I may as well point out, however, that theories so wild have recently been broached respecting Venus, that far more interesting explanations of the enigma than this optical one may be looked for presently. It has been gravely suggested by Mr. Jos. Brett, the artist, that Venus has a surface of metallic brilliancy, with a vitreous atmosphere,—which can only be understood to signify a glass case. This stupendous theory has had its origin in an observation of considerable interest which astronomers (it is perhaps hardly necessary to say) explain somewhat differently. When Venus has made her entry in part upon the sun's face at the beginning of transit, there is seen all round the portion of her disc which still remains outside the sun an arc of light so brilliant that it records its photographic trace during the instantaneous exposure required in solar photography. It is mathematically demonstrable that this arc of light is precisely what *should* be seen if

Venus has an atmosphere like our earth's. But mathematical demonstration is not sufficient (or perhaps we may say it is too much) for some minds. Therefore, to simplify matters, Venus has been provided with a mirror surface and a glass case. (See preceding essay, on Astronomical Paradoxes, for further details.)

The enigma next to be considered is of a more doubtful character than the myth relating to the satellite of Venus. Astronomers are pretty well agreed that Venus has no moon, but many, including some deservedly eminent, retain full belief in the story of the planet Vulcan.

More than seventeen years ago the astronomical world was startled by the announcement that a new planet had been discovered, under circumstances unlike any which had heretofore attended the discovery of fresh members of the solar system. At that time astronomers had already become accustomed to the discovery, year after year, of several asteroids, which are in reality planets, though small ones. In fact, no less than fifty-six of these bodies were then known, whereof fifty-one had been discovered during the years 1847-1858 inclusive, not one of these years having passed without the detection of an asteroid. But all these planets belonged to one family, and as there was every reason to believe that thousands more travel in the same region of the solar system, the detection of a few more among the number had no longer any special interest for astronomers. The discovery of the first known member of the family had indeed been full of interest, and had worthily inaugurated the present century, on the first day of which it was made. For it had been effected in pursuance of a set scheme, and astronomers had almost given up all hopes of success in that scheme when Piazzi announced his detection of little Ceres. Again the discovery of the next few members of the family had been interesting as revealing the existence of a new order of bodies in the solar system. No one had suspected the possibility that besides the large bodies which travel round the sun, either singly or attended by subordinate families of moons, there might be a ring of many planets. This was what the discovery of Ceres, Pallas, Juno, and Vesta seemed to suggest, unless —still stranger thought—these were but fragments of a mighty planet which had been shattered in long-past ages by some tremendous explosion. Since then, however, this startling theory has been (itself) exploded. Year after year new members of the ring of multitudinous planets are discovered, and that, not as was recently predicted, in numbers gradually decreasing, but so rapidly that more have been discovered during the last ten years than during the preceding twenty.

The discovery of the giant planet Uranus, an orb exceeding our earth twelve and a half times in mass and seventy-four times in volume, was a matter of much greater importance, so far as the dignity of the planetary system was concerned, for it is known that the whole ring of asteroids together does not equal one-tenth part of the earth in mass, while Uranus exceeds many times in volume the entire family of terrestrial planets—Mercury, Venus, the Earth, and Mars. The detection of Uranus, unlike that of Ceres, was effected by accident. Sir W. Herschel was looking for double stars of a particular kind in the constellation Gemini when by good fortune the stranger was observed.

The interest with which astronomers received the announcement of the discovery of Uranus, though great, was not to be compared with that with which they deservedly welcomed the discovery of Neptune. a larger and more massive planet, revolving at a distance one-half greater even than the mighty space which separates Uranus from the sun, a space so great that by comparison with it the range of 184,000,000 of miles, which forms the diameter of our earth's orbit, seems quite insignificant. It was not, however, the vastness of Neptune's mass or volume, or the awful remoteness of the path along which he pursues his gloomy course, which attracted the interest of astronomers, but the strangeness of the circumstances under which the planet had been detected. His influence had been felt for many years before astronomers thought of looking for him, and even when the idea had occurred to one or two, it was considered, and that, too, by an astronomer as deservedly eminent as Sir G. Airy, too chimerical to be reasonably entertained. All the world now knows how Leverrier, the greatest living master of physical astronomy, and Adams, then scarce known outside Cambridge, both conceived the idea of finding the planet, not by the simple method of looking for it with a telescope, but by the mathematical analysis of the planet's disturbing influence upon known members of the solar system. All know, too, that these mathematicians succeeded in their calculations, and that the planet was found in the very region and close to the very point indicated first by Adams, and later, but independently, and (fortunately for him more publicly) by Leverrier.

None of these instances of the discovery of members of the solar system resembled in method or details the discovery announced early in the year 1859. It was not amid the star-depths and in the darkness of night that the new planet was looked for, but in broad day, and on the face of the sun himself. It was not on the outskirts of the solar system that the planet was supposed to be travelling, but within the orbit of Mercury, hitherto regarded as of all planets the nearest to the sun. It was not hoped that any calculation of the perturbations of other planets would show the place of the stranger, though certain changes in the orbit of Mercury seemed clearly enough to indicate the stranger's existence.

Early in 1860 Leverrier had announced that the position of Mercury's path was not precisely in agreement with calculations based on the adopted estimates of the masses of those planets which chiefly disturb the motions of Mercury. The part of the path where Mercury is nearest to the sun, and where, therefore, he travels fastest, had slightly shifted from its calculated place. This part of the path was expected to move, but it had moved more than was expected; and of course Mercury having his region of swiftest motion somewhat differently placed than was anticipated, himself moved somewhat differently.

Leverrier found that to explain this feature of Mercury's motion either the mass of Venus must be regarded as one-tenth greater than had been supposed, or some unknown cause must be regarded as affecting the motion of Mercury. A planet as large as Mercury, about midway between Mercury and the sun, would account for the observed disturbance; but Leverrier rejected the belief that such a planet exists, simply because he could not 'believe that it would be invisible during total eclipses of the sun.' 'All difficulties disappear,' he added, 'if we admit, in place of a single planet, small bodies circulating between Mercury and the sun.' Considering their existence as not at all improbable, he advised astronomers to watch for them.

It was on January 2, 1860, that Leverrier thus wrote. On December 22, 1859, a letter had been addressed by a M. Lescarbault of Orgères to Leverrier, through M. Vallée, hon. inspector-general of roads and bridges, announcing that on March 26, 1859, about four in the afternoon, Lescarbault had seen a round black spot on the face of the sun, and had watched it as it passed across like a planet in transit—not with the slow motion of an ordinary sun-spot. The actual time during which the round spot was visible was one hour, seventeen minutes, nine seconds, the rate of motion being such that, had the spot crossed the middle of the sun's disc, at the same rate, the transit would have lasted more than four hours. The spot thus merely skirted the sun's disc, being at no time more than about one forty-sixth part of the sun's apparent diameter from the edge of the sun. Lescarbault expressed his conviction that on a future day, a black spot, perfectly round and very small, will be seen passing over the sun, and 'this point will very probably be the planet whose path I observed on March 26, 1859.' 'I am persuaded,' he added, 'that this body is the planet, or one of the planets, whose existence in the vicinity of the sun M. Leverrier had made known a few months ago' (referring to the preliminary announcement of results which Leverrier published afterwards more definitely).

Leverrier, when the news of Lescarbault's observation first reached him, was surprised that the observation should not have been announced earlier. He did not consider the delay sufficiently justified by Lescarbault's statement that he wished to see the spot again. He therefore set out for Orgères, accompanied by M. Vallée. 'The predominant feeling in Leverrier's mind,' says Abbé Moigno, 'was the wish to unmask an attempt to impose upon him, as the person more likely than any other astronomer to listen to the allegation that his prophecy had been fulfilled.'

'One should have seen M. Lescarbault,' says Moigno, 'so small, so simple, so modest, and so timid, in order to understand the emotion with which he was seized, when Leverrier, from his great height, and with that blunt intonation which he can command, thus addressed him: "It is then you, sir, who pretend to have observed the intra-mercurial planet, and who have committed the grave offence of keeping your observation secret for nine months. I warn you that I have come here with the intention of doing justice to your pretensions, and of demonstrating either that you have been dishonest or deceived. Tell me, then, unequivocally, what you have seen."' This singular address did not bring the interview, as one might have expected, to an abrupt end. The lamb, as the Abbé calls the doctor, trembling, stammered out an account of what he had seen. He explained how he had timed the passage of the black spot. 'Where is your chronometer?' asked Leverrier. 'It is this watch, the faithful companion of my professional journeys.' 'What! with that old watch, showing only minutes, dare you talk of estimating seconds. My suspicions are already too well confirmed.' 'Pardon me, I have a pendulum which beats seconds.' 'Show it me.' The doctor brings down a silk thread to which an ivory ball is attached. Fixing the upper end to a nail, he draws the ball a little from the vertical, counts the number of oscillations, and shows that his pendulum beats seconds; he explains also how his profession, requiring him to feel pulses and count pulsations, he has no difficulty in mentally keeping record of successive seconds.

Having been shown the telescope with which the observation was made, the record of the observation (on a piece of paper covered with grease and laudanum, and doing service as a marker in the 'Connaissance des Temps,' or French Nautical Almanac), Leverrier presently inquired if Lescarbault had attempted to deduce the planet's distance from the sun from the period of its transit. The doctor admitted that he had attempted this, but, being no mathematician, had failed to achieve success with the problem. He showed the rough draughts of his futile attempts at calculation on a board in his workshop, 'for,' said he naïvely, 'I am a joiner as well as an astronomer.'

The interview satisfied Leverrier that a new planet, travelling within the orbit of Mercury, had really been discovered. 'With a grace and dignity full of kindness,' says a contemporary narrative of these events,[1] 'he congratulated Lescarbault on the important discovery which he had made.' Anxious to obtain some mark of respect for the discoverer of Vulcan, Leverrier made inquiry concerning his private character, and learned from the village curé, the juge de paix, and other functionaries, that he was a skilful physician and a worthy man. With such high recommendations, M. Leverrier requested from M. Rouland, the Minister of Public Instruction, the decoration of the Legion of Honour for M. Lescarbault. The Minister, in a brief but interesting statement of his claim, communicated this request to the Emperor, who, by a decree dated January 25, conferred upon the village astronomer the honours so justly due to him. His professional brethren in Paris were equally solicitous to testify their regard; and MM. Felix Roubaud, Legrande, and Caffe, as delegates of the scientific press, proposed to the medical body, and to the scientific world in Paris, to invite Lescarbault to a banquet in the Hôtel du Louvre on January 18.

The announcement of the supposed discovery caused astronomers to re-examine records of former observations of black spots moving across the sun. Several such records existed, but they had gradually come to be regarded as of no real importance. Wolff of Zurich published a list of no fewer than twenty such observations made since 1762. Carrington added many other cases. Comparing together three of these observations, Wolff found that they would be satisfied by a planet having a period of revolution of 19 days, agreeing fairly with the period of rather more than 19½ days inferred by Leverrier for Lescarbault's planet.

[1] *North British Review* for August 1860.

But the entire set of observations of black spots require that there should be at least three new planets travelling between Mercury and the sun. Many observers also set themselves the task of searching for Vulcan, as the supposed new planet was called. They have continued fruitlessly to observe the sun for this purpose until the present time.

While the excitement over Lescarbault's discovery was at its height, another observer impugned not only the discovery but the honesty of the discoverer.

M. Liais, a French astronomer of considerable skill, formerly of the Paris Observatory, but at the time of Lescarbault's achievement in the service of the Brazilian Government, published a paper, 'Sur la Nouvelle Planète annoncée par M. Lescarbault,' in which he endeavoured to establish the four following points:—

First, the observation of Lescarbault was never made.

Secondly, Leverrier was mistaken in considering that a planet such as Vulcan might have escaped detection when off the sun's face.

Thirdly, that Vulcan would certainly have been seen during total solar eclipses, if the planet had a real objective existence.

Fourthly, M. Leverrier's reasons for believing that the planet exists are based on the supposition that astronomical observations are more precise than they really are.

Probably, Liais's objections would have had more weight with Leverrier had the fourth point been omitted. It was rash in a former subordinate to impugn the verdict of the chief of the Paris Observatory on a matter belonging to that special department of astronomy which an observatory chief might be expected to understand thoroughly. It is thought daring in the extreme for one outside the circles of official astronomy (as Newton in Flamstead's time, Sir W. Herschel in Maskelyne's, and Sir J. Herschel in the present century), to advance or maintain an opinion adverse to that of some official chief, but for a subordinate (even though no longer so), to be guilty of such rash procedure 'is most tolerable and not to be endured,' as a typical official has said. Accordingly, very little attention was paid by Leverrier to Liais's objections.

Yet, in some respects, what M. Liais had to say was very much to the point.

At the very time when Lescarbault was watching the black spot on the sun's face, Liais was examining the sun with a telescope of much greater magnifying power, and saw no such spot. His attention was specially directed to the edge of the sun (where Lescarbault saw the spot) because he was engaged in determining the decrease of the sun's brightness near the edge. Moreover, he was examining the very part of the sun's edge where Lescarbault saw the planet enter, at a time when it must have been twelve minutes in time upon the face of the sun, and well within the margin of the solar disc. The negative evidence here is strong; though it must always be remembered that negative evidence requires to be overwhelmingly strong before it can be admitted as effective against positive evidence. It seems at a first view utterly impossible that Liais, examining with a more powerful telescope the region where Lescarbault saw the spot, could have failed to see it had it been there; but experience shows that it is not impossible for an observer engaged in examining phenomena of one class to overlook a phenomenon of another class, even when glaringly obvious. All we can say is that Liais was not likely to have overlooked Lescarbault's planet had it been there; and we must combine this probability against Vulcan's existence with arguments derived from other con siderations. There is also the possibility of an error in time. As the writer in the 'North British Review' remarks, 'twelve minutes is so short a time that it is just possible that the planet may not have entered upon the sun during the time that Liais observed it.'

The second and third arguments are stronger. In fact, I do not see how they can be resisted.

It is, in the first place, clear from Lescarbault's account that Vulcan must have a considerable diameter—certainly if Vulcan's diameter in miles were only half the diameter of Mercury, it would have been all but impossible for Lescarbault with his small telescope to see Vulcan at all, whereas he saw the black spot very distinctly. Say Vulcan has half the diameter of Mercury, and let us compare the brightness of these two planets when at their greatest apparent distances from the sun, that is, when each looks like a half-moon. The distance of Mercury exceeds the estimated distance of Vulcan from the sun as 27 exceeds 10, so that Vulcan is more strongly illuminated in the proportion of 27 times 27 to 10 times 10, or 729 to 100—say at least 7 to 1. But having a diameter but half as large the disc of Vulcan could be but about a fourth of Mercury's at the same distance from us (and they would be at about the same distance from us when seen as half-moons). Hence Vulcan would be brighter than Mercury in the proportion of 7 to 4. Of course being so near the sun he would not be so easily seen; and we could never expect to see him at all, perhaps, with the naked eye—though even this is not certain. But Mercury, when at the same apparent distance from the sun, and giving less light than at his greatest seeming distance, is quite easily seen in the telescope. Much more easily, then, should Vulcan be seen, if a telescope were rightly directed at such a time, or when Vulcan was anywhere near his greatest seeming distance from the sun. Now it is true astronomers do not know precisely when or where to look for him. But he passes from his greatest distance on one side of the sun to his greatest distance on the other in less than ten days, according to the computed period, and certainly (that is, if the planet exists) in a very short time. The astronomer has then only to examine day after day a region of small extent on either side of the sun, for ten or twelve days in succession (an hour's observation each day would suffice), to be sure of seeing Vulcan. Yet many astronomers have made such search many times over, without seeing any trace of the planet. During total solar eclipses, again, the planet has been repeatedly looked for unsuccessfully—though it should at such a time be a very conspicuous object, when favourably placed, and could scarcely fail of being very distinctly seen wherever placed.

The fourth argument of Lescarbault's is not so effective, and in fact he gets beyond his depth in dealing with it. But it is to be noticed that a considerable portion of the discrepancy between Mercury's observed and calculated motions has long since been accounted for by the changed estimate of the earth's mass as compared with the sun's, resulting from the new determination of the sun's distance. However, the arguments depending on this consideration would not be suited to these pages.

There was one feature in Liais's paper which was a little unfortunate. He questioned Lescarbault's honesty. He said 'Lescarbault contradicts himself in having first asserted that he saw the planet enter upon the sun's disc, and having afterwards admitted to Leverrier that it had been on the disc some seconds before he saw it, and that he had merely inferred the time of its entry from the rate of its motion afterwards. If this one assertion be fabricated, the whole may be so.' 'He considers these arguments to be strengthened,' says the 'North British Review,' 'by the assertion which, as we have seen, perplexed Leverrier himself, that if M. Lescarbault had actually seen a planet on the sun, he could not have kept it secret for nine months.'

This charge of dishonesty, unfortunate in itself, had the unfortunate effect of preventing Lescarbault or the Abbé Moigno from replying. The latter simply remarked that the accusation was of such a nature as to dispense him from any obligation to refute it. This was an error of judgment, I cannot but think, if an effective reply was really available.

The Remarks with which the North British Reviewer closes his account may be repeated now, so far as they relate to the force of the negative evidence, with tenfold effect. 'Since the first notice of the discovery in the beginning of January 1860 the sun has been anxiously observed by astronomers; and the limited area around him in which the planet *must be*, if he is not upon the sun, has doubtless been explored with equal care by telescopes of high power, and processes by which the sun's direct light has been excluded from the tube of the telescope as well as the eye of the observer, and yet no planet has been found. This fact would entitle us to conclude that no such planet exists if its existence had been merely conjectured, or if it had been deduced from any of the laws of planetary distance, or even if Leverrier or Adams had announced it as the probable result of planetary perturbations. If the finest telescopes cannot rediscover a planet which with the small power used by Lescarbault has a visible disc, within so limited an area of which the sun is the centre, or rather within a narrow belt of that circle, we should unhesitatingly declare that no such planet exists. But the question assumes a very different aspect when it involves moral considerations. If,' proceeds the Reviewer, writing in August 1860, 'after the severe scrutiny which the sun and its vicinity will undergo before and after and during his total eclipse in July, no planet shall be seen; and if no round black spot distinctly separable from the usual solar spots shall be seen on the solar spots' (*sic*, presumably solar disc was intended), 'we will not dare to say that it does not exist. We cannot doubt the honesty of M. Lescarbault, and we can hardly believe that he was mistaken. No solar spot, no floating scoria, could maintain in its passage over the sun a circular and uniform shape, and we are confident that no other hypothesis but that of an intra-mercurial planet can explain the phenomena seen and measured by M. Lescarbault, a man of high character, possessing excellent instruments, and in every way competent to use them well, and to describe clearly and correctly the results of his observations. Time, however, tries facts as well as speculations. The phenomena observed by the French astronomer may never be again seen, and the disturbance of Mercury which rendered it probable may be otherwise explained. Should this be the case, we must refer the round spot on the sun to some of those illusions of the eye or of the brain which have sometimes disturbed the tranquillity of science.'

The evidence which has accumulated against Vulcan in the interval since this was written is not negative only, but partly positive, as the following instance, which I take from my own narrative at the time in a weekly journal, serves to show:—After more than sixteen years of fruitless watching, astronomers learned last August (1876) that in the month of April Vulcan had been seen on the sun's disc in China. On April 4, it appeared, Herr Weber, an observer of considerable skill, stationed at Pecheli, had seen a small round spot on the sun, looking very much as a small planet might be expected to look. A few hours later he turned his telescope upon the sun, and lo! the spot had vanished, precisely as though the planet had passed away after the manner of planets in transit. He forwarded the news of his observation to Europe. The astronomer Wolff, well known for his sun-spot studies, carefully calculated the interval which had passed since Lescarbault saw Vulcan on March 26, 1859, and to his intense satisfaction was enabled to announce that this interval contained the calculated period of the planet an exact number of times. Leverrier at Paris received the announcement still more joyfully; while the Abbé Moigno, who gave Vulcan its name, and has always staunchly believed in the planet's existence, congratulated Lescarbault warmly upon this new view of the shamefaced Vulcan. Not one of those who already believed in the planet had the least doubt as to the reality of Weber's observations, and of these only Lescarbault himself received the news without pleasure. He, it seems, has never forgiven the Germans for destroying his observatory and library during the invasion of France in 1870, and apparently would prefer that his planet should never be seen again rather than that a German astronomer should have seen it. But the joy of the rest and Lescarbault's sorrow were alike premature. It was found that the spot seen by Weber had not only been observed at the Madrid observatory, where careful watch is kept upon the sun, but had been photographed at Greenwich; and when the description of its appearance, as seen in a powerful telescope at one station, and its picture as photographed by a fine telescope at the other, came to be examined, it was proved unmistakably that the spot was an ordinary sun-spot (not even quite round), which had after a few hours disappeared, as even larger sun-spots have been known to do in even a shorter time.

It is clear that had not Weber's spot been fortunately seen at Madrid and photographed at Greenwich, his observation would have been added to the list of recorded apparitions of Vulcan in transit, for it fitted in perfectly with the theory of Vulcan's real existence. I think, indeed, for my own part, that the good fortune was Weber's. Had it so chanced that thick weather in Madrid and at Greenwich had destroyed the evidence actually obtained to show that what Weber described he really saw, although it was not what he thought, some of the more suspicious would have questioned whether, in the euphonious language of the North British Reviewer, 'the round spot on the sun' was not due 'to one of those illusions of the eye or of the brain which have sometimes disturbed the tranquillity of science.' Of course no one acquainted with M. Weber's antecedents would imagine for a moment that he had invented the observation, even though the objective reality of his spot had not been established. But if a person who is entirely unknown, states that he has seen Vulcan, there is antecedently some degree of probability in favour of the belief that the observation is as much a myth as the planet itself. Some observations of Vulcan have certainly been invented. I have received several letters purporting to describe observations of bodies in transit over the sun's face, either the rate of transit, the size of the body, or the path along which it was said to move, being utterly inconsistent with the theory that it was an intra-mercurial planet, while yet (herein is the suspicious circumstance of such narratives) the epoch of transit accorded in the most remarkable manner with the period assigned to Vulcan. A paradoxist in America (of Louisville, Kentucky) who had invented a theory of the weather, in which the planets, by their influence on the sun, were supposed to produce all weather-changes, the nearer planets being the most effective, found his theory wanted Vulcan very much. Accordingly, he saw Vulcan crossing the sun's face in September, which, being half a year from March, is a month wherein, according to Lescarbault's observation, Vulcan may be seen in transit, and by a strange coincidence the interval between our paradoxist's observation and Lescarbault's exactly contained a certain number of times the period calculated by Leverrier for Vulcan. This was a noble achievement on the part of our paradoxist. At one stroke it established his theory of the weather, and promised to ensure him text-book immortality as one of the observers of Vulcan. But, unfortunately, a student of science residing in St. Louis, after leaving the Louisville paradoxist full time to parade his discovery, heartlessly pointed out that an exact number of revolutions of Vulcan after Lescarbault's March observation, must of necessity have brought the planet on that side of the sun on which the earth lies in March, so that to see Vulcan so placed on the sun's face in September was to see Vulcan through the sun, a very remarkable achievement indeed. The paradoxist was abashed, the reader perhaps imagines. Not in the least. The planet's period must have been wrongly calculated by Leverrier—that was all: the real period was less than half as long as Leverrier had supposed; and instead of having gone a certain number of times round since Lescarbault had seen it, Vulcan had gone twice as many times round and half once round again. The circumstance that if Vulcan's period had been thus short, the time of crossing the sun's face would have been much less than, according to Lescarbault's account, it actually was, had not occurred to the Louisville weather-prophet.[1]

Leverrier's faith in Vulcan, however, has remained unshaken. He has used all the observations of spots which, like Weber's, have been seen only for a short time.

[1] He had, indeed, at an earlier stage, shown a marvellous ignorance of astronomy by the remark, which doubtless appeared to him a safe one, that when he saw a planet on the sun in September he supposed it was Mercury; a September transit of Mercury being as impossible as an eclipse of the sun during the moon's third quarter.

At least he has used all which have not, like Weber's, been proved to be only transient sun-spots. Selecting those which fit in well with Lescarbault's observation, he has pointed out how remarkable it is that they show this accord. The possibility that some of them might be explicable as Weber's proved to be, and that some even may have been explicable as completely, but less satisfactorily, in another way, seems to have been thought scarcely worth considering. Using the imperfect materials available, but with exquisite skill—as a Phidias might model an exquisite figure of materials that would presently crumble into dust —Leverrier came to the conclusion that Vulcan would cross the sun's disc on or about March 22, 1876. 'He, therefore,' said Sir G. Airy, addressing the Astronomical Society, 'circulated a despatch among his friends, asking them carefully to observe the sun on March 22.' Sir G. Airy, humouring his honoured friend, sent telegrams to India, Australia, and New Zealand, requesting that observations might be made every two hours or oftener. Leverrier himself wrote to Santiago de Chili and other places, so that, including American and European observations, the sun could be watched all through the twenty-four hours on March 21, 22, and 23. 'Without saying positively that he believed or disbelieved in the existence of the planet,' proceeds the report, 'Sir G. Airy thought, since M. Leverrier was so confident, that the opportunity ought not to be neglected by anybody who professed to take an interest in the progress of planetary astronomy.'

It is perhaps unnecessary to add that observations were made as requested. Many photographs of the sun also were taken during the hours when Vulcan, if he exists at all, might be expected to cross the sun's face. But the 'planet of romance,' as Abbé Moigno has called Vulcan, failed to appear, and the opinion I had expressed last

October ('English Mechanic and World of Science,' for October 27, 1876, p. 160), that Vulcan might perhaps better be called the 'planet of fiction' was *pro tanto* confirmed. Nevertheless, I would not be understood to mean by the word 'fiction' aught savouring of fraud so far as Lescarbault is concerned—I prefer the North Briton's view of Lescarbault's spot, that so to speak, it was

> . . . . the blot upon his brain,
> That *would* show itself without.

I have left small space to treat of other fancied discoveries among the orbs of heaven. Yet there are some which are not only interesting but instructive, as showing how even the most careful observers may be led astray. In this respect the mistakes into which observers of great and well deserved eminence have fallen are specially worthy of attention. With the description of three such mistakes, made by no less an astronomer than Sir W. Herschel, I shall bring this paper to a close.

When Sir W. Herschel examined the planet Uranus with his most powerful telescope he saw the planet to all appearance girt about by two rings at right angles to one another. The illusion was so complete that Herschel for several years remained in the belief that the rings were real. They were, however, mere optical illusions, due to the imperfect defining qualities of the telescope with which he observed the planet. Later he wrote that 'the observations which tend to ascertain' (indicate?) 'the existence of rings not being satisfactorily supported, it will be proper that surmises of them should either be given up, as ill-founded, or at least reserved till superior instruments can be provided.'

Sir W. Herschel was more completely misled by the false Uranian satellites. He had seen, as he supposed, no less than six of these bodies. As only two of these had been seen again, while two more were discovered by Lassell, the inference was that Uranus has eight satellites in all. These for a long time flourished in our text-books of astronomy; and many writers, confident in the care and skill of Sir W. Herschel, were unable for a long time to believe that he had been deceived. Thus Admiral Smyth, in his 'Celestial Cycle,' wrote of those who doubted the extra satellites:—'They must have but a meagre notion of Sir W. Herschel's powerful means, his skill in their application, and his method of deliberate procedure. So far from doubting there being six satellites' (this was before Lassell had discovered the other two) 'it is highly probable that there are still more.' Whewell, also, in his 'Bridgewater Treatise,' says, 'that though it no longer appears probable that Uranus has a ring like Saturn, he has at least five satellites which are visible to us, and we believe that the astronomer will hardly deny that he' (Uranus, not the astronomer), 'may possibly have thousands of smaller ones circulating about him.' But in this case Sir W. Herschel, anxiously though he endeavoured to guard against the possibility of error, was certainly mistaken. Uranus may, for anything that is known to the contrary, have many small satellites circulating about him, but he certainly has not four satellites (besides those known) which could have been seen by Sir W. Herschel with the telescope he employed. For the neighbourhood of the planet has been carefully examined with telescopes of much greater power by observers who with those telescopes have seen objects far fainter than the satellites supposed to have been seen by the elder Herschel.

The third of the Herschelian myths was the lunar volcano in eruption, which he supposed he had seen in progress in that part of the moon which was not at the time illuminated by the sun's rays. He saw a bright star-like point of light, which corresponded in position with the crater of the lunar mountain Aristarchus. He inferred that a volcano was in active eruption because the brightness of the point of light varied from time to time, and also because he did not remember to have seen it before under the same conditions. There is no doubt something very remarkable in the way in which this part of the moon's surface shines when not illumined by the sun. If it were always bright we should conclude at once that the earth-light shining upon it rendered it visible. For it must be remembered that the part of the moon which looks dark (or seems wanting to the full disc) is illuminated by our earth, shining in the sky of the moon as a disc thirteen times as large as that of the moon we see, and with the same proportion of its disc sunlit as is dark in the moon's disc. Thus when the moon is nearly new our earth is shining in the lunar skies as a nearly full moon thirteen times as large as ours. The light of this noble moon must illumine the moon's surface much more brightly than a terrestrial landscape is illumined by the full moon, and if any parts of her surface are very white they will shine out from the surface around, just as the snow-covered peak of a mountain shines out upon a moonlit night from among the darker hills and dales and rocks and forests of the landscape. But Herschel considered that the occasional brightness of the crater Aristarchus could not be thus explained. The spot had been seen before the time of Herschel's observations by Cassini and others. It has been seen since by Captain Kater, Francis Baily, and many others. Dr. Maskelyne tells us that in March 1794 it was seen by the naked eye by two persons.

Baily thus describes the appearance presented by this lunar crater on December 22, 1835: 'Directed telescope to the moon, and pointing it to the dark part in the vicinity of Aristarchus, soon saw the outline of that mountain very distinctly, formed like an irregular nebula. Nearly in the centre was a light resembling that of a star of the ninth or tenth magnitude. It appeared by glimpses, but at times was brilliant, and visible for several seconds together.'

There can be little doubt, however, that the apparent brightness of this lunar crater, or rather of its summit, is due to some peculiar quality in the surface, which may perhaps be covered by some crystalline or vitreous matter poured out in the far distant time when the crater was an active one. Prof. Shaler, who examined the crater when it was illuminated only by earthshine, with the fine 15-inch telescope of the Harvard Observatory (Cambridge U.S.), says that he has been able to recognise nearly all the craters over 15 miles in diameter in the dark part. 'There are several degrees of brightness,' he says, 'observable in the different objects which shine out by the earth-light. This fact probably explains the greater part of the perplexing statements concerning the illumination of certain craters. It certainly accounts for the volcanic activity which has so often been supposed to be manifested by Aristarchus. Under the illumination by the earth-light this is by far the brightest object on the dark part of the moon's face, and is visible much longer and with poorer glasses than any other object there.'

Here my record of astronomical myths must be brought to a close. It will be noticed that in every instance either the illusion has affected the actual observations of eminent and skilful astronomers, or has caused such astronomers to put faith for a while in illusory observations. Had I cared to include the mistakes which have been made by or have misled observers of less experience, I could have filled many sheets for each page of the present article. But it has seemed to me more instructive to show how error may affect the observations even of the most careful and deservedly eminent astronomers, how even the most cautious may be for a time misled by the mistakes of inferior observers, especially when the fact supposed to have been observed accords with preconceived opinions.

XII.

THE ORIGIN OF THE CONSTELLATION FIGURES.

ALTHOUGH the strange figures which astronomers still allow to straggle over their star maps no longer have any real scientific interest, they still possess a certain charm, not only for the student of astronomy, but for many who care little or nothing about astronomy as a science. When I was giving a course of twelve lectures in Boston, America, a person of considerable culture said to me, 'I wish you would lecture about the constellations; I care little about the sun and moon and the planets, and not much more about comets; but I have always felt great interest in the Bears and Lions, the Chained and Chaired Ladies, King Cepheus and the Rescuer Perseus, Orion, Ophiuchus, Hercules, and the rest of the mythical and fanciful beings with which the old astronomers peopled the heavens. I say with Carlyle, "Why does not some one teach me the constellations, and make me at home in the starry heavens, which are always overhead, and which I don't half know to this day."' We may notice, too, that the poets by almost unanimous consent have recognised the poetical aspect of the constellations, while they have found little to say about subjects which belong especially to astronomy as a science. Milton has indeed made an Archangel reason (not unskilfully for Milton's day) about the Ptolemaic and Copernican systems, while Tennyson makes frequent reference to astronomical theories. 'There sinks the nebulous star we call the Sun, if that hypothesis of theirs be sound,' said Ida; but she said no more, save 'let us down and rest,' as though the subject were wearisome to her. Again, in the Palace of Art the soul of the poet having built herself that 'great house so royal, rich, and wide,' thither—

> . . . when all the deep unsounded skies
>   Shuddered with silent stars, she clomb,
> And as with optic glasses her keen eyes
>   Pierced through the mystic dome,
> Regions of lucid matter taking forms,
>   Brushes of fire, hazy gleams,
> Clusters and beds of worlds and beelike swarms
>   Of suns, and starry streams :
> She saw the snowy poles of moonless Mars,
>   That marvellous round of milky light
> Below Orion, and those double stars
>   Whereof the one more bright
>   Is circled by the other.

But the poet's soul so wearied of these astronomical researches that the beautiful lines I have quoted disappeared (more's the pity) from the second and all later editions. Such exceptions, indeed, prove the rule. Poets have been chary in referring to astronomical researches and results, full though these have been of unspeakable poetry; while from the days of Homer to those of Tennyson, the constellations which 'garland the heavens' have always been favourite subjects of poetic imagery.

It is not my present purpose, however, to discuss the poetic aspect of the constellations. I propose to inquire how these singular figures first found their way to the heavens, and, so far as facts are available for the purpose, to determine the history and antiquity of some of the more celebrated constellations.

Long before astronomy had any existence as a science men watched the stars with wonder and reverence. Those orbs, seemingly countless—which bespangle the dark robe of night—have a charm and beauty of their own apart from the significance with which the science of astronomy has invested them. The least fanciful mind is led to recognise on the celestial concave the emblems of terrestrial objects, pictured with more or less distinctness among the mysterious star-groupings. We can imagine that long before the importance of the study of the stars was recognised, men had begun to associate with certain star-groups the names of familiar objects animate or inanimate. The flocks and herds which the earliest observers of the heavens tended would suggest names for certain sets of stars, and thus the Bull, the Ram, the Kids, would appear in the heavens. Other groups would remind those early observers of the animals from whom they had to guard their flocks, or of the animals to whose vigilance they trusted for protection, and thus the Bear, the Lion, and the Dogs would find their place among the stars. The figures of men and horses, and of birds and fishes, would naturally enough be recognised, nor would either the implements of husbandry, or the weapons by which the huntsman secured his prey, remain unrepresented among the star-groupings. And lastly, the altar on which the first-fruits of harvest and vintage were presented, or the flesh of lambs and goats consumed, would be figured among the innumerable combinations which a fanciful eye can recognise among the orbs of heaven.

In thus suggesting that the first observers of the heavens were shepherds, huntsmen, and husbandmen, I am not advancing a theory on the difficult questions connected with the origin of exact astronomy. The first observations of the heavens were of necessity made by men who depended for their subsistence on a familiarity with the progress and vicissitudes of the seasons, and doubtless preceded by many ages the study of astronomy as a science. And yet the observations made by those early shepherds and hunters, unscientific though they must have been in themselves, are full of interest to the student of modern exact astronomy. The assertion may seem strange at first sight, but is nevertheless strictly true, that if we could but learn with certainty the names assigned to certain star-groups, before astronomy had any real existence, we could deduce lessons of extreme importance from the rough observations which suggested those old names. In these days, when observations of such marvellous exactness are daily and nightly made, when instruments capable of revealing the actual constitution of the stars are employed, and observers are so numerous, it may seem strange to attach any interest to the question whether half-savage races recognised in such and such a star-group the likeness of a bear, or in another group the semblance of a ship. But though we could learn more, of course, from exacter observations, yet even such rough and imperfect records would have their value. If we could be certain that in long-past ages a star-group really resembled some known object, we should have in the present resemblance of that group to the same object evidence of the general constancy of stellar lustre, or if no resemblance could be recognised we should have reason to doubt whether other suns (and therefore our own sun) may not be liable to great changes.

The subject of the constellation-figures as first known is interesting in other ways. For instance, it is full of interest to the antiquarian (and most of us are to some degree antiquarians) as relating to the most ancient of all human sciences. The same mental quality which causes us to look with interest on the buildings raised in long-past ages, or on the implements and weapons of antiquity, renders the thought impressive that the stars which we see were gazed on perhaps not less wonderingly in the very infancy of the human race. It is, again, a subject full of interest to the chronologist to inquire in what era of the world's history exact astronomy began, the moon was assigned her twenty-eight zodiacal mansions, the sun his twelve zodiacal signs. It is well known, indeed, that Newton himself did not disdain to study the questions thus suggested; and the speculations of the ingenious Dupuis found favour with the great mathematician Laplace.

Unfortunately, the evidence is not sufficiently exact to be very trustworthy. In considering, for instance, the chronological inquiries of Newton, one cannot but feel that the reliance placed by him on the statements made by different writers is not justified by the nature of those statements, which were for the most part vague in the extreme. We owe many of them to poets who, knowing little of astronomy, mixed up the phenomena of their own time with those which they found recorded in the writings of astronomers. Some of the statements left by ancient writers are indeed ludicrously incongruous; insomuch that Grotius not unjustly said of the account of the constellations given by the poet Aratus, that it could be assigned to no fixed epoch and to no fixed place. However, this would not be the place to discuss details such as are involved in exact inquiries. I have indicated some of these in an appendix to my treatise on 'Saturn,' and others in the preface to my 'Gnomonic Star Atlas'; but for the most part they do not admit very readily of familiar description. Let us turn to less technical considerations, which fortunately are in this case fully as much to the point as exact inquiries, seeing that there is no real foundation for such inquiries in any of the available evidence.

The first obvious feature of the old constellations is one which somehow has not received the attention it deserves. It is as instructive as any of those which have been made the subject of profound research.

There is a great space in the heavens over which none of the old constellations extend, except the River Eridanus as now pictured, but we do not know where this winding stream of stars was supposed by the old observers to come to an end. This great space surrounds the southern pole of the heavens, and thus shows that the first observers of the stars were not acquainted with the constellations which can be seen only from places far south of Chaldæa, Persia, Egypt, India, China, and indeed of all the regions to which the invention of astronomy has been assigned. Whatever the first astronomers were, however profound their knowledge of astronomy may have been (as some imagine), they had certainly not travelled far enough towards the south to know the constellations around the southern pole. If they had been as well acquainted with geography as some assert, if even any astronomer had travelled as far south as the equator, we should certainly have had pictured in the old star charts some constellations in that region of the heavens wherein modern astronomers have placed the Octant, the Bird of Paradise, the Sword-fish, the Flying-fish, Toucan, the Net, and other uncelestial objects.

In passing I may note that this fact disposes most completely of a theory lately advanced that the constellations were invented in the southern hemisphere, and that thus is to be explained the ancient tradition that the sun and stars have changed their courses. For though all the northern constellations would have been more or less visible from parts of the southern hemisphere near the equator, it is absurd to suppose that a southern observer would leave untenanted a full fourth of the heavens round the southern or visible pole, while carefully filling up the space around the northern or unseen pole with incomplete constellations whose northern unknown portions would include that pole. Supposing it for a moment to be true, as a modern advocate of the southern theory remarks, that 'one of the race migrating from one side to the other of the equator would take his position from the sun, and fancy he was facing the same way when he looked at it at noon, and so would think the motion of the stars to have altered instead of his having turned round,' the theory that astronomy was brought to us from south of the equator cannot possibly be admitted in presence of that enormous vacant region around the southern pole. I think, however, that, apart from this, a race so profoundly ignorant as to suppose any such thing, to imagine they were looking north when in reality they were looking south, can hardly be regarded as the first founders of the science of astronomy.

The great gap I have spoken of has long been recognised. But one remarkable feature in its position has not, to the best of my remembrance, been considered—the vacant space is eccentric with regard to the southern pole of the heavens. The old constellations, the Altar, the Centaur, and the ship Argo, extend within twenty degrees of the pole, while the Southern Fish and the great sea-monster Cetus, which are the southernmost constellations on the other side, do not reach within some sixty degrees of the pole.

Of course, in saying that this peculiarity has not been considered, I am not suggesting that it has not been noticed, or that its cause is in any way doubtful or unknown. We know that the earth, besides whirling once a day on its axis, and rushing on its mighty orbit around the sun (spanning some 184,000,000 of miles) reels like a gigantic top, with a motion so slow that 25,868 years are required for a single circuit of the swaying axis around an imaginary line upright to the plane in which the earth travels. And we know that in consequence of this reeling motion the points of the heavens opposite the earth's poles necessarily change. So that the southern pole, now eccentrically placed amid the region where there were no constellations in old times, was once differently situated. But the circumstance which seems to have been overlooked is this, that by calculating backwards to the time when the southern pole was in the centre of that vacant region, we have a much better chance of finding the date (let us rather say the century) when the older constellations were formed, than by any other process. We may be sure not to be led very far astray; for we are not guided by one constellation but by several, whereas all the other indications which have been followed depend on the supposed ancient position of single constellations. And then most of the other indications are such as might very well have belonged to periods following long after the invention of the constellations themselves. An astronomer might have ascertained, for instance, that the sun in spring was in some particular part of the Ram or of the Fishes, and later a poet like Aratus might describe that relation (erroneously for his own epoch) as characteristic of one or other constellation; but who is to assure us that the astronomer who noted the relation correctly may not have made his observation many hundreds of years after those constellations were invented? Whereas, there was one period, and only one period, when the most southernmost of the old constellations could have marked the limits of the region of sky visible from some northern region. Thus, too, may we form some idea of the latitude in which the first observers lived.

For in high latitudes the southernmost of the old constellations would not have been visible at all, and in latitudes much lower than a certain latitude, presently to be noted, these constellations would have ridden high above the southern horizon, other star-groups showing below them which were not included among the old constellations.

I have before me as I write a picture of the southern heavens, drawn by myself, in which this vacant space—eccentric in position but circular in shape—is shown. The centre lies close by the Lesser Magellanic cloud—between the stars Kappa Toucani and Eta Hydri of our modern maps, but much neàrer to the last named. Near this spot, then, we may be sure, lay the southern pole of the star-sphere when the old constellations, or at least the southern ones, were invented. (If there had been astronomers in the southern hemisphere Eta Hydri would certainly have been their pole-star.)

Now it is a matter of no difficulty whatever to determine the epoch when the southern pole of the heavens was thus placed.[1] Between 2100 and 2200 years before the Christian era the southern constellations had the position described, the invisible southern pole lying at the centre of tne vacant space of the star-sphere—or rather of the space free from constellations. It is noteworthy that for other reasons this period, or rather a definite epoch within it, is indicated as that to which must be referred the beginning of exact astronomy. Amongst others must be mentioned this—that in the year 2170 B.C. *quam proximè*, the Pleiades rose to their highest above the horizon at noon (or techni-

[1] It is, by the way, somewhat amusing to find Baron Humboldt referring a question of this sort to the great mathematician Gauss, and describing the problem as though it involved the most profound calculations. Ten minutes should suffice to deal with any problem of the kind.

cally made their noon culmination), at the spring equinox. We can readily understand that to minds possessed with full faith in the influence of the stars on the earth, this fact would have great significance. The changes which are brought about at that season of the year, in reality, of course, because of the gradual increase in the effect of the sun's rays as he rises higher and higher above the celestial equator, would be attributed, in part at least, to the remarkable star-cluster coming then close by the sun on the heavens, though unseen. Thus we can readily understand the reference in Job to the 'sweet influences of the Pleiades.' Again at that same time, 2170 B.C. when the sun and the Pleiades opened the year (with commencing spring) together, the star Alpha of the Dragon, which was the pole-star of the period, had that precise position with respect to the true pole of the heavens which is indicated by the slope of the long passage extending downwards aslant from the northern face of the Great Pyramid; that is to say, when due north below the pole (or at what is technically called its sub-polar meridional passage) the pole-star of the period shone directly down that long passage, and I doubt not could be seen not only when it came to that position during the night, but also when it came there during the day-time.

But some other singular relations are to be noted in connection with the particular epoch I have indicated.

It is tolerably clear that in imagining figures of certain objects in the heavens, the early observers would not be apt to picture these objects in unusual positions. A group of stars may form a figure so closely resembling that of a familiar object that even a wrong position would not prevent the resemblance from being noticed, as for instance the 'Chair,' the 'Plough,' and so forth. But such cases are not numerous; indeed, to say the truth, one must 'make believe a good deal' to see resemblance between the star-groups and *most* of the constellation-figures, even under the most favourable conditions. When there is no very close resemblance, as is the case with all the large constellations, position must have counted for something in determining the association between a star-group and a known object.

Now the constellations north of the equator assume so many and such various positions that this special consideration does not apply very forcibly to them. But those south of the equator are only seen above the southern horizon, and change little in position during their progress from east to west of the south point. The lower down they are the less they change in position. And the very lowest—such as those were, for instance, which I have been considering in determining the position of the southern pole—are only fully visible when due south. They must, then, in all probability, have stood upright or in their natural position when so placed, for if they were not rightly placed then they only were so when below the horizon and consequently invisible.

Let us, then, inquire what was the position of the southernmost constellations when fully seen above the southern horizon at midnight.

The Centaur stood then as he does now, upright; only—whereas now in Egypt, Chaldæa, India, Persia, and China, only the upper portions of his figure rise above the horizon, he then stood, the noblest save Orion of all the constellations, with his feet (marked by the bright Alpha and Beta still belonging to the constellation, and by the stars of the Southern Cross which have been taken from it) upon the horizon itself. In latitude twenty degrees or so north he may still be seen thus placed when due south.

The Centaur was represented in old times as placing an offering upon the altar, which was pictured, says Manilius, as bearing a fire of incense represented by stars. This to a student of our modern charts seems altogether perplexing. The Centaur carries the wolf on the end of his spear; but instead of placing the wolf (not a very acceptable meat offering, one would suppose) upon the altar, he is directing this animal towards the base of the altar, whose top is downwards, the flames represented there tending (naturally) downwards also. It is quite certain the ancient observers did not imagine anything of this sort. As I have said, Aratus tells us the celestial Centaur was placing an offering *upon* the altar, which was therefore upright, and Manilius describes the altar as

Ferens thuris, stellis imitantibus, ignem,

so that the fire was where it should be, on the top of an upright altar, where also on the sky itself were stars looking like the smoke from incense fires. Now that was precisely the appearance presented by the stars forming the constellation at the time I have indicated, some 2170 years B.C. Setting the altar upright above the southern horizon (that is, inverting the absurd picture at present given of it) we see it just where it should be placed to receive the Centaur's offering. A most remarkable portion of the Milky Way is then seen to be directly above the altar in such a way as to form a very good imitation of smoke ascending from it. This part of the Milky Way is described by Sir J. Herschel, who studied it carefully during his stay at the Cape of Good Hope, as forming a complicated system of interlaced streaks and masses which covers the tail of Scorpio' (extending from the altar which lies immediately south of the Scorpion's Tail). The Milky Way divides, in fact, just above the altar as the constellation was seen 4000 years ago above the southern horizon, one branch being that just described, the other (like another stream of smoke) 'passing,' says Herschel, 'over the stars Iota of the Altar, Theta and Iota of the Scorpion, etc., to Gamma of the Archer, where it suddenly collects into a vivid oval mass, so very rich in stars, that a very moderate calculation makes their number exceed 100,000.' Nothing could accord better with the descriptions of Aratus and Manilius.

But there is another constellation which shows in a more marked way than either the Centaur or the Altar that the date when the constellations were invented must have been near that which I have named. Both Ara and Centaurus look now in suitable latitudes (about twenty degrees north) as they looked in higher latitudes (about forty degrees north) 4000 years ago. For, the reeling motion of our earth has changed the place of the celestial pole in such a way as only to depress these constellations southwards without much changing their *position;* they are nearly upright when due south now as they were 4000 years ago, only lower down. But the great ship Argo has suffered a much more serious displacement. One cannot now see this ship *like* a ship at any time or from any place on the earth's surface. If we travel south till the whole constellation comes into visibility above the southern horizon at the proper season (January and February for the midnight hours) the keel of the ship is aslant, the stern being high above the waist (the fore part is wanting). If we travel still further south, we can indeed reach places where the course of the ship is so widened, and the changes of position so increased, that she appears along part of her journey on an even keel, but then she is high above the horizon. Now 4000 years ago she stood on the horizon itself at her southern culmination, with level keel and upright mast.

In passing I may note that for my own part I imagine

that this great ship represented the Ark, its fore part being originally the portion of the Centaur now forming the horse, so that the Centaur was represented as a man (not as a man-horse) offering a gift on the Altar. Thus in this group of constellations I recognise the Ark, and Noah going up from the Ark towards the altar 'which he builded unto the Lord; and took of every clean beast, and of every clean fowl, and offered burnt offerings on the altar.' I consider further that the constellation-figures of the Ship, the Man with an offering, and the Altar, painted or sculptured in some ancient astrological temple, came at a later time to be understood as picturing a certain series of events, interpreted and expanded by a poetical writer into a complete narrative. Without venturing to insist on so heterodox a notion, I may remark as an odd coincidence that probably such a picture or sculpture would have shown the smoke ascending from the Altar which I have already described, and in this smoke there would be shown the bow of Sagittarius; which, interpreted and expanded in the way I have mentioned, might have accounted for the 'bow set in the clouds, for a token of a covenant.' It is noteworthy that all the remaining constellations forming the southern limit of the old star-domes or charts, were watery ones—the Southern Fish, over which Aquarius is pouring a quite unnecessary stream of water, the Great Sea Monster towards which in turn flow the streams of the River Eridanus. (The equator, too, was then occupied along a great part of its length by the great sea serpent Hydra, which reared its head above the equator, very probably indicated then by a water horizon, for nearly all the signs below it were then watery.) At any rate, as the length of Hydra then lay horizontally above the Ship, whose masts reached it, we may well believe that this part of the picture of the heavens showed a sea-horizon and a ship, the great sea serpent lying along the horizon. On the back of Hydra is the Raven, which again may be supposed by those who accept the theory mentioned above to have suggested the raven which went forth to and fro from the ark. He is close enough to the rigging of Argo to make an easy journey of it. The dove, however, must not be confounded with the modern constellation Columba, though this is placed (suitably enough) near the Ark. We must suppose the idea of the dove was suggested by a bird pictured in the rigging of the celestial ship. The sequence in which the constellations came above the horizon as the year went round corresponded very satisfactorily with the theory, fanciful though this seem to some. First Aquarius pouring streams of water, the three fishes (Pisces and Piscis australis), and the great sea monster Cetus, showing how the waters prevailed over the highest hills, then the Ark sailing on the waters, a little later the Raven (Corvus), the man descending from the ark and offering a gift on the Altar, and last the Bow set amid the clouds.

The theory just described may not meet with much favour. But wilder theories of the story of the deluge have been adopted and advocated with considerable confidence. One of the wildest, I fear, is the Astronomer-Royal's, that the deluge was simply a great rising of the Nile ; and Sir G. Airy is so confident respecting this that he says, 'I cannot entertain the smallest doubt that the flood of Noah was a flood of the Nile ;' precisely as he might say, 'I cannot entertain the smallest doubt that the earth moves round the sun.' On one point we can entertain very little doubt indeed. If it ever rained before the flood, which seems probable, and if the sun ever shone on falling rain, which again seems likely, nothing short of a miracle could have prevented the rainbow from making its appearance before the flood. The wildest theory that can be invented to explain the story of the deluge cannot be wilder than the supposition that the rays of sunlight shining on falling raindrops could have ever failed to show the prismatic colours. The theory I have suggested above, without going so far as strongly to advocate it, far less insist upon it, is free at any rate from objection on this particular score, which cannot be said of the ordinary theory. I am not yet able, however, to say that 'I cannot entertain the smallest doubt' about my theory.

We may feel tolerably sure that the period when the old southern constellations were formed must have been between 2400 and 2000 years before the present era, a period, by the way, including the date usually assigned to the deluge,—which, however, must really occupy our attention no further. In fact, let us leave the watery constellations lying below the equator of those remote times and seek at once the highest heavens above them.

Here, at the northern pole of these days, we find the great Dragon, which in any astrological temple of the time must have formed the highest or crowning constellation, surrounding the very key-stone of the dome. He has fallen away from that proud position since. In fact, even 4000 years ago he only held to the pole, so to speak, by his tail, and we have to travel back 2000 years or so to find the pole situate in a portion of the length of the Dragon which can be regarded as central. One might almost, if fancifully disposed, recognise the gradual displacement of the Dragon from his old place of honour, in certain traditions of the downfall of the great Dragon whose 'tail drew the third part of the stars of heaven.'

The central position of the Dragon, for even when the pole-star had drawn near to the Dragon's tail the constellation was still central, will remind the classical reader of Homer's description of the Shield of Hercules—

The scaly horror of a dragon, coil'd
Full in the central field, unspeakable,
With eyes oblique retorted, that ascant
Shot gleaming fire. (*Elton's translation.*)

I say Homer's description, for I cannot understand how any one who compares together the description of the Shield of Achilles in the Iliad and that of the Shield of Hercules in the fragmentary form in which we have it, can doubt for a moment that both descriptions came from the same hand. (The theory that Hesiod composed the latter poem can scarcely be entertained by any scholar.) As I long since pointed out in my essay 'A New Theory of Achilles' Shield' ('Light Science,' first series), no poet so inferior as actually to borrow Homer's words in part of the description of the Shield of Hercules could have written the other parts not found in the Shield of Achilles. 'I cannot for my own part entertain the slightest doubt'—that is to say, I think it altogether probable—that Homer composed the lines supposed to describe the Shield of Hercules long before he introduced the description, pruned and strengthened, into that particular part of the Iliad where it served his purpose best. And I have as little doubt that the original description, of which we only get fragments in either poem, related to something far more important than a shield. The constellations are not suitable adornments for the shield of fighting man, even though he was under the special care of a celestial mother and had armour made for him by a celestial smith. Yet we learn that Achilles' shield displayed—

The starry lights that heav'n's high convex crown'd
The Pleiads, Hyads, and the northern beam,
And great Orion's more refulgent beam,—
To which, around the cycle of the sky,
The bear revolving, points his golden eye,—
Still shines exalted.

And so forth. The Shield of Hercules displayed at its centre the polar constellation the Dragon. We read also that—

> There was the knight of fair-hair'd Danae born.
> Perseus.

Orion is not specially mentioned, but Orion, Lepus, and the Dogs seem referred to :—

> Men of chase
> Were taking the fleet hares ; two keen-toothed dogs
> Bounded beside.

Homer would find no difficulty in pluralising the mighty Hunter and the hare into huntsmen and hares when utilising a description originally referring to the constellation.

I conceive that the original description related to one of those zodiac temples whose remains are still found in Egypt, though the Egyptian temples of this kind were probably only copies of more ancient Chaldæan temples. We know from Assyrian sculptures that representations of the constellations (and especially the zodiacal constellations) were common among the Babylonians; and, as I point out in the essay above referred to, 'it seems probable that in a country where Sabæanism or star-worship was the prevailing form of religion, yet more imposing proportions would be given to zodiac temples than in Egypt.' My theory, then, respecting the two famous 'Shields' is that Homer in his eastern travels visited imposing temples devoted to astronomical observation and star-worship, and that nearly every line in both descriptions is borrowed from a poem in which he described a temple of this sort, its domed zodiac, and those illustrations of the labours of different seasons and of military or judicial procedures which the astrological proclivities of star-worshippers led them to associate with the different constellations. For the arguments on which this theory is based I have not here space. They are dealt with in the essay from which I have quoted.

One point only I need touch upon here, besides those I have mentioned already. It may be objected that the description of a zodiac temple has nothing to connect it with the subject of the Iliad. This is certainly true; but no one who is familiar with Homer's manner can doubt that he would work in, if he saw the opportunity, a poem on some subject outside that of the Iliad, so modifying the language that the description would correspond with the subject in hand. There are many passages, though none of such length, in both the Iliad and the Odyssey, which seem thus to have been brought into the poem; and other passages not exactly of this kind yet show that Homer was not insensible to the advantage of occasionally using memory instead of invention.

Any one who considers attentively the aspect of the constellation Draco in the heavens, will perceive that the drawing of the head in the maps is not correct; the head is no longer pictured as it must have been conceived by those who first formed the constellation. The two bright stars Beta and Gamma are now placed on a head in profile. Formerly they marked the two eyes. I would not lay stress on the description of the Dragon in the Shield of Hercules, 'with eyes oblique retorted, that ascant shot gleaming fire;' for all readers may not be prepared to accept my opinion that that description related to the constellation Draco. But the description of the constellation itself by Aratus suffices to show that the two bright stars I have named marked the eyes of the imagined monster—in fact, Aratus's account singularly resembles that given in the Shield of Hercules. 'Swol'n is his neck,' says Aratus of the Dragon—

> . . . Eyes charg'd with sparkling fire
> His crested head illume. As if in ire.

> To Helice he turns his foaming jaw,
> And darts his tongue, barb'd with a blazing star.

And the dragon's head with sparkling eyes can be recognised to this day, so soon as this change is made in its configuration, whereas no one can recognise the remotest resemblance to a dragon's head in profile. The star barbing the Dragon's tongue would be Xi of the Dragon according to Aratus's account, for so only would the eyes be turned towards Helice the Bear. But when Aratus wrote, the practice of separating the constellations from each other had been adopted; in fact, he derived his knowledge of them chiefly from Eudoxus, the astronomer and mathematician, who certainly would not have allowed the constellations to be intermixed. In the beginning, there are reasons for believing it was different, and if a group of stars resembled any known object it would be called after that object, even though some of the stars necessary to make up the figure belonged already to some other figure. This being remembered, we can have no difficulty in retorting the Dragon's head more naturally—not to the star Xi of the Dragon, but to the star Iota of Hercules. The four

*

stars are situated thus, * * the larger ones representing

*

the eyes; and so far as the head is concerned it is a matter of indifference whether the lower or the upper small star be taken to represent the tongue. But, as any one will see who looks at these stars when the Dragon is best placed for ordinary (non-telescopic) observation, the attitude of the animal is far more natural when the star Iota of Hercules marks the tongue, for then the creature is situated like a winged serpent hovering above the horizon and looking downwards, whereas when the star Xi marks the tongue, the hovering Dragon is looking upwards and is in an unnaturally constrained position. (I would not, indeed, claim to understand perfectly all the ways of dragons; still it may be assumed that a dragon hovering above the horizon would rather look downwards in a natural position than upwards in an awkward one.)

The star Iota of Hercules marks the heel of this giant, called the Kneeler (Engonasin) from time immemorial. He must have been an important figure on the old zodiac temples, and not improbably his presence there as one of the largest and highest of the human figures may have caused a zodiac-dome to be named after Hercules. The Dome of Hercules would come near enough to the title, 'The Shield of Hercules,' borne by the fragmentary poem dealt with above. The foot of the kneeling man was represented on the head of the dragon, the dragon having hold of the heel. And here, again, some imagine that a sculptured representation of these imagined figures in the heavens may have been interpreted and expanded into the narrative of a contest between the man and the old serpent the dragon, Ophiuchus the serpent-bearer being supposed to typify the eventual defeat of the dragon. This fancy might be followed out like that relating to the deluge; but the present place would be unsuitable for further inquiries in that particular direction

Some interest attaches to the constellation Ophiuchus, to my mind, in the evidence it affords respecting the way in which the constellations were at first intermixed. I have mentioned one instance in which, as I think, the later astronomers separated two constellations which had once been conjoined. Many others can be recognised when we compare the actual star-groups with the constellation-figures as at present depicted. No one can recognise the poop of a ship in the group of stars now assigned to the stern of Argo, but if we include the stars of the Greater Dog, and others close by, a well-shaped poop can be clearly seen. The head of the Lion of our maps is as the head of a dog, so far as stars are concerned; but if stars from the Crab on one side and from Virgo on the other be included in the figure, and especially Berenice's hair to form the tuft of the lion's tail, a very fine lion with waving mane can be discerned, with a slight effort of the imagination. So with Bootes the herdsman. He was of old 'a fine figure of a man,' waving aloft his arms, and, as his name implies, shouting lustily at the retreating bear. Now, and from some time certainly preceding that of Eudoxus, one arm has been lopped off to fashion the northern crown, and the herdsman holds his club as close to his side as a soldier holds his shouldered musket. The constellation of the Great Bear, once I conceive the only bear (though the lesser bear is a very old constellation), has suffered wofully. Originally it must have been a much larger bear, the stars now forming the tail marking part of the outline of the back; but first some folks who were unacquainted with the nature of bears turned the three stars (the horses of the plough) into a long tail, abstracting from the animal all the corresponding portion of his body, and then modern astronomers finding a great vacant space where formerly the bear's large frame extended, incontinently formed the stars of this space into a new constellation, the Hunting Dogs. No one can recognise a bear in the constellation as at present shaped, but any one who looks attentively at the part of the skies occupied by the constellation will recognise (always 'making believe a good deal') a monstrous bear, with the proper small head of creatures of the bear family, and with exceedingly well-developed plantigrade feet. Of course this figure cannot at all times be recognised with equal facility; but before midnight during the last four or five months in the year, the bear occupies positions favouring his recognition, being either upright on his feet, or as if descending a slope, or squatting on his great haunches. As a long-tailed animal the creature is more like one of those wooden toy-monkeys which used to be made for children, and may be now, in which the sliding motion of a ringed rod carried the monkey over the top of a stick. The little bear has I think been borrowed from the dragon, which was certainly a winged monster originally.

Now the astronomers who separated from each other, and in so doing spoiled the old constellation-figures, seem to have despaired of freeing Ophiuchus from his entanglements. The Serpent is twined around his body, the Scorpion is clawing at one leg. The constellation makers have *per fas et nefas* separated Scorpio from the Serpent Holder, spoiling both figures. But the Serpent has been too much for them, insomuch that they have been reduced to the abject necessity of leaving one part of the Serpent on one side of the region they allow to Ophiuchus, and the other part of the Serpent to the other.

A group of constellations whose origin and meaning are little understood remains to be mentioned. Close by the Dragon is King Cepheus, beside him his wife Cassiopeia (the Seated Lady), near whom is Andromeda the Chained Lady. The Sea Monster Cetus is not far away, though not near enough to threaten her safety, the Ram and Triangle being between the monster's head and her feet, the Fishes intervening between the body of the monster and her fair form. Close at hand is Perseus, the Rescuer, with a sword (looking very much like a reaping-hook in all the old pictures) in his right hand, and bearing in his left the head of Medusa. The general way of accounting for the figures thus associated has been by supposing that, having a certain tradition about Cepheus and his family, men imagined in the heavens the pictorial representation of the events of the tradition. I have long believed that the actual order in this and other cases was the reverse of this, that men imagined certain figures in the heavens, pictured these figures in their astronomical temples or observatories, and made stories to fit the pictures afterwards, probably many generations afterwards. Be this as it may, we can at present give no satisfactory explanation of the group of constellations.

Wilford gives an account, in his 'Asiatic Researches,' of a conversation with a pundit or astronomer respecting the names of the Indian constellations. 'Asking him,' he says, 'to show me in the heavens the constellation Antarmada, he immediately pointed to Andromeda, though I had not given him any information about it beforehand. He afterwards brought me a very rare and curious work in Sanscrit, which contained a chapter devoted to *Upanachatras*, or extra-zodiacal constellations, with drawings of *Capuja* (Cepheus) and of *Casyapi* (Cassiopeia) seated and holding a lotus-flower in her hand, of Antarmada charmed with the Fish beside her, and last of *Paraseia* (Perseus), who, according to the explanation of the book, held the head of a monster which he had slain in combat; blood was dropping from it, and for hair it had snakes.' Some have inferred from the circumstance that the Indian charts thus showed the Cassiopeian set of constellations, that the origin of these figures is to be sought in India. But probably both the Indian and the Greek constellation-figures were derived from a much older source.

The zodiacal twelve are in some respects the most important and interesting of all the ancient constellations. If we could determine the origin of these figures, their exact configuration as at first devised, and the precise influences assigned to them in the old astrological systems, we should have obtained important evidence as to the origin of astronomy itself. Not indeed that the twelve signs of the zodiac were formed at the beginning or even in the early infancy of astronomy. It seems abundantly clear that the division of the zodiac (which includes the moon's track as well as the sun's) had reference originally to the moon's motions. She circuits the star-sphere in about twenty-seven days and a third, while the lunation or interval from new moon to new moon is, as we all know, about twenty-nine days and a half in length. It would appear that the earliest astronomers, who were of course astrologers also, of all nations—the Indian, Egyptian, Chinese, Persian, and Chaldæan astronomers—adopted twenty-eight days (probably as a rough mean between the two periods just named) for their chief lunar period, and divided the moon's track round the ecliptic into twenty-eight portions or mansions. How they managed about the fractions of days outstanding—whether the common lunation was considered or the moon's motion round the star-sphere—is not known. The very circumstance, however, that they were for a long time content with their twenty-eight lunar mansions shows that they did not seek great precision at first. Doubtless they employed some rough system of 'leap-months' by which, as occasion required, the progress of the month was reconciled with the progress of the moon, just as by our leap-years the progress of the year is reconciled with the progress of the sun or seasons.

The use of the twenty-eight-day period naturally suggested the division of time into weeks of seven days each. The ordinary lunar month is divided in a very obvious manner into four equal parts by the lunar aspects. Every one can recognise roughly the time of full moon and the times of half moon before and after full, while the time of new moon is recognised from these two last epochs. Thus the four quarters of the month, or roughly the four weeks of the month, would be the first time-measure thought of;—after the day, which is the necessary foundation of all time measures. The nearest approach which can be made to a quarter-month in days is the week of seven days; and although some little awkwardness arose from the fact that four weeks differ appreciably from a lunar month, this would not long prevent the adoption of the week as a measure of time. In fact, just as our years begin on different days of the week without causing any inconvenience, so the ancient months might be made to begin with different week-days. All that would be necessary to make the week measure fairly well the quarters of the month, would be to start each month on the proper or nearest week-day. To inform people about this, some ceremony could be appointed for the day of the new moon, and some signal employed to indicate the time when this ceremony was to take place. This—the natural and obvious course—we find was the means actually adopted, the festival of the new moon and the blowing of trumpets in the new moon being an essential part of the arrangements adopted by nations who used the week as a chief measure of time. The seven days were not affected by the new moons so far as the nomenclature of these days, or special duties connected with any one of them, might be concerned.

Originally the idea may have been to have festivals and sacrifices at the time of new moon, first quarter, full moon, and third quarter; but this arrangement would naturally (and did, as we know, actually) give way before long to a new moon festival regulating the month and seventh-day festivals, each class of festival having its appropriate sacrifices and duties. This, I say, was the natural course. Its adoption *may* have been aided by the recognition of the fact that the seven planets of the old system of astronomy might conveniently be taken to rule the days and the hours in the way described in the essay on astrology. That that nomenclature and that system of association between the planets and the hours, days, and weeks of time-measurement was eventually adopted, is certain; but whether the convenience and apparent mystical fitness of this arrangement led to the use of weekly festivals in conjunction with monthly ones, or whether those weekly festivals were first adopted in the way described above, or whether (which seems altogether more likely) both sets of considerations led to the arrangement, we cannot certainly tell. The arrangement was in every way a natural one; and one may say, considering all the circumstances, that it was almost an inevitable one.

There was, however, another possible arrangement, viz., the division of time into ten-day periods, three to each month, with corresponding new moon festivals. But as the arrival of the moon at the *thirds* of her progress are not at all so well marked as her arrival at the quarters, and as there is no connection between the number ten and the planets, this arrangement was far less likely to be adopted than the other. Accordingly we find that only one or two nations adopted it. Six sets of five days would be practically the same arrangement; five sets of six for each month would scarcely be thought of, as with that division the use of simple direct observations of the moon for time measurement, which was the real aim of all such divisions, would not be convenient or indeed even possible for the generality of persons. Few could tell easily when the moon is two-fifths or four-fifths full, whereas every one can tell when she is half-full or quite full (the requisite for weekly measurement); and it would be possible to guess pretty nearly when she is one-third or two-thirds full, the requisite for the tridecennial division.

My object in the above discussion of the origin of the week (as distinguished from the origin of the Sabbath, which I considered in the essay on astrology), has been to show that the use of the twelve zodiacal signs was in every case preceded by the use of the twenty-eight lunar mansions. It has been supposed that those nations in whose astronomy the twenty-eight mansions still appear, adopted one system, while the use of the twelve signs implies that another system had been adopted. Thus the following passage occurs in Mr. Blake's version of Flammarion's 'History of the Heavens:'—'the Chinese have twenty-eight constellations, though the word *sion* does not mean a group of stars, but simply a mansion or hotel. In the Coptic and ancient Egyptian the word for constellations has the same meaning. They also have twenty-eight, and the same number is found among the Arabians, Persians, and Indians. Among the Chaldæans or Accadians we find no sign of the number twenty-eight. The ecliptic, or "yoke of the sky," with them, as we see in the newly-discovered tablet, was divided into twelve divisions, as now, and the only connection that can be imagined between this and the twenty-eight is the opinion of M. Biot, who thinks that the Chinese had originally only twenty-four mansions, four more being added by Chenkung, 1100 B.C., and that they corresponded with the twenty-four stars, twelve to the north and twelve to the south, that marked the twelve signs of the zodiac amongst the Chaldæans. But under this supposition the twenty-eight has no reference to the moon, whereas we have every reason to believe it has.' The last observation is undoubtedly correct—the twenty-eight mansions have been mansions of the moon from the beginning. But in this very circumstance, as also in the very tablets referred to in the preceding passage, we find all the evidence needed to show that originally the Chaldæans divided the zodiac into twenty-eight parts. For we find from the tablets that, like the other nations who had twenty-eight zodiacal mansions, the Chaldæans used a seven-day period, derived from the moon's motions, every seventh day being called *sabbatu*, and held as a day of rest. We may safely infer that the Chaldæan astronomers, advancing beyond those of other nations, recognised the necessity of dividing the zodiac with reference to the sun's motions instead of the moon's. They therefore discarded the twenty-eight lunar mansions, and adopted instead twelve solar signs; this number twelve, like the number twenty-eight itself, being selected merely as the most convenient approximation to the number of parts into which the zodiac was naturally divided by another period. Thus the twenty-eighth part of the zodiac corresponds roughly with the moon's daily motion, and the twelfth part of the zodiac corresponds roughly with the moon's monthly motion; and both the numbers twenty-eight and twelve admit of being subdivided, while twenty-nine (a nearer approach than twenty-eight to the number of days in a lunation) and thirteen (almost as near an approach as twelve to the number of months in a year) do not.

It seems to me highly probable that the date to which all inquiries into the origin of the constellations and the zodiacal signs seems to point—viz. 2170 B.C.—was the date at which the Chaldæan astronomers definitely adopted the new system, the lunisolar instead of lunar division of the zodiac and of time. One of the objects which the architects of the Great Pyramid (not the king who built it) may have had was not improbably this—the erection of a building indicating the epoch when the new system was entered upon, and defining in its proportions, its interior passages, and other features, fundamental elements of the new system. The great difficulty, an overwhelming difficulty it has always seemed to me, in accepting the belief that the year 2170 B.C. defined the beginning of exact astronomy, has been this, that several of the circumstances insisted upon as determining that date imply a considerable knowledge of astronomy. Thus astronomers must have made great progress in their science before they could select as a day for counting from, the epoch when the slow reeling motion of the earth (the so-called precessional motion) brought the Pleiades centrally south, at noon, at the time of the vernal equinox. The construction of the Great Pyramid, again, in all its astronomical features, implies considerable proficiency in astronomical observation. Thus the year 2170 B.C. may very well be regarded as defining the introduction of a new system or astronomy, but certainly not the beginning of astronomy itself. Of course we may cut the knot of this difficulty, as Prof. Smyth and Abbé Moigno do, by saying that astronomy began 2170 B.C., the first astronomers being instructed supernaturally, so that the astronomical Minerva came into full-grown being. But I apprehend that argument against such a belief is as unnecessary as it would certainly be useless.

And now let us consider how this theory accords with the result to which we were led by the position of the great vacant space around the southern pole. So far as the date is concerned, we have already seen that the epoch 2170 B.C. accords excellently with the evidence of the vacant space. But this evidence, as I mentioned at the outset, establishes more than the date; it indicates the latitude of the place where the most ancient of Ptolemy's forty-eight constellations were first definitely adopted by astronomers. If we assume that at this place the southernmost constellations were just fully seen when due south, we find for the latitude about thirty-eight degrees north. (The student of astronomy who may care to test my results may be reminded here that it is not enough to show that every star of a constellation would when due south be above the horizon of the place—what is wanted is, that the whole constellation when towards the south should be visible at a single view. However, the whole constellation may not have included all the stars now belonging to it.) The station of the astronomers who founded the new system can scarcely have been more than a degree or two north of this latitude. On the other side, we may go a little further, for by so doing we only raise the constellations somewhat higher above the southern horizon, to which there is less objection than to a change thrusting part of the constellations below the horizon. Still it may be doubted whether the place where the constellations were first formed was less than 32 or 33 degrees north of the equator. The Great Pyramid, as we know, is about 30 degrees north of the equator; but we also know that its architects travelled southwards to find a suitable place for it. One of their objects may well have been to obtain a fuller view of the star-sphere south of their constellations. I think from 35 to 39 degrees north would be about the most probable limits, and from 32 to 41 degrees north the certain limits of the station of the first founders of solar zodiacal astronomy.

What their actual station may have been is not so easily established. Some think the region lay between the sources of the Oxus (Amoor) and Indus, others that the station of these astronomers was not very far from Mount Ararat —a view to which I was led long ago by other considerations discussed in the first appendix to my treatise on 'Saturn and its System.'

At the epoch indicated, the first constellation of the zodiac was not, as now, the Fishes, nor, as when a fresh departure was made by Hipparchus, the Ram, but the Bull, a trace of which is found in Virgil's words—

> Candidus auratis aperit cum cornibus annum
> Taurus.

The Bull then was the spring sign, the Pleiades and ruddy Aldebaran joining their rays with the sun's at the time of the vernal equinox. The midsummer sign was the Lion (the bright Cor Leonis nearly marking the sun's highest place). The autumn sign was the Scorpion, the ruddy Antares and the stars clustering in the head of the Scorpion joining their rays with the sun's at the time of the autumnal equinox. And lastly the winter sign was the Water Bearer, the bright Fomalhaut conjoining his rays with the sun's at midwinter. It is noteworthy that all these four constellations really present some resemblance to the objects after which they are named. The Scorpion is in the best drawing, but the Bull's head is well marked, and, as already mentioned, a leaping lion can be recognised. The streams of stars from the Urn of Aquarius and the Urn itself are much better defined than the Urn Bearer.

I have not left myself much space to speak of the finest of all the constellations, the glorious Orion—the Giant in his might, as he was called of old. In this noble asterism the figure of a giant ascending a slope can be readily discerned when the constellation is due south. At the time to which I have referred the constellation Orion was considerably below the equator, and instead of standing nearly upright when due south high above the horizon, as now in our northern latitudes, he rose upright above the south-eastern horizon. The resemblance to a giant figure must then have been even more striking than it is at present (except in high northern latitudes, where Orion, when due south, is just fully above the horizon). The giant Orion has long been identified with Nimrod; and those who recognise the antitypes of the Ark in Argo, of the old dragon in Draco, and of the first and second Adams in the kneeling Hercules defeated by the serpent and the upright Ophiuchus triumphant over the serpent, may, if they so please, find in the giant Orion, the Two Dogs, the Hare, and the Bull (whom Orion is more directly dealing with), the representations of Nimrod, that mighty hunter before the Lord, his hunting dogs, and the animals he hunted. Pegasus, formerly called the Horse, was regarded in very ancient times as the Steed of Nimrod.

In modern astronomy the constellations no longer have the importance which once attached to them. They afford convenient means for naming the stars, though I think many observers would prefer the less attractive but more business-like methods adopted by Piazzi and others, according to which a star rejoices in no more striking title than 'Piazzi XIIIh. 273,' or 'Struve, 2819.' They still serve, however, to teach beginners the stars, and probably many years will pass before even exact astronomy dismisses them altogether to the limbo of discarded symbolisms. It is, indeed, somewhat singular that astronomers find it easier to introduce new absurdities among the constellations than to get rid of these old ones. The new and utterly absurd figures introduced by Bode still remain in many charts despite such inconvenient names as *Honores Frederici*, *Globum Ærostaticum* and *Machina Pneumatica*; and I have very little doubt that a new constellation, if it only had a specially inconvenient title, would be accepted. But when Francis Baily tried to simplify the heavens by removing many of Bode's absurd constellations, he was abused by many as violently as though he had proposed the rejection of the Newtonian system. I myself tried a small measure of reform in the three first editions of my 'Library Atlas,' but have found it desirable to return to the old nomenclature in the fourth.

THE END.